FAITH
AND
HISTORY

A COMPARISON OF CHRISTIAN
AND MODERN VIEWS OF HISTORY

BY

REINHOLD NIEBUHR

NEW YORK
CHARLES SCRIBNER'S SONS

To My Colleagues on the Faculty
and
To the Students of Union Theological Seminary

*In their fellowship the exposition of doctrine is
subjected to critical understanding. Thus the sun
and the rain is provided, without which no fruit of
mind and spirit can ripen.*

PREFACE

THE theme of this volume was first presented as the Lyman Beecher Lectures On Preaching at the Yale Divinity School in 1945. Some of the same lectures were given, by arrangement, under the Warrack Lectureship On Preaching at the Universities of Glasgow and Aberdeen in Scotland in the winter of 1947. Some of the chapters were used as the basis of lectures given under the Olaf Petri Foundation of the University of Uppsala in Sweden. I sought to develop various portions of a general theme in these various lectureships. In this volume I have drawn these lectures into a more comprehensive study of the total problem of the relation of the Christian faith to modern conceptions of history. While the total work, therefore, bares little resemblance to the lectures, it does contain consideration of the specific problems which were dealt with in the lectures. I shall not seek to identify this material by chapters as I subjected the whole to reorganization.

Two of these lectureships usually deal with the art of preaching, though not a few of the actual lectures have been concerned with the preacher's message. Since I had no special competence in the art of homiletics I thought it wise to devote the lectures to a definition of the apologetic task of the Christian pulpit in the unique spiritual climate of our day. Since several of the Beecher lecturers in the past half-century sought to accommodate the Christian message to the prevailing evolutionary optimism of the nineteenth and early twentieth centuries, I thought it might be particularly appropriate to consider the spiritual situation in a period in which this evolutionary optimism is in the process of decay. This volume is written on the basis of the faith that the Gospel of Christ is true for men of every age and that Jesus Christ is "the same yesterday, today and forever." It is, nevertheless, the task of the pulpit to relate the ageless Gospel to the special problems of each age. In doing so, however, there is always a temptation to capitulate to the characteristic prejudices of an age.

The preaching of the Gospel was not immune to this temptation in the past centuries. The real alternative to the Christian faith elaborated by modern secular culture was the idea that history is itself Christ, which is to say that historical development is redemptive. Typical modern theology accommodated itself to this secular scheme of redemption much too readily. Meanwhile the experiences of contemporary man have refuted the modern faith in the redemptive character of history itself. This refutation has given the Christian faith, as presented in the Bible, a new relevance. It is not the thesis of this new volume that this new relevance could establish the truth of the Christian Gospel in the mind of modern man. The truth of the Christian faith must, in fact, be apprehended in any age by repentance and faith. It is, therefore, not made acceptable by rational validation in the first instance.

It is important, nevertheless, for the preacher of the Gospel to understand, and come to terms with, the characteristic credos of his age. It is important in our age to understand how the spiritual complacency of a culture which believed in redemption through history is now on the edge of despair.

I should like to express my gratitude to Dean Luther A. Weigle and the faculty of the Yale Divinity School for the invitation to this historic lectureship, and to the faculty and the students of the school for their kindness to me during the course of the convocation at which the lectures were delivered. I am also deeply indebted to many of my colleagues on the faculty of Union Theological Seminary for helpful criticisms on various chapters of the book; and especially to Professor Richard J. Kroner, Mr. Roger L. Shinn, and Professor John E. Smith of Barnard College for a critical scrutiny of the entire manuscript. My secretary, Mrs. Nola Meade, deserves special gratitude for painstaking work on the manuscript; as does also Mr. Langdon Gilkey, for preparing the index.

REINHOLD NIEBUHR

Union Theological Seminary
New York City
January 1949

CONTENTS

FAITH
AND
HISTORY

CHAPTER I

~~~~~~

The Current Refutation of the Idea of Redemption through Progress

I

IT would have been difficult for the generations of the twentieth century to survive the hazards and to face the perplexities of our age in any event, since every problem of human existence had been given a wider scope than known in previous ages. But our perplexities became the more insoluble and the perils to which we were exposed became the more dangerous because the men of this generation had to face the rigors of life in the twentieth century with nothing but the soft illusions of the previous two centuries to cover their spiritual nakedness. There was nothing in the creeds and dogmas of these centuries which would have enabled modern men either to anticipate or to understand the true nature of the terrors and tumults to which they would be exposed.

The history of mankind exhibits no more ironic experience than the contrast between the sanguine hopes of recent centuries and the bitter experiences of contemporary man. Every technical advance, which previous generations regarded as a harbinger or guarantor of the redemption of mankind from its various difficulties, has proved to be the cause, or at least the occasion, for a new dimension of ancient perplexities.

A single article of faith has given diverse forms of modern culture the unity of a shared belief. Modern men of all shades of opinion agreed in the belief that historical development is a redemptive process. It was the genuine achievement of modern historical science to discover that human culture is subject to indeterminate development. Natural science added the discovery that nature, as well as human culture and institutions, undergoes an evolutionary process. Thus the static conception of history which characterized the Middle Ages as well as antiquity was breached. It would be more accurate to say that the discoveries of the historical and natural sciences gave modern men a final justification for a new faith which had been developing since the Renaissance. Joachim of Flores had given the first intimation of it in the late Middle Ages when he transmuted Christian eschatology into the hope of a transfigured world, of a future age of the Holy Spirit, in which the antinomies and ambiguities of man's historic existence would be overcome in history itself.

The Renaissance, which ostensibly restored classical learning, was actually informed by a very unclassical sense of history. It retained, or returned to, the cyclical interpretation of history, as known in the classical age; but historical cycles became spirals of advance in Renaissance historiography. Its passion for a return to old disciplines was submerged by its enthusiasm for man's new and growing powers. This enthusiasm was increased as evidence accumulated that among man's unique gifts belonged the capacity to increase his freedom and power indeterminately. Had not human institutions developed from crude and barbaric beginnings to their present proud estate? The nineteenth century added to this new certainty not only the assurance that nature itself was subject to growth but also the obvious achievements of applied science. The phenomenal technical advances of the century, outstripping the slow conquest of nature of all previous eras, seemed to be the final proof of the validity of modern man's new faith in history. The classical conception of time as a cycle of endless recurrences was finally overcome. Time was no longer a mystery which required explanation. It became the principle of interpretation by which the mystery of life was comprehended. History was no longer an enigma. It became the assurance of man's redemption from his every ill.

The modern age is variously described as an age of science or as an age of reason. Confidence in the power of reason, and particularly in the inductive and empirical strategy of the rational faculty, is indeed a characteristic of our age. But the classical ages also believed in the power and virtue of reason. Modern culture is distinguished by its confidence, both in the growing power of reason and in its capacity, when rightly disciplined, to assure the development of every human power and virtue.

The dominant note in modern culture is not so much confidence in reason as faith in history. The conception of a redemptive history informs the most diverse forms of modern culture. The rationalist, Leibnitz, shared it with the romanticist, Herder. Kant's critical idealism was not so obviously informed by the new historical sense as the thought of Hegel, who had reinterpreted Platonism to conform to the historical consciousness of modernity; but Kant was as certain as Hegel of a movement of history toward increasing rationality. J. S. Mill's utilitarianism stood in sharp contradiction to Kant's ethics; but Mill agreed with Kant that history was moving toward a universal concord of life with life. The difference between the French Enlightenment's materialism and the idealism of the German Enlightenment made no appreciable difference in the common historical optimism of both. The French physiocrats believed that progress would be assured by the removal of the irrelevancies of historical restraints from the operation of the laws of nature; while Comte thought it would be achieved by bringing social process under the control of an elite of social scientists. But this contrast between determinism and voluntarism (which is, incidentally, never composed in modern culture) had no influence upon the shared belief in progress. There is only a slight difference in optimism between the deterministic thought of Herbert Spencer and the modern voluntarism of John Dewey.

Even Karl Marx, who introduced a provisional historical catastrophism to challenge the optimism of bourgeois life, did not shake the modern conception of a redemptive history basically. He saw in the process of historical development certain "dialectical" elements not observed in bourgeois theories. He knew that there is disintegration as well as increasing integration in history; that there is death as well as growth. But he also believed that a new life and a new age would rise out of the death of an old one with dialectical necessity. Catastrophe was the certain prelude of redemption in his scheme of salvation. The ultimate similarity between Marxist and bourgeois optimism, despite the provisional catastrophism of the former, is, in fact, the most telling proof of the unity of modern culture. It is a unity which transcends warring social philosophies, conflict between which contributed to the refutation of a common hope.

The goal toward which history was presumably moving was variously defined. The most unreflective forms of historical optimism in the nineteenth century assumed that increasing physical comfort and well-being were the guarantee of every other form of advance. Sometimes the enlarging human community was believed to be developing inevitably toward a universal community, for "clans and tribes, long narrowly self-regarding, are finally enlarged and compacted into nations; and nations move inevitably, however slowly, into relations with one another, whose ultimate goal is the unification of mankind." [1] It may be recorded in passing that scarcely a single student in the modern era noted the marked difference between the task of unifying tribes, nations and empires and the final task of the unification of mankind. In the former case there is always some particular force of geography, language, common experience or the fear of a common foe which furnishes the core of cohesion. In the latter case unity must be achieved in defiance of the unique and particularistic forces of historical concretion.

Sometimes, as in H. G. Wells' *Outline of History*, the historical process is assumed to be moving toward the democratization, as well as the universalization, of the human community. The democratic culmination, toward which history was presumably moving was frequently defined in contradictory terms. Libertarians thought they saw a movement toward increasing liberty while equalitarians and collectivists thought they could discern a movement toward more intense social cohesion.

Nor was there agreement about the cause of historical advance.

[1] Edmund Noble, *Purposive Evolution*, p. 418.

Social Darwinism as well as other forms of naturalism looked upon historical development as a mere extension of natural evolution. The Darwinists saw the guarantee of progress in the survival of the fittest. Others discerned a movement in both nature and history from consistent egoism to a greater and greater consideration of the interests of others.[2]

More frequently historical development was regarded not so much as an extension of forces operative in nature as a negation of natural impulses through the growth of mind. The method of reason's triumph over the irrationalities of nature was, however, variously interpreted. The French Enlightenment assigned reason the primary function of discerning the "laws of nature" and of destroying man's abortive efforts to circumvent these laws. Comte, on the other hand, believed that a scientific political program would bring the irrational factors in man's common life under rational control. Condorcet believed that justice would triumph when universal education destroyed the advantage which the shrewd had over the simple. Or it was assumed that increasing rationality would gradually destroy the irrational (primarily religious) justifications of special privilege.[3] Or that increasing reason would gradually prompt all men to grant their fellowmen justice, the power of logic requiring that the interests of each individual be brought into a consistent scheme of value.[4] More recently the psychological sciences have hoped for the increasing control or elimination of self-regarding impulses and the extension of human sympathy through the rational control of man's sub-rational life.

Though modern culture is predominantly rationalistic, so that even naturalistic philosophies place their primary confidence in

---

[2] Prince Kropotkin in *Mutual Aid* traced the development from limited mutual aid in the animal world to wider and wider extensions of mutuality. Leslie Stephens described an evolutionary development of conscience as the "gradual growth of social tissue." (*The Science of Ethics*, p. 120.)

W. K. Clifford equated an evolutionary development of the moral sense with the growth of a "tribal self." (*Lectures and Essays*, II, p. 110.)

[3] This is the thesis of Robert Briffault's *Rational Evolution*.

[4] L. T. Hobhouse bases his confidence in progress upon this argument in *Principles of Social Justice, The Rational Good,* and *Development and Purpose.*

increasing rationality, the subordinate romantic distrust of reason
must not be obscured. Romanticism in its most consistent form has
a preference for the primitive, which implies a pessimistic estimate of
the growth of civilization. Rousseau's dictum that men were born
free and are now everywhere in chains led to a provisional pessimism;
but this did not prevent him from elaborating a system of historical
optimism, based on confidence in the possibility of bringing all competing wills into the concurrence of a general will. Bergson's distrust
of reason likewise failed to arrest his optimistic conclusions about
historical development. He placed his confidence in the growth of
a mystical capacity, which would lift men from particular to universal loyalties.[5]

The fact that the prevailing mood of modern culture was able to
transmute the original pessimism of romanticism into an optimistic
creed proves the power of this mood. Only occasionally the original
pessimism erupts in full vigor, as in the thought of a Schopenhauer
or Nietzsche. The subjugation of romantic pessimism, together with
the transmutation of Marxist catastrophism establishes historical
optimism far beyond the confines of modern rationalism. Though
there are minor dissonances the whole chorus of modern culture
learned to sing the new song of hope in remarkable harmony. The
redemption of mankind, by whatever means, was assured for the
future. It was, in fact, assured by the future.

II

There were experiences in previous centuries which might well
have challenged this unqualified optimism. But the expansion of
man's power over nature proceeded at such a pace that all doubts
were quieted, allowing the nineteenth century to become the "century of hope" [6] and to express the modern mood in its most extravagant terms. History, refusing to move by the calendar, actually permitted the nineteenth century to indulge its illusions into the
twentieth. Then came the deluge. Since 1914 one tragic experience

[5] *Cf.* Henri Bergson, *Two Sources of Religion and Morality.*
[6] *Cf.* F. S. Marvin, *The Century of Hope.*

has followed another, as if history had been designed to refute the vain delusions of modern man.

The "laws" and tendencies of historical development proved in the light of contemporary experience to be much more complex than any one has supposed. Every new freedom represented a new peril as well as a new promise. Modern industrial society dissolved ancient forms of political authoritarianism; but the tyrannies which grew on its soil proved more brutal and vexatious than the old ones. The inequalities rooted in landed property were levelled. But the more dynamic inequalities of a technical society became more perilous to the community than the more static forms of uneven power. The achievement of individual liberty was one of the genuine advances of bourgeois society. But this society also created atomic individuals who, freed from the disciplines of the older organic communities, were lost in the mass; and became the prey of demagogues and charlatans who transmuted their individual anxieties and resentments into collective political power of demonic fury.

The development of instruments of communication and transportation did create a potential world community by destroying all the old barriers of time and space. But the new interdependence of the nations created a more perplexing problem than anyone had anticipated. It certainly did not prompt the nations forthwith to organize a "parliament of man and federation of the world." Rather it extended the scope of old international frictions so that a single generation was subjected to two wars of global dimensions. Furthermore the second conflict left the world as far from the goal of global peace as the first. At its conclusion the world's peace was at the mercy of two competing alliances of world savers, the one informed by the bourgeois and the other by the proletarian creed of world redemption. Thus the civil war in the heart of modern industrial nations, which had already brought so much social confusion into the modern world, was re-enacted in the strife between nations. The development of atomic instruments of conflict aggravated the fears not only of those who lacked such instruments, but of those who had them. The fears of the latter added a final ironic touch to the whole destiny of modern man. The possession of power has never annulled the fears of those who wield it, since it prompts them to anxiety over its possible loss. The possession of a phenomenal form of destructive power in the modern day has proved to be so fruitful of new fears that the perennial ambiguity of man's situation of power and weakness became more vividly exemplified, rather than overcome. Thus a century which was meant to achieve a democratic society of world-scope finds itself at its half-way mark uncertain about the possibility of avoiding a new conflict of such proportions as to leave the survival of mankind, or at least the survival of civilization, in doubt.

The tragic irony of this refutation by contemporary history of modern man's conception of history embodies the spiritual crisis of our age. Other civilizations have assumed their own indestructibility, usually indulging in pretensions of immortality in a "golden age," precisely when their ripeness was turning into over-ripeness and portents of their disintegration were becoming discernible. It remained for the culture of the Renaissance and Enlightenment to raise this *Hybris* of civilizations to a new and absurd height by claiming to have found the way of arresting the decay not merely of a particular civilization but of civilization as such. Was not the "scientific conquest of nature" a "sure method" by which the "wholesale permanent decay of civilization has become impossible"? [7] Had not the scientific method established the dominion of man over nature in place of "the dominion of man over the labor of others" which was the "shaky basis" of older civilizations?

Contemporary experience represents a *Nemesis* which is justly proportioned in its swiftness and enormity to the degree of *Hybris* which had expressed itself in modern life. In one century modern man had claimed to have achieved the dizzy heights of the mastery both of natural process and historical destiny. In the following century he is hopelessly enmeshed in an historical fate, threatening mutual destruction, from which he seems incapable of extricating himself. A word of Scripture fits the situation perfectly: "He that sitteth in the heavens shall laugh: the Lord shall have them in derision" (Psalms 2:4).

[7] John Dewey, in *International Journal of Ethics*, April 1916, p. 313.

The modern experience belongs in the category of pathos or irony rather than tragedy, because contemporary culture has no vantage point of faith from which to understand the predicament of modern man. It is therefore incapable either of rising to a tragic defiance of destiny, as depicted in Greek drama, or of achieving a renewal of life through a contrite submission to destiny, as in Christian tragedy. Subsequent centuries (if, indeed, there be survivors capable of reflecting upon the meaning of the experience of this age) may discern in it the pathos characteristic of Thomas Hardy's novels. For the actors in the drama are enmeshed in an inscrutable fate, which either drives them to despair or for which they find false interpretations.

Most of the explanations of contemporary catastrophe are derived from principles of interpretation which were responsible for modern man's inability to anticipate the experiences which he now seeks to comprehend. A culture, rooted in historical optimism, naturally turns first of all to the concepts of "retrogression" and "reversion" to explain its present experience. Thus Nazism is interpreted as a "reversion to barbarism" or even as a "reversion to the cruelty of the Middle Ages." We are assured that mankind has no right to expect an uninterrupted ascent toward happiness and perfection. Comfort is drawn from the figure of a "spiral" development. This is usually accompanied by the assurance that no recession ever reaches the depth of previous ones and that each new "peak" achieves a height beyond those of the past. This spiral version of the concept of progress is hardly more adequate than the simpler version; for both the failures and achievements of advanced civilizations are incommensurable with those of simpler societies. To call them better or worse by comparison is almost meaningless. Insofar as comparisons can be made it is idle to regard the tyrannies and anarchies which result from the breakdown of an advanced and highly integrated civilization as preferable to the social confusion of more primitive societies.

An equally favored mode of reassurance is to take a long view of history, to enlarge upon the millennia of pre-historic barbarism which preceded the known, and comparatively brief, period of civilized life, and to express the hope that present misfortunes belong to the period of civilization's infancy which will be forgotten in the unimagined heights of perfection which will be achieved in the unimagined subsequent ages. So James Bryce wrote in the period of disillusionment, following the first world war: "Shaken out of that confident hope in progress . . . mankind must resume its efforts toward improvement in a chastened mood, . . . consoled by the reflection that it has taken a thousand years to emerge from savagery and less than half that time to rise above the shameless sensualities of the ancient world and the ruthless ferocity of the Dark Ages." [8]

A modern biologist seeks comfort in a similar logic: "When world wide wars, with their indescribable sufferings and horrors, brutalities and tyrannies shake one's faith in human progress, it is comforting to take a long view of cosmic evolution and remember that the longest wars are but a fraction of a second on the clock of life on earth, and that 'eternal process moving on' is not likely to stop today or tomorrow." [9]

These comforting assurances rest upon the dubious assumption that the "shameless sensualities" of the ancient world and the "ruthless ferocity" of the Dark Ages have no counterpart in modern life. The belief that human brutality is a vestigial remnant of man's animal or primitive past represents one of the dearest illusions of modern culture, to which men cling tenaciously even when every contemporary experience refutes it.

The appeal to future millennia of the world's history, in comparison with which past history is but a brief episode and its periods of conflict but seconds on the clock of time, is hardly reassuring when for instance the history of warfare in this brief episode is considered. For that history contains the development from partial and limited to total wars; and the evolution of means of combat from spears to atomic bombs. To be sure historical development contains creative movements as well as progress in means of destruction. But the fact that history contains such developments as progress in the lethal efficacy of our means of destruction and the increasing consistency of

[8] *Modern Democracies*, Vol. II, p. 607 (1921).
[9] Edward G. Conklin, *Man: Real and Ideal*, pp. 205–206.

tyrannical governments must prove the vanity of our hope in historical development as such. The prospect of the extension of history into untold millennia must, if these facts are considered, sharpen, rather than assuage, man's anxiety about himself and his history.

A more favored explanation of present catastrophies is to hold the "cultural lag" responsible for them, which means to attribute them to the failure of man's social wisdom to keep pace with his technical advances. This explanation has the merit of being quite true as an interpretation of specific evils, arising from specific maladjustments between a culture and its social institutions, or between the economic and technical arrangements of an era and its political forms. It nevertheless hides a profound illusion with reference to the total situation.

One of the most potent causes of historical evil is the inability of men to bring their customs and institutions into conformity with new situations. Political institutions developed in a pastoral society maintain themselves stubbornly in an agrarian economy; and agrarian institutions are projected into a commercial age. In a period of rapid technical advance these maladjustments are a source of great social confusion. It is obvious, for instance, that the sometimes extravagant individualism of the commercial age is not an adequate social philosophy for the intense social cohesion of a new industrial age; and that the national sovereignties of the past must be abridged to permit the growth of international political institutions, consonant with the economic interdependence of modern nations. All this is clear.

The error embodied in the theory of the cultural lag is the modern assumption that the "cultural lag" is due merely to the tardiness of the social sciences in achieving the same standards of objectivity and disinterestedness which characterize the natural sciences. This belief embodies the erroneous idea that man's knowledge and conquest of nature develops the wisdom and the technics required for the knowledge and the conquest of human nature.

It is man in the unity of his being who must come to terms with his fellowmen and, for that matter, with himself. Scientific knowledge of what human nature is and how it reacts to various given social situations will always be of service in refashioning human conduct. But ultimately the problems of human conduct and social relations are in a different category from the relations of physical nature. The ability to judge friend or foe with some degree of objectivity is, in the ultimate instance, a moral and not an intellectual achievement, since it requires the mitigation of fears and prejudices, envies and hatreds which represent defects, not of the mind, but of the total personality. Moreover, the ability to yield to the common good, to forego special advantages for a larger measure of social justice, to heal the breach between warring factions by forgiveness, or to acknowledge a common human predicament between disputants in a social situation, is the fruit of a social wisdom to which science makes only ancillary contributions. This type of wisdom involves the whole of man in the unity of his being. The modern belief that "scientific objectivity" may be simply extended from the field of nature to the field of history obscures the unity of the self which acts, and is acted upon, in history. It also obscures the ambiguity of the human self; for the self as the creature of history is the same self which must be the creator of history. The creaturely limitations which corrupt his actions as creator are, however, never the limitations of mere ignorance. The self as creator does not master the self as creature merely by the extension of scientific technics. The hope that everything recalcitrant in human behaviour may be brought under the subjection of the inclusive purposes of "mind" by the same technics which gained man mastery over nature is not merely an incidental illusion, prompted by the phenomenal achievements of the natural sciences. It is the culminating error in modern man's misunderstanding of himself. Thus the principle of comprehension by which modern culture seeks to understand our present failure belongs to the misunderstanding about man's life and history which contributed to that failure. The spiritual confusions arising from this misunderstanding constitute the cultural crisis of our age, beyond and above the political crisis in which our civilization is involved.

The contradiction between the hopes of yesterday and the realities of today has created something like despair in those parts of the world where past stabilities have been most seriously shaken; and it is generating a kind of desperate complacency in those parts of the world in which the crisis of the age is dimly, though not fully, sensed.

The time is ripe, at any rate, to survey both the modern and the Christian and classical ideas of man's relation to history. Such a study may reveal the roots of modern misconceptions about man's history more clearly and it may restore the relevance of previous answers to the problem of human destiny, which were prematurely discarded.

CHAPTER II

~~~~~~

The History of the Modern Conception of History

I

A RIDE at extravagant speed in a modern motor vehicle may end in disaster even if the driver of the vehicle is not informed by a philosophy which regards movement and speed as the highest desiderata. Modern technical civilization might have failed to bring the vast new powers over nature under social control, even if it had not been animated by a culture which assumed historical development to be the answer to the problem of human existence. But a philosophy which places a premium upon movement and speed will probably not inculcate the caution which the driver of a high-powered vehicle ought to possess. The uncritical confidence in historical development as a mode of redemption may have, likewise, contributed to our present disaster by heightening the historical dynamism of western civilization to the point where it became a kind of demonic fury. We certainly can not deny that the center of modern disorder lies within the very portion of the world which took a more affirmative attitude toward the drama of human history than the waking-sleeping cultures of the orient; and that this affirmative attitude became transmuted into an idolatrous confidence in historical growth in the past two centuries of secularization.

Western culture embodies three approaches toward the vexing problem of the nature of human history: 1) The approach of Greek classicism which equated history with the world of nature and sought emancipation of man's changeless reason from this world of change; 2) the Biblical-Christian approach which found man's historic existence both meaningful and mysterious and which regarded the freedom of man, which distinguished history from nature, as the source of evil as well as of good; 3) and the modern approach which regarded the historical development of man's power and freedom as the solution for every human perplexity and as the way of emancipation from every human evil.

These three approaches have a significant relationship to each other which must be examined more carefully if we would understand the predicament of modern culture. For the dynamism of western culture was made possible by the triumph of the Biblical-Christian sense of history as a realm of meaning over the ahistorical culture of classicism. The unanticipated disaster which followed upon this dynamism is, on the other hand, related to the triumph of the modern view of history over the Biblical-Christian. For the Christian view of life and history recognized the peril, as well as the creativity, of human freedom, while the modern view had an uncritical confidence in the enlargement of human freedom. The three views of history which have matured in western culture are all answers to problems and perplexities which are consequent upon the radical nature of human freedom. Man's freedom is unique because it enables him, though in the temporal process, also to transcend it by conceptual knowledge, memory and a self-determining will. Thus he creates a new level of coherence and meaning, which conforms neither to the world of natural change nor yet to the realm of pure Being in which Greek idealism sought refuge from the world of change. This is the realm of history.

Man not only creates the historical realm through his freedom, but he is himself subject to development through history because historical processes extend the power of his freedom indeterminately. It was this extension of human powers which modern culture recognized more clearly than any previous culture. It was so impressed by its discovery that it arrived at the false conclusion that the indeterminate extension of human capacities would eventually alter the human situation. It would emancipate man from his ambiguous position as both creature and creator of history and enable him to become the unambiguous master of historical destiny.

II

The classical culture, elaborated by Plato, Aristotle and the Stoics, is a western and intellectual version of a universal type of ahistorical spirituality. Brahmin and Buddhistic mysticism are oriental and non-rational versions of the same general attitude toward life. The common characteristic in all of these approaches is that a rigorous effort is made to disassociate what is regarded as a timeless and divine element in human nature from the world of change and temporal flux. The mystical, predominantly oriental, versions seek this divine and changeless element in a level of consciousness which transcends every particularity of finite existence, including the particularity of the individual ego. The rational, predominantly western-classical, version finds the divine and immortal element in human nature primarily in the power of human reason, more specifically in man's capacity for conceptual knowledge. This capacity, when rigorously purged of the taints and corruptions of the passions and senses of man's physical existence, lifts man into a timeless realm. It relates him to the world of change only in the sense that conceptual knowledge enables him to discern the changeless patterns and structures which underlie the world of change, the world of "coming-to-be" and "passing away."

In both oriental and western-classical thought the temporal world is comprehended in terms of cycles of endless recurrences. The world of history is also equated with this realm of natural cycles. The identification of natural with historical time determines the non-historical character of this form of spirituality. History is a realm of ambiguity. It is, for the classical mind, intelligible only as it participates in the cycle of birth and death which characterizes nature. In their analysis of individual life classical and mystical interpretations tend to separate the freedom of man too absolutely from his nature as a creature of nature and to obscure the interpenetration of a unique human freedom with the impulses of nature. Their corresponding interpretations of human history ignore, or fail duly to appreciate, the dimension of the historical in which human freedom is mixed with natural necessity.

The unique freedom of man transmutes every physical impulse and gives it a wider range and a more complex relation to other impulses than known in the animal world. Yet the natural basis of the impulse is never annulled. Thus animal gregariousness is transmuted in human life to become the basis of an endless variety of human communities of wider and wider scope. But the simple "consciousness of kind" remains a potent aspect of man's communal existence to the desperation of those who would like to create a universal community without the irrelevance of particular communities.

In a similar fashion, the sex impulse, which has the sole function of procreation in animal existence, helps to create the human family and remains operative in the wider kinship groups. It is therefore one of the sources of man's communal existence. It is furthermore one of the creative roots of the aesthetic and religious life. It may also, as all other human impulses, become the perverse center of man's existence, thereby devouring and corrupting other creative capacities. Yet no spiritual transfiguration of man's sexual life can either negate or obscure the natural root from which it is derived. Significantly when the mystics, seeking to renounce natural impulses for the sake of obtaining a pure equanimity of spirit, make a report of their state of bliss they find difficulty in eliminating tell-tale notes of eroticism from the account.

Other impulses of nature are subject to similar transmutations. The various impulses are related to each other, moreover, in such an endless profusion of interpenetrations that modern psychologists rightly question the validity of the concept "instinct" because it connotes a too complete independence of particular impulses. The degree of freedom compounded with the stuff of nature may vary endlessly in specific acts and emotions, in types of conduct and in patterns of behaviour. But these variations move within one constant pattern, namely that both freedom and necessity are involved in

every human action and in every historical concretion and con-
figuration. It is this mixture of freedom and necessity which gives the
realm of history its particular character of meaning and obscurity,
of partial but not complete intelligibility.

The non-historical forms of spirituality both in the Orient and in
Greek rationalism emphasize that aspect of man's freedom which is
expressed in his ability to rise above the flux of temporal events. But
they do not see that other aspects of the same freedom enable him to
create a new order of reality, which, though grounded in a temporal
flux, is not completely governed by natural necessity, since human
agents have the power to change the natural course. This distinctive
realm is most succinctly defined simply as "history." Man has an
ambiguous position in this realm because he is both the creature and
the creator of its course. It is a realm of coherence and meaning but
it is not simply intelligible. The freedom of the human agent introduces complex and incalculable factors into the flow of cause and
effect. There are events in history which could be fully understood
only if the secret motives of the human agents could be fully known.

It is significant that neither mysticism nor classical rationalism is
particularly interested in the power of memory as one of the facets of
man's freedom. In mysticism the evidence of man's unique freedom
lies in a level of consciousness above the temporal flux. Classical
rationalism, on the other hand, finds man's unique freedom primarily
in his capacity for conceptual knowledge, by which he discerns the
changeless patterns and structures which underlie the world of
change. The significance of memory as one aspect of what Christian
thought has defined as the "image of God" in man was first given
due appreciation in western thought by Augustine, who also first
elaborated the sense of history, derived from Biblical thought, into
the philosophical speculations of the West. Memory represents man's
capacity to rise above, even while he is within, the temporal flux. It
proves that time is in him as surely as he is in time. The most obvious
definition of "history" is that it is a record or memory of past events.
More profoundly considered it is a dimension of existence in which
present realities can be rightly interpreted only through the memory
of past events. Since both present and past realities did not follow

necessarily from previous events, the bewildering mixture of freedom and necessity in every historical concretion is rightly understood only if the particular and unique acts which constitute the flow of events are remembered in their uniqueness. The memory of how things came to be prevents the present reality from appearing as an event of pure natural necessity. Thus nations have a memory of the unique events of their origin and history, which furnishes the frame for a structure of meaning, distinguishing their history from the history of other nations and establishing a level of meaning above that of natural necessity.

While memory of unique decisions in the past prevents the past from appearing to the present as irrevocable, the capacity to live in the past by memory also emancipates the individual from the tyranny of the present. He can choose, if he wants, to reverse a present trend of history in favor of some previous trend. He can, if he wishes, seek asylum from present tumults in a past period of history, or use the memory of a past innocency to project a future of higher virtue. Memory is, in short, the fulcrum of freedom for man in history. That is why the study of history is an emancipating force in human life. The less disclosed the past and the human contrivance which entered into present realities, the more do present facts appear in the guise of irrevocable facts of nature.

While memory and its weaker twin of foresight represent the freedom of man over the flux of temporal events, it is not true, as Augustine thought, that the past is present to us only in this freedom, and that the present is merely an infinitesimal point between the "past which is not now and the future which is not yet." [1] Actually the past is present to us not only in our memory of its events but in the immediacy of the accomplished events which it places upon our doorsteps. We do not merely remember the accident we had in our childhood but we have a scar upon our forehead as a "reminder." We do not merely remember that our fathers brought slaves to this country from Africa. We are reminded of their action by our colored fellow-citizens. The problems which arise from the actions of our fathers remind us that past actions are not simply revocable. We can

[1] Augustine, *Confessions*, II, 18.

not simply undo what our fathers have done, even though our fathers might have had the freedom to take another course of action. Thus the past is present to us in varying degrees of revocable tentativity and irrevocable finality. The individual can not change present facts which have their origin in the locus of his birth or childhood, or the economic social or ethnic status of his parents. Yet he does have a limited freedom to change his national loyalty, or rise above the social status of his parents, or add the knowledge of new languages to the language of his childhood. The forces of language and custom, of laws and institutions, of cultural and political traditions are all propulsive forces from the past into the present, in which freedom and necessity are variously mixed. Some of them are facts of nature which are completely immutable. Some of them are facts of history in which human contrivance has been mixed with natural necessity in the past but which impinge nevertheless upon the present with irrevocable force. No statesman in modern Europe can undo the complex of facts which resulted from Hitler's political adventures, however much he may have freedom to choose between new alternatives which arise from the irrevocable facts thus created. Some of the facts of history are revocable if challenged with sufficient initiative, though irrevocable if accepted with complacency.

Thus the complex of events which constitute history represent a bewildering confusion of destiny and freedom, which conform to the patterns of neither logical nor natural coherence. They are comprehended as a unity by memory but not by logic.

Memory is thus that aspect of human freedom which is most determinative in the construction of historical reality. It gives meaning to historical events without reducing them to natural necessity and recurrence; and it thereby gives the agent of action a dimension of freedom in the present moment which proves history to be a realm of freedom as well as of destiny.

III

The Biblical-Christian historical spirituality triumphed over classicism in western culture when it became apparent that the classical doctrine of recurrence made it impossible for men to deal creatively with the endlessly novel situations and vitalities which arise in history. To look to the past for guidance in these novel situations means to deal with only one of the two dimensions of historical reality, the dimension of necessity which creates the factors of recurrence. But even perennially recurring factors in history appear in new dimensions in new situations. It was impossible for classicism, particularly Stoic spirituality, to deal with this aspect of history. In Charles Cochrane's searching study of the decline of classical spirituality and the triumph of the Christian faith over it, the decay of classical spirituality is attributed to the inadequacy of the doctrine of recurrence. It prompted the Stoic political scientists and statesmen of the late Roman Republic and Early Empire to seek solutions for the ever more complex problems of Roman civilization by abortive effort to rejuvenate the virtues, and to reenact the policies, of the past. Cochrane sees Augustine's *Civitas Dei* as the most significant milestone in the gradual triumph of the Christian faith over classical paganism. This triumph was most obviously occasioned by the breakdown of the Roman civilization, Augustine's masterpiece having, in fact, the immediate and superficial objective of proving that the Christian faith was not doomed by the destruction of Rome.[2] But more profoundly considered it marked the triumph of the Christian faith over the culture which informed the Roman civilization, the inadequacies of which made it impossible to deal creatively with new problems of freedom and order which arose after it became apparent that Augustus' imperial solution for the problem of order had only temporary but not permanent validity.

The Christian faith is, however, not merely a faith which gives meaning to history through memory, contrasted with a philosophy which seeks abortively to give it meaning by forcing it into the mold of natural recurrence. Memory alone can not produce a universe of meaning above the level of the life of the individual or a tribe or nation. Religions of memory, whether tribal or imperial, can not rise to the level of envisaging the story of mankind in its totality. Neither can

[2] *Cf.* Charles Cochrane, *Christianity and Classical Culture, A Study of Thought and Action from Augustus to Augustine.* Oxford Press.

they deal with the threat to life's meaning arising from the fact that the freedom of man contains the possibility of defying and destroying the coherence of life. Ahistorical forms of spirituality attribute evil to the chaos of nature and find emancipation from evil in the realm of pure spirit or pure reason. Primitive forms of historical spirituality do not deal with the problem of evil profoundly because they conceive evil to be the power of the foe or competitor and regard the triumph over the foe as tantamount to redemption. The significance of Christianity as a "high" religion is partly derived from the two facts, 1) that it comprehends the whole of history, and not only the story of a particular people in its universe of meaning, and 2) that it deals with the problems of evil ultimately and not merely from the standpoint of what may appear to be evil to a particular individual or collective agent in human history in the actions of competitors and foes.

Christianity embodies the whole of history in its universe of meaning because it is a religion of revelation which knows by faith of some events in history, in which the transcendent source and end of the whole panorama of history is disclosed. Christian faith fully appreciates the threat of meaninglessness which comes into history by the corruption of human freedom. But it does not succumb to the despairing conclusion that history is merely a chaos of competing forces. It has discerned that the divine power which is sovereign over history also has a resource of mercy and love which overcomes the rebellion of human sin, without negating the distinctions between good and evil, which are the moral content of history. The revelations of God in history, are, in fact, according to the Biblical faith, evidences of a divine grace which both searches out the evil character of human sin and overcomes it.

These two aspects of the Christian faith must be explicated more fully in turn. Let us consider first the relation of memory to universal history. The most obvious basis of coherence for a particular "story" recorded in memory is simply the identity of the rememberer. I remember my own story of development from infancy to maturity and have a sense of an identical self moving through this development. Thus also a nation or tribe knows its own story and gives coherence to the various events of its history by the simple fact that these events are remembered as happening to it as tribe or nation. But this coherence is obviously minimal. Individuals and nations seek a deeper or higher dimension of meaning than the mere record of their continuance in time. They require some structure of meaning which will give various events a place in a comprehensive story. Invariably they select some particular events of their history as symbolic for their whole story, as giving the key for the comprehension of the whole. More specifically they endow some particular hero of their history with this revelatory function. Very frequently the hero is the "father" of the nation, the contriver of its unity, the victor over the foes of its infant strength. Naturally this hero is mythical or semi-mythical, not merely because he appears before scientific history is known, as Sargon in the Babylonian myths, or Romulus and Remus in the Roman myths of national genesis; but also because he must bear the entire structure of meaning. Thomas Masaryk and George Washington are "fathers" of their country in a late, rather than early, period of civilization. They are partly mythical figures even though the light of mature rather than infant memory illumines them, because the nation requires that they be symbolic of the whole structure of meaning by which it seeks to explain its history to itself. The significant figure need not belong to the nation's infancy. Lincoln has become for obvious reasons a more adequate symbol of the meaning of America's national existence than Washington. The symbol may also be an event rather than a person, as the granting of the Magna Carta in the history of modern democratic England.

Nations may be content to emphasize their historic continuity, without giving it a special meaning. The power of the dynastic principle is certainly partly derived from the need of nations to comprehend their continuity through the history of their dynasty. Yet nations generally seek to comprehend their story as something more than merely an unbroken continuity. They would like to believe that it "stands" for something beyond themselves, that it embodies an idea of "freedom" or "order," or some other value. These concepts of meaning usually do not break radically with the egocentricity of men and of nations. They are usually the basis for imperial pretensions. The nation which claims to embody values beyond its own life also claims the right to bestow these values upon others by its power.

The Biblical faith expresses a radical departure from both the high religions which can not incorporate history into the meaning of life and the low religions which can incorporate only the history of a tribe, nation or empire. Yet early Biblical history has many facets which relate it to lower particularistic religion. The canon of the faith contains an "Old Testament" in which we find the usual "story" of a particular people, seeking to comprehend their history in terms of their origin. Their God is the God of "Abraham, Isaac and Jacob," who seems to be, on some levels of their history, simply their champion against competitors and foes, both allowing and enjoining them to the most ruthless actions in order to encompass the defeat of the foe and to establish their own security.

The radically new dimension in this "story" of a people is that the God of this people is conceived, seemingly at the very beginning, as not their God but the God who singled them out for a special destiny. The "fact" of history by which they give meaning to their history is God's "covenant" with Israel, in which, by a special act of divine grace, this people is singled out for a special mission. The particular event which becomes the center of historical interpretation, from which history is finally interpreted backward to creation and forward to the messianic reign, is the Sinaitic covenant. God's promise to Abraham seems to be an even earlier beginning of the story, which may represent a different tradition or which may be the consequence of a natural inclination to trace the strand of meaning as far back as possible. There are never any absolutely new beginnings in history. Insofar as they are radically new, the historian, particularly the devout historian who is dealing with profound meanings, will look for an earlier beginning in order to place the crucial event in a larger setting.

At any rate the "covenant" is the point of remembrance in the history of a nation, which compels the nation, or the prophetic interpreters of the nation's mission and destiny, to envisage the total panorama of history. The prophetic movement in Israel explicates and enlarges the meaning of this covenant. This is done in such a way that one can never be quite certain whether the prophets explicated what was implicit in the covenant relation or enlarged the meaning in such a way that it was in their thought that it achieved its radical significance. The second interpretation of prophetism can not be completely valid because the covenant is presupposed in prophetic thought. The prophets could not have thought as they did without its presupposition. Insofar as the prophets clarified the idea of the covenant, "revelation" has a cultural and social history. Insofar as they explicated what was presupposed, revelation is a mystery, discerned by faith. It is the presupposition of cultural history in a religion rooted in such radical revelation.

While the destiny of Israel continues to remain in the center of the story, the prophets significantly enlarged the frame of history to include all national stories, the rise and fall of empires, and ultimately both the origin and the end of man's existence on this earth. Some prophets never freed themselves of the hope that the triumph of Israel over all its foes would be the climax of the whole story of mankind. That is a nice symbol of the fact that a religion, which breaks radically with particular and idolatrous conceptions of the meaning of life, can never carry through consistently what it has established in basic principle. Even a Christian missionary enterprise can never completely overcome certain imperialistic corruptions which arise from the historic relation of the missionary enterprise to particular powerful nations and cultures.

The prophetic explication of the original revelation, the first "covenant" moves by tortuous historical development toward the "second covenant," toward an event and a person in history, in which the destiny of a single nation is clearly transcended, and in terms of which other nations and peoples interpret, not their own story but the total story of mankind.

Prophetism moves toward that climax primarily through a consideration of the second great problem about the meaning of history: the problem of historical evil. Biblical faith is the apprehension of a God who is not the extension of a nation's power or the instrument of a nation's policy. He is, in fact, not known through the enlargement of any human value or virtue. The worship of this

God involves the disclosure of a corruption of evil in human life, which can be attributed neither to the sloth of nature nor to the defects of foe or competitor. It is in man in himself, and not in nature; and it is in all men, and not merely in the foe who challenges our life.

The prophets are more conscious of the sins of Israel than of the sins of other nations, precisely because of their confidence in Israel's special mission. Biblical faith finally interprets this evil as so universal a corruption of human freedom that it is symbolized as having infected the first man. Adam fell into evil when he refused to accept the limits which the Creator had set for his power and wisdom, and sought to be like God. Ever since men and nations have been prompted by pride to introduce the evils of contention and domination into the world. They have rent and torn the whole fabric of human togetherness because they made themselves the false centers of the whole of existence. These proud actions result in consequences which echo down the ages. The children suffer for the sins of the fathers, because generations are bound to each other in one unbroken chain of life.

The universality of this corruption of evil raises the question whether history has any moral meaning. Do not the strong men and nations regard their own will as the source of law and their own interests as the criterion of right? Is there any sovereignty over history strong enough to overcome this rebellion against the moral content of life? And is there any love great enough to give meaning to the life of the innocent victims of the cruelties and the contumelies of proud men and nations? These questions were asked more and more searchingly by the Old Testament prophets; and they looked for an answer to the questions in a future messianic reign.

The Christian faith begins with, and is founded upon, the affirmation that the life, death, and resurrection of Christ represent an event in history, in and through which a disclosure of the whole meaning of history occurs, and all of these questions are answered. The interpretation of history in the light of this event creates a structure of meaning in which the history of a particular nation, as the center of the whole of history is unequivocally transcended. This "second covenant" between God and His people is not between God and any particular people but with all those of any nation who are "called," that is, who are able to apprehend by faith that this person, drama and event of history discloses the power and the love which is the source and the end of the whole historical drama. Insofar as this is an event, the revelatory depth and height of which must be apprehended by faith, it is not the basis of a "philosophy of history" at which one might arrive by analyzing the sequences and recurrences, the structures and patterns of history. But insofar as history becomes meaningful by being oriented toward the revelation of this event, the event is the source of "wisdom" and of "truth."

The conception of a divine sovereignty over history which is not immediately apparent in the structures and recurrences of history establishes a dimension in which there can be meaning, though the facts of history are not related to each other in terms of natural or logical necessity. The freedom of God over and beyond the structures of life makes room for the freedom of man. All forms of naturalistic or spiritualistic determinism are broken. History is conceived meaningfully as a drama and not as a pattern of necessary relationships which could be charted scientifically. The clue to the meaning of the drama is in the whole series of revelatory events, "God's mighty acts," culminating in the climax of revelation in the life, death, and resurrection of Christ. In these mighty acts the mysterious design of the sovereignty which controls historical destiny is clarified.

The interpretation of history from the standpoint of this revelation leads to a full understanding of the reality of evil. Evil is a force within history itself and not the intrusion of the necessities of nature into the historical. The drama of history contains a subordinate conflict between good and evil forces in history. Ultimately the drama consists of God's contest with all men, who are all inclined to defy God because they all tend to make their own life into the center of history's meaning. An outer limit is set for this human defiance of the divine will by the fact that God's power, revealed in the structures of existence, leads to the ultimate self-destruction of forms of life which make themselves into their own end by either isolation or dominion. But it is not denied that any particular period of history is morally obscure because of the seeming impunity of the proud and the powerful who exploit the weak, and the general self-seeking of all men who defy the sovereignty of God. Ultimately this rebellion of man against God is overcome by divine power, which includes the power of the divine love. The "foolishness of the Cross" as the ultimate source of wisdom about life consists precisely in the revelation of a depth of divine mercy within and above the "wrath" of God. By this love God takes the evils and sins of man into and upon Himself. Whenever men penetrate through the illusions and self-deceptions of life to confront this God, as revealed in Christ, finding His judgment upon their sin not less but more severe, because of the disclosure of the love which prompts it, they may be converted and renewed. History is thus a realm of endless possibilities of renewal and rebirth. The chain of evil is not an absolute historical fate.

Yet even men and nations, thus redeemed, are never free of the taint of rebellion against God. Ultimately, therefore, only the divine forgiveness toward all men can overcome the confusion of human history and make this whole drama meaningful. According to the New Testament, men who are armed with this clue to the meaning of the whole of life and history will face all the future possibilities and perils of history without fear. They will not be surprised or dismayed by anything, knowing "that neither life nor death . . . will separate them from the love of God which is in Christ Jesus our Lord." The New Testament faith anticipates that man's defiance of God will reach the highest proportions at the end of history. Precisely in "the last days perilous times will come" when men shall be "lovers of their own selves, covetous, boasters, proud, blasphemers, disobedient to parents, unthankful, unholy . . . traitors, heady, high-minded, lovers of pleasure rather than lovers of God" (II Timothy 3:2, 4). This expectation of heightening forms of human defiance of God in history, which is also clearly expressed by Jesus himself in his warning of false Christs and false prophets (Matthew 24) is a symbol of the tremendously wide frame of meaning which the Christian faith has for the stuff of history. It envisages antinomies, contradictions, and tragic realities within the framework without succumbing to despair.

Life and history were understood in the western world within this framework for centuries after the Christian faith triumphed over classicism. This triumph did not take place without the incorporation of some classical elements into the structure of meaning; but it is beyond the scope of the present treatise to analyze these in detail. The Augustinian interpretation of history, upon which the dogmatic theological structure of medieval Christianity rests, did, for instance, exempt the church from the ambiguities and contradictions of history more absolutely than the prophets of Israel exempted their own nation. Thereby new errors were introduced into the interpretation of history. When the Reformation rejected this idolatry of the church it frequently slipped into an eschatology in which the meaning, given to life by God's final triumph over evil, was emphasized at the expense of the proximate and tentative meanings, arising from the renewal and the reconstruction of life at any point in history where the love and the power of God are acknowledged. Catholicism tended to interpret history statically from the standpoint of a supposed triumph over evil in the historic Christian community. The Reformation interpreted history dynamically but in negative terms. It lived in the expectation of the ultimate climax of history but was less able than Catholicism to impart meaning to the proximate tasks and fulfillments, judgments and renewals which occur in the drama.

But these particular differences and difficulties are of little moment in the present context. It is more important to note that any and all Christian interpretations of history were reduced to seeming irrelevance by currents of modern culture which had their rise in the Renaissance and which culminated in the eighteenth and nineteenth centuries. These currents of thought ostensibly rejected the Christian faith because its simple symbols did not correspond to the realities of nature or history, disclosed by the natural and historical sciences. But we can not understand the spiritual problem of our age if we fail to apprehend a profounder cause for the triumph of modern culture over the Christian faith. That cause was the introduction of a new and more plausible version of the classical idea of simple rational intelligibility as the key to historical meaning. The modern version was more plausible because it rested upon the new appreciation of the significance of time and the realization that there is actual growth and development in both nature and history. This new view of a moving, a growing, a developing world seemed to resolve every perplexity about life and to hold the promise of emancipation from every evil.

The temporal process itself ceased to be a mystery which required such explanations as either Aristotle or the Biblical concept of creation made. Natural causation and *durée* became, rather, the principle of explanation for life and history. The vast panorama of historical occurrences ceased to be a mystery, difficult to comprehend meaningfully because it contained a simple pattern of intelligibility. Amidst all the confusion of the rise and fall of empires, of civilizations and cultures, one clear pattern was discernible: history was the story of man's increasing power and freedom. The ambiguity of man's position as both a creature and creator of historical events ceased to be a problem because the historical process seemed to be moving toward man's emancipation from this ambiguity by endowing him with the freedom and the power of unambiguous mastery over his own destiny. The obscurity which evil introduces into history ceased to be a problem because modern culture returned to the classical view of evil as an intrusion of natural chaos into the rational ends of history; but, unlike classical culture, it found the possibilities of the growth of reason to be limitless. It therefore interpreted history as a movement toward the final triumph of rational order over the primitive chaos. Modern culture is always an essentially temporalized version of the classical answer to the problems of human existence. Anaxagoras had said: "In the beginning everything was in confusion; then Mind came and ordered the chaos." The modern version is: "In the beginning everything is in confusion; but Mind grows progressively to order the chaos."

We have already noted that the facts of contemporary experience are in glaring contradiction to this interpretation of history. The purpose of this treatise is to present the Christian interpretation of history in the light of this refutation through experience of modern views of history; and to reexamine the Christian view from the standpoint of what is true in the modern discovery of historical growth and development.

This apologetic task requires that the issue be joined not only with a secular culture, the hopes of which have proved illusory, but also with two contrasting versions of the Christian faith. One of these merely clothed the modern secular faith in traditional Christian phrases; and the other sought to prove the truth of the Christian faith by denying and defying the fact of development in nature and in history, which modern culture disclosed.

The prestige of the idea of salvation through history has been so great that the portion of the Christian church in most intimate contact with modern culture practically capitulated to the modern scheme of salvation, seeking to save the relevance of Christianity by making it appear to be an anticipation of the modern idea of progress. Since the Christian claim of a unique (*einmalig*) revelation is particularly embarrassing in an historical culture it was thought well to equate revelation with history (Herder); or to make history the bearer of progressive revelations (Ritschl); or to regard revelation as an anticipation of the truth to be found progressively by reason (Lessing); or to regard Christ as the religious symbol of history itself (Hegel); or to equate the record of revelation with the story of man's developing religious consciousness (Wellhausen). Christ became either the anticipation, the symbol, or the culmination of the growing spiritualization of religion and of human life. The whole unique Christian interpretation of the relation between the divine mystery and human life was thereby obscured. The Biblical idea that the vanity of the imagination of man, rather than the paucity of his intellectual faculties, is the primary veil between God and man also was rejected.

Modern liberal or "progressive" versions of the Christian faith were particularly embarrassed by the traditional Biblical-Christian doctrine of sin. This doctrine contained the belief that evil in human history was due to a corruption of human freedom and not to a "lag" of nature. It asserted that the corruption arose at the point of man's unwillingness to abide by the limits of his creaturely existence.

It was therefore a particularly inconvenient interpretation of evil in a culture which believed in the achievement of good through the unlimited extension of all human powers. But it could be reinterpreted to mean exactly what modern culture meant. A modern liberal theologian accomplishes the task of reinterpretation in this fashion: "Now we know that the natural impulses of man stem from brutal ancestry; and religion faces the Herculean task of making moral and spiritual ideals flourish above the beastly strain of savage blood, inherited, perhaps, from Neanderthal man." [8]

These modern forms of Christian apologetics disavowed every depth of meaning and every unique insight of the Christian faith which did not conform to the modern idea of redemption through history. They were content to teach the modern, rather than the Christian, faith if only they would be allowed to tell the story through the pictures and symbols, the concepts and images drawn from the ·Scripture, and tortured to yield the same plan of salvation in which the modern man already believed.

Actually the Biblical account of the human predicament and the Biblical answer to that predicament are not invalidated by the newly discovered fact of historical development. On the contrary, the Biblical faith penetrates to the ultimate issues of life in such a way that it reveals the modern scheme of salvation to be merely another of many efforts which men make to evade the embarrassing truth that they are themselves the authors of most of the evils from which they suffer.

It is as important to challenge the errors of an atrophied Christian orthodoxy as to refute the mistakes of a too compliant Christian liberalism. Christian faith is tempted more easily to cultural obscurantism than the less history-conscious faiths of the orient. The temptation arises from the fact that its symbols of the ultimate describe, not some eternal unity, devoid of the concrete and discordant stuff of temporal existence, but a transfiguration of history. A rationalistic age would have been impatient with the Christian truth in any event. That truth finds man's historic existence potentially meaningful but does not confine the meaning of life to

[8] Shirley Jackson Case, *Christian Philosophy of History*, p. 213.

that existence. This is not sufficiently neat for a culture which equates rational intelligibility with ultimate meaning. But the Christian truth was frequently made completely unavailable to modern men by a theological obscurantism which identified the perennially valid depth of Christian symbols with the pre-scientific form in which they were expressed.

Thus the idea of the divine creation of the world, which, when taken profoundly, describes the limits of the world's rationality and the inadequacy of any "natural" cause as a sufficient explanation for the irrational givenness of things, is frequently corrupted into a theory of secondary causation and thereby comes in conflict with a valid scientific account of causation on the natural level. This corruption of religion into a bad science has aroused the justified protest of a scientific age. It also helped to tempt science to become a bad religion by offering natural causation as an adequate principle of ultimate coherence.

Theological literalism also corrupts the difficult eschatological symbols of the Christian faith. In these the fulfillment of life is rightly presented, not as a negation but as a transfiguration of historical reality. If they are regarded as descriptions of a particular end in time, the real point of the eschatological symbol is lost. It ceases to symbolize both the end and the fulfillment of time, or to point to both the limit and the significance of historical development as the bearer of the meaning of life.

In the same manner a symbolic historical event, such as the "fall" of man, loses its real meaning when taken as literal history. It symbolizes an inevitable and yet not a natural corruption of human freedom. It must not, therefore, be regarded either as a specific event with which evil begins in history nor yet as a symbol of the modern conception of evil as the lag of nature and finiteness.

In a similar fashion the affirmation of the Christian faith that the climax of the divine self-revelation is reached in a particular person and a particular drama of his life, in which these particular events become revelatory of the meaning of the whole of life, is falsely rationalized so that the Jesus of history who is known as the Christ by faith, is interpreted as an inhuman and incredible personality with alleged powers of omniscience within the conditions of finiteness. In this way the ultimate truth about God and His relation to men, which can be appropriated only in repentance and faith, is made into a "fact" of history.

These errors of a literalistic orthodoxy tend to obscure the real issues between Christianity and modern culture as surely as the premature capitulation of liberal Christianity to modern culture. The Christian truth is presented as a "dated" bit of religious fantasy which is credible only to the credulous and which may be easily dismissed by modern man.

Christian theology has every reason to be humble when it considers the errors of cultural obscurantism which were allowed to confuse the issue between Christ and the religion which regards history itself as the redeemer. It is nevertheless the duty of the Christian church to penetrate to the profounder religious problem, which underlies the confusions in this modern debate, so that a world which is on the edge of despair may again hear the message of the Gospel and understand its saving power for man in any historic situation and more particularly in his present situation.

The truth of the Christian Gospel does not lie in the false absolutes with which fundamentalism seeks to defy the indubitable fact that both nature and human history are in process. Yet there is a perennially valid truth in the Gospel which clarifies a perennial human predicament and may redeem man from the constant tendency to aggravate his predicament by false efforts to escape from it. In order to state that truth with any degree of persuasiveness it is necessary to analyze the modern hope of redemption more carefully and to discover how such implausible hopes of redemption through historic process should have been generated by the indubitable evidence that all nature and all human life are subject to historic development.

CHAPTER III

Time as the Stage of History

I

THE drama of history is played upon the stage of time. All historical actions take place against the background of an inexorable forward movement from past to future. This flux of temporal events is a mystery beyond and behind the mystery and the meaning of history. "Stage" and "background" are only partially adequate symbols for depicting the relation of time to history. For time is both the stage and the stuff of history. Insofar as human agents have the freedom to stand above the flux of natural events and create forms and institutions not governed by natural necessity and not limited to the life spans of nature, time is the stage of history. Insofar as these human agents are themselves subject to natural flux and their historic achievements and institutions are also subject to decay and mortality (though possessing a longer life span than the vitalities of nature), time is part of the stuff of history. It is the woof of its fabric, and human freedom is the warp.

The relation of time to history makes history a double enigma. Behind its mystery and meaning is the mystery of time. The mystery and meaning of time is logically prior to the mystery and meaning of history; but chronologically the meaning of history becomes the object of human attention before the mystery of time is considered. Primitive totemism and the imperial religions of ancient civilizations

35

are religious efforts to grasp the meaning of the history of a tribe,
nation or empire. Chronologically the creation myths are late in the
history of culture.[1] They appear at the point where the interpretation of the life and history of a nation and empire becomes related to
a vaguely discerned universal history.

In Biblical religion the interpretation of the meaning of history is
also much older than the interpretation of time. The principle of
meaning for the history of the children of Israel is given by the idea
of God's covenant with Israel. The idea of a covenant between a
God who is not owned or chosen by Israel but who chooses Israel
contains the germs of a conception of universal history which the
prophets explicate. The ascription of the creation of the world to
this God is, however, a fairly late interest in prophetism. The Second
Isaiah is the first prophet to be particularly concerned to reinforce
the concept of the divine sovereignty over historical destiny with the
idea of the majesty of the divine Creator of the world (Isaiah 40–45).

In modern culture the idea of progress was substituted for the idea
of providence a full century before the concept of evolution was
substituted for the idea of creation. The historic development of
human institutions and the emergence of novelty in historic time was
more obvious and therefore more quickly discerned than the fact
that the forms of nature were also subject to temporal mutation. It
is significant, however, that the latter discovery placed the final seal
upon the idea of a progressive history just as the concept of the
divine creation of the world finally established the faith in a divine
sovereignty over historical destiny in prophetism.

The question about time is how change is related to the changeless. The problem of history is how the freedom of human agents
is related to the changes of history which are beyond the power of
the human will. Without a discernible relation of change to the

---

[1] In Egypt a fully developed creation myth appears first in the Memphite
theology in which creation is ascribed to Ptah, the earth-god. Creation is
viewed as a "spiritual act" and "divinity is recognized beyond and not in the
phenomena." H. Frankfort, *Ancient Egyptian Religion*, p. 23.

The Babylonian creation epic of the seventh century B.C. describes the divine
creation of the world out of a primeval chaos (Tiamat). God is the artificer
who fashions primeval stuff in the usual early concepts of creation.

changeless the temporal mutations which furnish the woof of the fabric of history would be pure caprice; and human thought and action are not possible in chaos but only in a system of coherence. Without some relation between human freedom and the inexorable changes of history, human action would result in caprice and chaos in history. Thus the power or the order which informs natural change is recognized to be the clue to the enigma of the relation of historic changes through human action to natural and inexorable changes. The problem of Providence represents the more perplexing enigma because it is concerned with the paradoxical relation of human freedom to that which is beyond the power of the human will. But the history of culture proves that every effort to solve it must penetrate to the mystery of Creation. Human freedom makes history into something more than natural time. But the mystery of time underlies the mystery of history.

We are seeking in this treatise to understand how modern culture could have arrived at so dubious a conclusion, that history is the solution of all human problems, from so indubitable a fact, that both nature and human institutions are subject to temporal development. This analysis requires that we inquire into the conception of time which informs modern ideas of history and compare this modern idea of time with the classical and the Christian view of time and creation. In brief summary the situation is this: classical culture regarded neither time nor history as self-explanatory. Time was made intelligible in terms of its relation to a world of changeless forms; and history was made intelligible by its unqualified identification with natural time. In modern culture both time and history are regarded as self-explanatory. They do not require explanation but become the principle of explanation by which life is given meaning. The affinity between modern culture and classicism lies in their common belief in the simple intelligibility of time and history. The profound difference between them lies in the fact that modern culture finds time and history to be self-explanatory while classical culture can make them intelligible only with reference to a world of changelessness.

Christian faith finds neither time nor history self-explanatory.

The mystery of divine Providence gives meaning to history and the mystery of creation gives meaning to time. Christian faith distinguishes itself from both classical and modern culture by discerning mystery, and finding no simple intelligibility, in either time or history. It distinguishes itself from classical culture by making a sharp distinction between history and time, regarding historical time as moving toward a significant future rather than being involved merely in the recurrences of natural time. In this emphasis Christian faith has an affinity with the modern sense of history. It is indeed the soil out of which the modern historical consciousness grew. It distinguishes itself from modern culture (and has some affinities with classical culture) in its belief that both time and history point beyond themselves to a more ultimate source of meaning.

II

The approach of the classical world toward both time and history is determined by the profound metaphysical impulse to resolve life's mysteries into rational intelligibility. Beginning with Parmenides this impulse toward intelligibility takes the form of seeking to penetrate through the world of contingency and change to the realm of Being. Only this world of Being is real, for it alone is intelligible, for, in the words of Parmenides, "thinking and being are one and the same." Parenthetically it may be remarked that when being is abstracted from becoming it stands on the abyss of non-being, a fact which persuaded Hegel to invent a dialectic in order to comprehend the world of becoming as rational because it embodied being and non-being in a synthesis. For classical culture the world of change and becoming was intelligible and real insofar as it participated in the changeless world through a cycle of changeless recurrence. For it time is the cycle of "coming to be and falling-away," of birth and death, of growth and decay. Aristotle defined the relation of time to eternity in terms which became authoritative for the whole of classical culture: "Coming to be and passing away will, as we have said, always be continuous and will never fail. . . . For in all things, as we affirm, nature strives after 'the better.' Now 'being' is better than 'not-being'; but not all things can possess being, since they are too far away from the 'originative source.' God therefore adopted the remaining alternative and fulfilled the perfection of the universe by making coming-to-be uninterrupted; for the greatest possible coherence would thus be secured to existence because 'coming-to-be' should itself come to be uninterruptedly in closest possible approximation to eternal being." [2]

There is a subordinate thesis in classical culture that the world of change gradually falls into decay, or into non-being through the cycles of coming to be and falling away. "For the ancients," declares Bergson, "time is theoretically negligible because the duration of a thing only manifests the degradation of its essence." [3] Combined with Christian pessimism this thought became determinative for the interpretation of history in the later Middle Ages. It furnished the primary target for the rising historical optimism of modern culture.[4] But the dominant conception of the classical world is the cyclical interpretation of time. In Plato's thought the cycle of growth and decay of sensible things is determined by their participation in the changeless forms which are their real being. "These ideas," in the words of Bergson, "Aristotle rolled into a ball and set above the physical world a Form that was found to be the Form of Forms, the Idea of Ideas, or to use his own words, the Thought of Thought, in other words God." [5]

The rational intelligibility of the world of change through its participation in the changeless world is reinforced by Plato's faith that the universe is filled with every conceivable kind and form of living thing, required to explicate the goodness of God. Thus the irrationality of the givenness of things is completely overcome and all things are brought into the realm of the rationally intelligible.

The Greek concept of rational causation is, in effect, a rationalized

<hr />

[2] *De generatione et corruptione*, 336b, pp. 25-35.
[3] Henri Bergson, *Creative Evolution*, p. 342.
[4] *Cf.* George Hakewill, *An Apologie or Declaration of the Power of God in the Government of the World, consisting in an examination of and censure of the common error concerning nature's perpetual and universal decay* (1627-35). *Cf.* also John B. Bury, *The Idea of Progress,* Chs. 1 and 2.
[5] Bergson, *ibid.*, p. 323.

version of those creation myths in which the divine creator is conceived as the artificer who forms some given stuff already to hand. While Greek naturalism regarded natural causation as a sufficient principle of explanation, the main current of classical thought found the creative source of sensible things in the form and structure, in the *Nous* or *Logos* which forms chaos into order and gives the unformed matter or *Hyle* its form. This version of the creation of the temporal world makes the sensible world intelligible by reason of its relation to the world of eternal forms; which means it is not intelligible in and of itself. Thus the mystery of creation or of the relation of time to eternity is banished. In this simply intelligible world the mystery of *dynamis,* of the propulsive force from past to future, is obscured and the question of the origin of the stuff which is formed by *Nous* is left unanswered.

The conception of time as a cycle of recurrence excludes the emergence of novelty in the world. God as Prime Mover is required to explain the world of movement and change; but the temporal process makes eternal potencies actual in endless recurrence. Aristotle does not deny the emergence of contingent elements in the temporal order; but these are not subject to scientific knowledge. Only that which is necessary is subject to such knowledge; and the necessary, according to Aristotle, "must be cyclical—i.e. must return upon itself. . . . It is in circular movement and cyclical coming-to-be that the 'absolutely necessary' is to be found. . . . For since the revolving body is always setting something else in motion, the movement of the things it moves must also be circular." [6]

Greek naturalism had a different conception of cause, but not of time, than Plato and Aristotle. "Nothing new happens in the universe," declared Epicurus, "if you consider the infinite time past." [7] The Roman naturalist, Lucretius, had the same view; and related his cyclical conception to his proof for the finite character of the physical world. "Since I see the chiefest members and parts of the world are destroyed and begotten anew," he wrote, "I may be sure that for heaven and earth as well there has been a time of beginning

[6] *De generatione et corruptione,* 338a, 5—338b, 3.
[7] *Fragments,* 55.

and a time of destruction." [8] Lucretius, incidentally, traced the development of mankind from barbarism to civilization in what would seem to constitute the frame of a progressive view of history. But his knowledge of actual historical developments did not break his cyclical concepts of history. Thus also the historian Thucydides pictured the history of Athens in a provisionally progressive frame; but the decay of Athens prompted a return to the cyclical view. Thus the classical conception of time determines the classical view of history even though the emergence of novelty in history came to be known while the emergence of novelty in nature remained unknown.

The Stoic view did not depart from the general classical pattern. "The rational soul," wrote Marcus Aurelius, "wanders round the whole world and through the encompassing void and gazes on infinite time and considers the periodic destructions and rebirths of the universe and reflects that our posterity will see nothing new and that our ancestors saw nothing that we have not seen." [9]

III

It was Christian faith rather than modern science which first breached the classical conception of time. But there will be value in ignoring chronology for the moment to consider the modern view of time in terms of its affinities with and its sharp contrast to the classical view. The modern and the classical view of time have a common desire to render the temporal process rationally intelligible while the Biblical faith seeks to understand it from the standpoint of the mystery of creation. In classical thought the temporal process is made intelligible through its relation to the eternal world. In modern thought it is presumably self-explanatory. The radical contrast between the two views lies in the modern emphasis upon the emergence of novelty in both the historical and the natural process, leading to the conviction that "duration means the invention and creation of forms, the continual elaboration of the absolutely new." [10]

The discovery of new emergents was first apparent in the historical

[8] *On The Nature of Things*, Book v, 240.
[9] *Meditations*, xi 1.
[10] Bergson, *ibid.*, p. 11.

process. When natural science discovered that natural forms were also subject to mutation it seemed that the keystone for the arch of a new temple of meaning for life and history had been placed.

The modern view is distinguished from the classical conception in its belief that time and the world of change are not mysteries which require explanation by reference to a changeless world but are, rather, the clue to the mystery of the origin and the end of life. It is profoundly related to the classical world in its conception of a rationally intelligible world from which mystery is banished.

The mystery of *Genesis* and creation is solved by the general confidence, induced by the prestige of the natural sciences, in natural causation as a sufficient explanation of all phenomena appearing in the temporal process. Modern culture is not consistently naturalistic; but the tremendous achievement of modern science in tracing the natural or "secondary" causes of the phenomena of nature and history creates a general inclination to regard the temporal process as self-explanatory, which means to regard the natural cause of a subsequent event as a sufficient explanation of the new occurrence.[11]

[11] Sir Edmund Whitaker describes this modern development as consisting in dropping "the material, formal and final causes [of Aristotle], of which indeed most of the modern physicists have never heard, and taking the word *cause* to mean what Aristotle had called efficient cause." "This would be typically represented by a dynamic force acting on a particle at a point." *Space and Spirit*, p. 87.

J. L. Stocks makes the same point: "The efficient cause," he writes, "may still perhaps be distinguished at least in academic circles which defer to the old tradition, from formal, material and final cause; but in fact these other three applications are felt to be archaic and artificial. When cause was used without qualification in what was felt as its proper and natural sense it was used of an event which made possible or necessary a subsequent event." *Time, Cause and Eternity*, p. 35.

The general tendencies in modern thought are most accurately described by Jean Wahl: "Surveying the history of the idea of causality from Aristotle to Kant and Comte, we may say that at first (with Aristotle) there were four causes; then there were, with the classical conceptions of Descartes, Leibnitz, and Spinoza, two causes, the formal and the efficient, united as closely as possible; and then in the third stage there remained only one cause, the efficient cause, more rationally founded with Kant and more empirically founded with Comte and the empiricists. . . . The history of the philosophical theory of causality is the history of a diminishing number of causes and finally even the vanishing idea of cause. . . . The nineteenth century witnessed the replacement of the idea of cause by the idea of law, of necessary conditions and of functional relations." *The Philosopher's Way*, p. 111.

The inclination of modern culture to exalt time into the position of God, by making it the clue to the mystery of existence, is most consistently expressed by Bergson. He criticizes modern science as a modified form of Aristotelianism because of its interest in causes. This error, in Bergson's opinion, is due to a "cinematographic view" of the whole complex interwovenness of moving reality through which transient forms are given the appearance of permanence. Actually, according to Bergson, it is the movement, *durée* itself, which is the clue to the mystery of life. This reality can not be penetrated by physics but only "by a second type of knowledge" which would "transport us by an effort of sympathy into the inwardness of becoming." If such knowledge "were to succeed it would be reality itself which it would clasp in its final embrace." [12] The sense of religious awe before the divine is explicit. Thus the conception of time as God undergirds the conception of history as redeemer in modern thought.

A consistent naturalism and a Bergsonian worship of *duré* represent the most typical but not the only modern attitudes toward time. The Hegelian attitude toward the temporal and historical process is governed by a frame of thought in which Christian and classical concepts are related to, but not annulled, by the modern temper. In Hegel's thought time is not God; but God requires time to become truly God, i.e. to achieve self-conscious freedom. Thus the time process is not self-explanatory but requires the presupposition of what Whitehead has defined as the "primordial" God. But God is himself altered by the temporal process, so that the true nature of God can be understood only in terms of the end as well as the genesis of the temporal process. The real God is the "consequent God." Frequently in modern forms of idealism the temporal growth of God is described as the increasing power of Mind over mechanism. Thus L. T. Hobhouse is "led to conceive the world process as a development of organic harmony through the extension and control of Mind, operating under mechanical conditions, which it comes by degrees to master." [13]

---

[12] Bergson, *ibid.*, p. 342.
[13] *Development and Purpose*, p. 372.

This is clearly a new temporal version of the old classical concept of the creative power of *Nous* over chaos. The emphasis is not upon the mystery of new emergents in history but upon the gradual sub-jugation of the chaos of conflicting mechanisms to the more in-clusive purposes of mind. Hobhouse's conceptions are clearly drawn from the study of history rather than nature. God's growing mind is obviously the counterpart of the growing "mind of humanity" which, "grasping the conditions of its own development and the true goal of its actions, opened to itself the prospect of dominating the actual future of the race and securing the harmony which is its ideal." [14]

The growth which gives meaning to both the natural and the historical process is the growth of reason. The process is thus reduced to rational intelligibility; and two further mysteries are also resolved. The mystery of evil is resolved by the supposition that it represents life's and nature's provisional fragmentariness and that the growth of reason gradually overcomes all that is contradictory and at cross purposes in nature or history.

The mystery of the end of the process is also resolved. The end of the time process is the triumph of *Nous* over chaos. There are versions of the modern trust in time in which the end is the only remaining mystery. In S. Alexander's *Space, Time and Deity* the real God, i.e. the real principle of meaning for life, is obviously the process itself. Yet Alexander defines God as the mystery of the culmination of the process. "Deity," he declares, "is the next higher empirical quality to mind which the universe is engaged in bring-ing to birth. That the universe is pregnant with such a quality we are speculatively assured. . . . Deity is the quality which attends upon or, more strictly, is equivalent to, previous or lower existences of the order of mind, which itself rests upon a lower basis of qualities and emerges when certain complexities and refinements and arrange-ments have been reached." [15] Alexander's god as *Omega* stands in nice contrast to the *Alpha* of Aristotle's Prime Mover. In one case

[14] *Ibid.*, p. 370.
[15] *Space, Time and Deity*, II, p. 347.

everything is intelligible except the beginning; and in the other case everything is intelligible except the end.

André Gide's non-philosophical espousal of the creed propounded by Alexander proves, however, that the God of the end or Whitehead's consequent God is not easily avowed without implying the primordial God. Gide confesses in his journals: "If I had to formulate a credo I would say: God is not behind us. He is to come. He must be sought not at the beginning but at the end of evolution. He is terminal, not initial. He is the supreme and final point toward which all nature tends in time." But Gide inadvertently invokes the "primordial" God even as he tries to center his thought upon the "consequent" God. For he continues: "Since time does not exist for him it is a matter of indifference to him whether the evolution of which he is the summit, follows or precedes and whether he determines it by propulsion or attraction." [16]

These various interpretations reveal that modern culture, despite its diversities, has a common confidence in the temporal process as that which gives meaning to our existence. Insofar as God is what we must certainly rely upon, it is time that is God. But they also reveal that it is not quite as simple to reduce meaning to rational intelligibility as is assumed in the most consistent naturalism. There is always a mystery of origin or end, of *Alpha* or *Omega* which obtrudes. The philosophies which are most directly under the scientific interest in tracing particular causes can banish mystery by dealing only with particular causal sequences and relationships, which science is able to trace. But if they are consistent they are also pluralistic, making no claims to an adequate account of the whole complex interwovenness of moving reality. They renounce the final mystery behind every problem of meaning by raising no ultimate questions. If, as in the case of Bergson, they seek to grasp the meaning of the whole, the time process itself becomes a mystery which must be mystically, rather than scientifically, apprehended. If, as in the case of the Hegelians, a primordial mystery is acknowledged but the temporal process is reduced to logical intelligibility, it is pre-

[16] *The Journals of André Gide*, Vol. II, p. 122.

sumed to end in a triumph of mind which is in glaring contradiction to the known facts of history. If, as in the case of Alexander and Gide, mystery is reserved for the end, it is impossible to express such a conception without resorting to the presupposition of the primordial God. Thus time proves itself an inadequate divinity, a simple intelligible principle of meaning, even if we did not have empirical evidence that history is an inadequate Christ or redeemer.

IV

From the standpoint of either classical or modern culture the Biblical idea of the creation of the world by God's almighty word is a dated bit of religious fantasy which served mankind tolerably well until the intellect became sufficiently discerning to fashion concepts of rational and natural causation. Actually belief in divine creation points to a realm of mystery which is at once the beginning and the end of any system of meaning and which prevents it from being reduced to a too simple system of rational intelligibility. The inadequacy of such systems of intelligibility become particularly apparent when the history of man, which developes on the stage of time, is interpreted through such systems. For classical thought reduces it too simply to natural recurrence and modern thought is betrayed into utopian illusions about history.

In Biblical thought God is not, however, pure mystery. There is a provisional and residual mystery in the divine. But God makes Himself known. His sovereignty over history is disclosed in specific events and acts which are revelatory of the meaning of the whole process. But these revelations of sovereignty presuppose the divine power over the whole created world; and in the Biblical idea of the world's creation by God the emphasis is upon mystery. It calls attention to a depth of reality where mystery impinges upon meaning. The Biblical idea of God's relation to the world through His being the Creator is a necessary presupposition for the whole Christian view of life and history. The concept of creation establishes a necessary distinction between the derived and underived world. It agrees with classical, as against modern, thought that the temporal process is not self-derived, self-explanatory or self-fulfilling. It recognizes a depth of mystery of creation within and above the chain of natural causation. But unlike classical thought it does not regard the temporal world as merely a corruption of the eternal world. The God of Biblical faith includes *Logos* and is manifested in form and structure. But he is power as well as form and structure. Thus the forms and structures of the world cease to be the final clue to the mystery of life. Being sensible of a mystery of creation beyond mind and *Logos*, the Christian view does not lead to the premature deification of mind. Thereby it escapes both the classical and the modern error of regarding the source of evil as residing in the recalcitrance of the mechanisms, the passions, the necessities and the limitations of matter or of the physical. This difference becomes of tremendous importance in the analysis of historical evil. For both classical and modern culture equate evil with finiteness; and modern culture erroneously believes that the extension of rational freedom gradually overcomes historic evil.

While the Biblical idea of creation did not anticipate the modern discovery of the emergence of novelty in time, it is actually much more compatible with the view of an evolutionary process than the Greek concept of temporal recurrence. This compatibility was unfortunately obscured both by the theological obscurantism which used the Biblical idea of creation to refute the indubitable discoveries of modern science in the field of natural causation and by the theological liberalism which simply equated God with the evolutionary process.

The creation myths of Genesis, undoubtedly related in some way to the Babylonian creation epic, do not depart from the general character of the creation myths of early religion. They assume a primitive chaos ("the earth was without form, and void" Genesis 1:2) which is formed by God's creative word. But prophetic thought, particularly that of the Second Isaiah, interprets the mystery of the divine creation more ultimately. God is no longer the artificer who forms the formless stuff. He is the source of every aspect of existence. In the words of Psalm 104, "God laid the foundations of the earth" and is not merely the former of its formless stuff. Ultimately Christian theology elaborated the logic of this idea into the concept of creation *ex nihilo*. The assertion that God created the world out of nothing is a logically absurd concept which calls attention to the limits of rationality in dealing with the mystery of origin. It is not in conflict with the slogan of science: *ex nihilo nihil fit*. For that slogan emphasizes the chain of natural causation within the temporal process, while the Christian concept of creation *ex nihilo* calls attention to the fact that the temporal process is not self-explanatory, though there are always particular explanations for particular events. The two ideas are not contradictory but complementary, provided one understands that the concept *ex nihilo* marks the limits of rationality and is the dividing line between intelligibility and mystery. "The idea of creation," declares Erich Frank, in one of the most illuminating studies of the relation of religious to scientific ideas, "does not infringe upon the precincts of natural science. It is a religious idea and its realm is so far remote from that of science that a confusion of the two spheres would endanger not only scientific understanding but religious truth as well. . . . This religious idea, though it can not be defined in its positive content, is all the more important as a negative concept, as a philosophical warning that nothing in the world should be considered absolute. For if we assume that the world and man are created by God, neither the world nor man can be independent in their existence, but must be relative, contingent, and accidental. In other words they can not have their origin or meaning within themselves." [17]

Though the idea of creation is not in conflict with any scientific account of natural causation, which accurately describes the relation of an antecedent cause to a subsequent event, yet without the idea the antecedent cause tends falsely to become the sufficient cause of the subsequent event. This logic, when consistent, would exclude precisely the emergence of the novel in time, which it has been the achievement of modern culture to discern. "We must provide," declares Whitehead, "a ground for the limitation which stands

[17] *Philosophical Understanding and Religious Truth*, pp. 56–58. Used by permission of Oxford University Press.

among the attributes of substantial activity. This attribute provides the limitation for which no reason can be given, for all reasons flow from it. God is the ultimate limitation and His existence the ultimate irrationality." [18] It is only from the standpoint of this faith in the divine creation of the world that the world can be comprehended as meaningful without giving the structures and coherences by which it is made intelligible a false absoluteness and without regarding the irrationality of the givenness of things as proof of their illusoriness.

Professor Lovejoy in his searching analysis of the thesis of the world's rational intelligibility in both its classical and its modern versions, arrives at the conclusion that the history of the idea "is the history of a failure. . . . The experiment, taken as a whole, constitutes one of the most grandiose enterprises of the human intellect. But as the consequences of this most persistent and most comprehensive of hypotheses became more and more explicit, the more apparent became the difficulties; and when they were fully drawn out they showed the hypothesis of the absolute rationality of the cosmos to be unbelievable." [19]

Professor Lovejoy does not seek to account for the remarkable persistence of the thesis of the world's rational intelligibility. But it is not too difficult to see in this effort a typical instance of man's tendency to overreach the limits of his powers and thereby to obscure the ambiguity of his situation as both a creature of time and a creator of history in time. Insofar as he transcends the temporal process he can discern many meanings in life and history by tracing various coherences, sequences, causalities and recurrences through which the events of history are ordered. But insofar as man is himself in the temporal process which he seeks to comprehend, every sequence and realm of coherence points to a more final source of meaning than man is able to comprehend rationally.

Thus it is possible to trace the temporal process back to God's creation; but it is not possible, as Christian theology frequently attempts, to begin with God and to prove rationally that His good-

[18] Alfred N. Whitehead, *Science and the Modern World*, p. 249.
[19] Arthur O. Lovejoy, *The Great Chain of Being*, p. 329.

ness or His power or His love require that He create the world. Augustine seeks to comprehend the antinomies and contradictions which arise from such efforts, but finally gives up. He asserts "that we can reasonably say that there was another time when this time was not; but the merest simpleton could not say that there was a time when there was no time." The Lordship of God requires, for Augustine, that God be Creator eternally. "For if we point to a time when the works of God were begun it would be believed that He considered His past eternal leisure to be inert and indolent." Augustine thus asserts that, "if God has always been Lord He has always had creatures under His dominion." It would thus appear that creation was necessary for the perfection of God. But Augustine ultimately retreats from this effort to make mystery intelligible and humbly confesses: "If I make this reply to those who demand to know how He was always Lord and always creator, if there were not always a subject creation, and how this was created and not rather co-eternal with its creator . . . I fear I may be accused of recklessly affirming what I know not instead of teaching what I know." [20]

Thomas Aquinas is less circumspect. He boldly asserts on the one hand that the goodness of God is self-sufficient and does not require the creation for its perfection: "Since the goodness of God is perfect and can exist without other things, inasmuch as no perfection can accrue to Him from them, it follows that for Him to will things other than Himself is not absolutely necessary." Yet He does "will things other than Himself insofar as they are ordered to His own goodness as their end." [21] And it would seem from many assertions in Aquinas that he wills them "necessarily" even though the necessity is one which springs from his own nature.[22]

There is no rational solution for this problem. Its difficulties mark the limit between rational intelligibility and mystery when man seeks to reach beyond the bounds of his own finiteness.

[20] *De civitate Dei,* Bk. XII, 15 and 16.
[21] *Summa theol.,* I, Quest. 19.3.
[22] Whether and to what extent a contradiction is involved here has been exhaustively debated by Arthur O. Lovejoy and Anton N. Pegis in *Philosophy and Phenomenological Research,* September, 1948.

V

The significance of the realm of mystery which stands at both the beginning and the end of man's effort to comprehend the coherences and sequences of his world rationally, has been discredited in an age of science. Such an age naturally assumes that man's capacity to chart the scientifically observable structures and coherences of nature proves his ability to give a simple rational answer to the problem of the meaning of his existence. But it must be noted also that the response of faith to the realm of mystery and meaning has also been discredited by the general idea of a progressive development of culture in which faith preceded philosophy as philosophy preceded science. The idea of progress seemed to have invalidated faith, and any of the meaning of life which faith discerns, simply because there is a development in history from religion to metaphysics and from metaphysics to science. Auguste Comte's description of the three ages of the world, the theological, the metaphysical and the scientific, correctly traces a general movement in the history of culture; for religion is the mother of metaphysics as metaphysics is the mother of science. But the value judgments in Comte's scheme are as mistaken as they are typical of the mood of modern culture. Comte assumes, as does modern culture generally, that theology fumbles incoherently for the truth, that metaphysics subjects the irrational notions of theology to rational analysis and thus acts as a midwife for the birth of science which traces all the world's coherences empirically and thus gives a final authoritative account both of the meaning of the whole and of the relation of all the parts.

The whole temper and mood of a progressive and history-minded culture naturally prompts it to believe that the final fruit of a culture must be the profoundest expression of it. This is a very dubious conclusion. It may be just as important to move back from the sophistication of maturity to the naïveté of childhood for the sake of achieving the highest wisdom, as to move from the naïveté of childhood to the sophistication of maturity.

Unquestionably the notions of primitive religion are naïve. They do not comprehend life or the world in any great breadth of meaning or coherence. They establish little realms and structures of coherence with some little idolatrous center of meaning as god. But there is depth in these structures of meaning, if not breadth. The simplest animism is seeking to comprehend the relation of the human world to the world of nature; and the most primitive totemism, in seeking to comprehend the meaning of a tribe's or clan's history, has some dark awareness of a power more potent than human decisions being operative in it.

Gradually these little islands of meaning are related to larger and larger realms of coherence. Man's growing reason insists on great and greater consistency in relating realms of supernal mystery to each other and to the structures of coherence which are empirically observed in nature and in history. This is the movement toward breadth which broadly characterizes the metaphysical impulse, and which moves toward a monistic and comprehensive system of intelligibility. It is on the whole a rational movement, though it must be noted that the rigorous monotheism of the Hebrew prophets exploits resources within religion itself while Greek monism is primarily a rational achievement, which gradually overcomes the inconsistencies of contradictory interpretations of life's and the world's coherence by the power of logic.

The scientific impulse to find particular causes for particular phenomena, and to analyze the detailed coherences of nature and history by empirical observation is inherent in and dependent upon the philosophical search for "first principles"; but it can not be denied that, on the whole, it flowers later. If Aristotle embodied both impulses most perfectly in classical culture and laid the foundation for modern science in many a shrewd scientific observation, it is true, nevertheless, that only modern culture developed the scientific disciplines in their fullest scope. The general consequence of scientific analysis is to add detail to the depth and breadth of previous culture. Sometimes the analysis of detailed coherences, empirically observed, changes the picture of the whole. The modern conceptions of time and history, for instance, are primarily the products of empirical observation. The idea of evolution is the fruit of science and not of philosophy or religion, though it may be questioned if it could have arisen if a religion with an affirmative attitude toward history had not laid the foundation for it. But usually scientific observation fills in the picture, previously outlined. It may well be that, even as modern historical consciousness required the soil of a prophetic-Christian attitude toward history, so also modern science required an attitude toward nature which could be furnished only by the Christian idea of creation. For that idea made it possible to view nature as neither divine nor corrupt; and therefore as subject to analysis without the danger of impiety on the one hand and as worthy of analysis on the other.

But the dependence of science upon previous philosophical and religious foundations is only a part of the situation obscured by the modern confidence in science as the profoundest, because it is the latest, fruit of culture. The other part is the tendency of a culture preoccupied with detailed analysis to obscure the ultimate issues of life and to give shallow answers to ultimate questions. One need enumerate only a few of the illusions of a scientific culture to illustrate the point. Does it not incline to interpret the penumbra of mystery which surrounds every realm of meaning as nothing but the residual ignorance which the advancing frontiers of scientific knowledge will gradually obliterate? Does it not thereby obscure the ambiguity of the human situation? Does it not incline to build metaphysical systems upon the erroneous confidence in natural cause as the final and adequate principle of meaning? Are not the historical sciences easily persuaded that the frameworks of meaning which they use as a loom upon which to weave the detailed facts of history into a pattern are the consequence, rather than the presupposition, of their scientific pursuit? And do not the various sciences, pretending to be presuppositionless, insinuate metaphysical presuppositions into their analyses which are most congenial to the type of reality subject to their analysis? Do they not therefore require the criticism of wider philosophical disciplines?

These inadequacies suggest that there must be a movement from science to philosophy to counteract the movement from philosophy to science. In the same manner when philosophy approaches the ultimate issues of life and finds itself incapable of overcoming the ultimate ambiguities of human existence, it is forced to recognize the realm of mystery as both the fulfillment and negation of the realm of meaning and to acknowledge the function of faith as both the fulfillment and the negation of reason.

It is as true of the kingdom of truth as of the kingdom of heaven that "except we be as little children" we can not enter therein. It is the illusion of a progressive culture that the movement from childhood toward maturity is always a movement toward larger life and profounder wisdom. That movement is actually toward both life—and death. Death in the realm of culture means a sophistication which either loses interest in the ultimate issues of life because of a too great preoccupation with immediate issues, or, even worse, which imagines that a cumulation of detailed answers to detailed questions solves the ultimate issues of life.

There is, of course, no easy road from maturity back to childhood. A too simple return to the innocency of childhood results in obscurantism in the realm of culture and social primitivism in the realm of man's moral life. Yet the return is both possible and necessary.

The way to it lies in a wisdom which recognizes the limits of human knowledge and a humility which knows the limits of all human powers.

CHAPTER IV

~~~~~~

Similarities and Differences between Classical and Modern Ideas of Meaning in History

I

HISTORY is the fruit and the proof of man's freedom. Historical time is to be distinguished from natural time by the unique freedom which enables man to transcend the flux of time, holding past moments in present memory and envisaging future ends of actions which are not dictated by natural necessity. History is organically related to natural time insofar as man is involved in the natural flux and does not rise above it. All the structures of history are a complex unity of the natural and the spiritual, even as individual man exhibits this unity. History is thus a proof of the creatureliness of man as well as of his freedom.

Man's freedom over time, exhibited in his memory of past events and his desires and ambitions beyond the present moment, results in historical structures and configurations, institutions and cultures which, though subject to mortality, have a longer life span than the organisms of nature. The freedom of human agents in the temporal process creates novelties of such dimension and at such a tempo as to distinguish historical change radically from the slow mutations of forms known in nature. It also creates a new dimension of causality of endless complexity and depth. To the degree that men are not free, their actions, both individual and collective, may be predicted with something of the assurance with which a natural scientist charts the recurrences of nature. Insofar as they are free, causal sequences

55

in history reach a height and complexity in which the full understanding of the character of an event would require the knowledge of the secret motive of the agent of the action. History is thus comprised of causalities and sequences, coherences and structures which are not easily comprehended as meaningful. They are too varied and unique to fit into any simple pattern of meaning. The freedom of the human agents of action results in diverse and novel modes of behavior and action which make scientific generalizations, based upon the observation of recurrence, much more dubious and hazardous than the generalizations which constitute the stuff of natural science.

The ultimate question raised by the facts of freedom and necessity in history is how human freedom is related to the patterns and structures of historical existence. If human freedom were absolute, human actions would create a realm of confusion. If the patterns and structures, whether natural or historical, were absolute, human freedom would be annulled. The uniqueness of human freedom makes it impossible to regard the structures and sequences of pure nature as the basis of the pattern of meaning for life. But where then is the center of meaning to be found for both individual life and for the total human enterprise? It is because the answer to this question is so difficult and extends the bounds of meaning from the confines of the simply intelligible to the realm of mystery that both classical and modern naturalism have sought to confine the meaning of human existence rigorously to the realm of nature. If this procedure is carried through rigorously, as in classical naturalism, the freedom of man is annulled and all characteristically human desires and ambitions are regarded as aberrations. If it is not carried through rigorously, as it is not in modern history-minded naturalism, an endless confusion results about what is "natural" and what is "human."

The simple alternative to the effort to confine human life and ambitions to the limits of nature is to make reason itself the principle of its meaning. The assumption which underlies this solution is that the freedom which lifts man above the level of natural necessity also contains a higher principle of order within itself. This con-

fidence in the inherent rationality of human freedom, this certainty
that the realm above natural necessity is inevitably a realm of a
wider and more inclusive harmony, prevents both classical and
modern rationalism from taking the evil, which occurs in human
history, seriously.

The difficulty with this confidence is that men, in the unity of
their freedom and finiteness, are something more and something less
than *Nous* or *Logos;* and the something more or less which they
are is intimately and organically related to the processes of
their mind. Insofar as human selfhood is something more than mind,
man may use his freedom to defy the canons of logic. Insofar as he
is something less, man is involved in the processes of nature which
he seeks to comprehend rationally.

Man transcends nature, time and history sufficiently to be able
to develope rational structures of meaning for his individual and
collective life. But insofar as he is involved in the flux of time and
history, the flux of history must have some other meaning than that
which he can give it, as a creature involved in it. This is the significance of religious ideas of providence in which, by faith, a center,
source and end of the historical process more powerful than the
human agent and more omniscient than the human observor is presupposed. The apprehension of such a center of meaning by faith is
a necessary corollary of the preservation of the sense of the unity of
man in his finiteness and freedom; and of the unity and meaningfulness of history, despite its ambiguity, as more than natural and
less than purely rational. Something of the wisdom of this faith is
involved in the most primitive totemistic interpretation of the history
of a tribe or clan; for that interpretation seeks to relate a flux of
tribal life to a more absolute center of meaning beyond itself. It
achieves its final universal expression in the Biblical faith which is
par excellence a religion of both history and revelation, able to
affirm the meaning of historical existence in its unity because it discerns by faith revelations of the center of its meaning, beyond coherences of nature and the rationally ambiguous coherences of history. Man's historic existence can not have meaning without faith.
But before we seek to explicate this thesis more fully it is necessary

to portray the classical and the modern attempt to give life meaning through the affirmation of a rational intelligibility, transcending history (as in classical thought) or to assert the rational intelligibility of history itself (as in modern thought). As between these two alternatives modern culture is superior to classical thought insofar as it finds positive meaning, and is able to do justice to the emergence of novelty, in history as well as in natural time. But it falls into an even more grievous error than classical thought; for it equates historical growth with redemption from evil and thereby makes historical development too simply meaningful. Both the classical and the modern versions of history's rational intelligibility can not do full justice, either to the multifarious vitalities and configurations of history or to the tragic antinomies of life which are the consequence of the corruption of freedom.

II

Classical rationalism tends, as we have seen, to equate historical time with time in nature. When this identification is carried through consistently historical events are reduced to the inferior realm of "coming-to-be and passing away." They are meaningful only in the sense that the recurrent cycles are rationally intelligible. They offer no hope for the fulfillment of the unique capacities of human personality. That fulfillment is possible only through emancipation from the cycle of natural-historical recurrences. This logic drives classical thought into its negative attitude toward the realm of history. But it also has a provisionally affirmative attitude, which is expressed in the effort to bring the irrational stuff of man's individual and collective life under the dominion of reason, thereby bringing it into conformity with the cosmic order. This provisional affirmation of the historical is naturally stronger in Roman Stoicism than in Greek rationalism because of the strong practical and political interests of Roman culture. But in neither Rome nor Greece is this affirmative attitude strong enough finally to challenge the otherworldly pinnacle of classical spirituality. The otherworldliness of classicism has affinities with the eschatological climax of Biblical interpretations of history; but the differences between them are important. The Biblical transcendent ends of life are also otherworldly in the sense that they picture fulfillments beyond the possibilities of nature-time. But they represent transfigurations of the stuff of history while the otherworldliness of classicism negates the conditions of history.

Plato's historical interest is most perfectly embodied in the *Republic* where he seeks to construct a rational communal order in which the rational soul will have the best opportunity of flowering. Significantly the philosophers must be the rulers of this commonwealth: "Inasmuch as philosophers only are able to grasp the eternal and unchangeable; and those who wander in the region of the many and the variable are not philosophers, I must ask you which of the two classes should be rulers of our State? . . . And are not those who are verily and indeed wanting in the knowledge of the true being of each thing, and who have in their souls no clear pattern, and are unable as with a painter's eye to look at the absolute truth, and to that original to repair . . . are not such persons, I ask, simply blind?" [1]

Plato is of different minds about the possibility of establishing the perfect harmony of justice in any historic community. Even in the *Republic* he comes to a very pessimistic conclusion at the end of Book 9 and declares: "In heaven, . . . there is laid up a pattern of it [the ideal city] which he who desires may behold, and beholding, may set his own house in order. But whether such an one exists, or ever will exist in fact, is no matter; for he will live after the manner of that city, having nothing to do with any other." [2]

Plato's renunciation of the historical as an inferior world of change and illusion and his faith in the fulfillment of life through emancipation from the historical is unambiguous in the *Phaedo*:

"Were we not saying," he declares, "long ago that the soul, when using the body as an instrument of perception, that is to say when using the sense of sight and hearing or some other sense (for the meaning of perceiving through the body is perceiving through the

[1] *Republic*, 484.
[2] *Republic*, 594.

senses) . . . were we not saying that the soul too is then dragged by the body into the region of the changeable and wanders and is confused; the world spins round her and she is like a drunkard when under their influence.

"But when returning into herself, she reflects, then she passes into the other world, the region of purity and eternity and immortality and unchangeableness, which are her kindred and with them she ever lives when she is by herself and is not let or hindered; then she ceases from her erring ways and being in communion with the unchanging is unchanging. . . . The soul which is pure at departing draws after her no bodily taint, having never voluntarily during her life had a connection with the body, which she is ever avoiding, herself gathered into her self; and making such abstraction her perpetual study (which means that she has been a perpetual disciple of philosophy) and therefore has in fact always been engaged in the practice of dying. For is not the philosophy the study of death?" [8]

In these words of Plato we have the classical attitude toward history in its most consistent form. The rigorous separation between soul and body, the one involved in and the other above change, is clear. The fulfillment of life comprises both the knowledge of unchanging truth and the achievement of pure being, for the soul "being in communion with the unchanging is unchanging." The denial of the unity of man in his freedom and finiteness is explicit, and the identification of the world of history with natural time is equally unambiguous.

Aristotle's interest in the historical is more robust than Plato's. He is more fully aware than Plato of the contingent and the particular as objects of deliberation for the practical wisdom of the statesman.

---

[8] The *Phaedo*. In this passage the conditioned or finite character of the bodily senses is regarded as the hazard to the truth.

In a previous argument in the *Phaedo*, Plato sees the passions and the lusts of the body as the source of error: "While we are in the body and while the soul is mingled with this mass of evil our desire will not be satisfied; and our desire is for the truth. . . . For the body is a source of endless trouble . . . by filling us as full of loves and lusts, and fears, and fancies, and idols, and every sort of folly, prevents our ever having, as people say, so much as a thought. From whence come wars and fightings and factions? Whence but from the body and the lusts of the body?"

He separates such wisdom much more rigorously from the pure wisdom "which must be intuitive reason combined with scientific knowledge" [4] than most modern theories of historical science; and suggests its relation to animal shrewdness since "some even of the lower animals have practical wisdom, *viz.*, those which have the power of foresight with regard to their own life." [5] The distinction is similar to Whitehead's differentiation between the pragmatic reason which Ulysses shares "with the foxes" and the speculative reason which Plato shares "with the gods." [6]

But Aristotle's attitude toward the rational task of bringing the irrational stuff of men's historic life into a system of order is nevertheless not less, but rather more, affirmative than Plato's. Aristotle believes that though the *Polis* is natural in the sense that it is prior to the individual because "the individual, when isolated is not self-sufficing . . . but like a part in relation to the whole," nevertheless the organization of the commonwealth in its final perfection is a rational achievement so that though "a social instinct is implanted by nature, yet he who founded the first state is the greatest of benefactors." The *Polis* is the very source of that order and justice without which man is "the most unholy and savage of animals." [7]

The dependence of individual virtue or *Arete* upon social order and justice, conceived not as a creative and mutual relation between persons, but as the conformity of all vital capacities to sharply defined rational principles of order, is a characteristic emphasis of classical thought. Thus historical institutions and constructions represent tentative approximations of the cosmic order, the achievement of permanence within the transient.

But this affirmative attitude toward the historical is finally transcended in Aristotle as well as in Plato. Political and military actions, according to Aristotle, may be "distinguished by nobility and greatness" but "they aim at an end and are not desirable for their own

[4] *Nicomachean Ethics*, VI, 7, 1141a, 15.
[5] *Ibid.*, 1141a, 25.
[6] *The Function of Reason*, pp. 7 ff.
[7] *Politics*, 1253a, 25–35.

sakes" whereas the "activity of reason which is contemplative seems both to be superior in serious worth and to aim at no end beyond itself." [8] The contemplation of pure being represents a higher virtue than the rational organization of the changing world. It is a perfection in which the merely human is transcended and the divine achieved: "for it is not in so far as he is a man that he will live so, but in so far as something divine is present in him; and by so much as this is superior to our composite nature, is its activity superior to the exercise of the other kind of virtue. If reason is divine, then, in comparison with man, the life according to it is divine in comparison with human life. We must not follow those who advise us, being men, to think of human things and, being mortal, of mortal things, but must so far as we can, make ourselves immortal." [9]

Here we have the clearest final rejection of the realm of the historical, so characteristic of classical thought. It is also quite clear that the fulfillment of life requires emancipation from the historical and that the possibility of such emancipation lies in a dimension of a rational freedom which is in man and yet not of man. It is the gift of *Nous* which relates him to the immortal world. This rigorous dualism, which modern culture persistently but erroneously ascribes to Christianity, is the price in classical culture for the construction of a realm of intelligibility in two dimensions: one for rational man above the flux of time and one for history reduced to the dimension of natural time. The Christian attitude toward it is admirably, though somewhat extravagantly, expressed by Tertullian. He recognizes that the wholeness and unity of man is imperiled by this kind of intelligibility. "The soul," he declares, "comes before letters . . . and man himself before the philosopher and the poet." Life in its wholeness is threatened by the philosophers and is understood by the simple faith and wisdom of "the uncultivated soul, such as those have who have nothing else, whose whole experience has been gleaned on the street-corners and cross-roads and in the industrial plant." It is this "secret deposit of congenital and inborn knowledge" which guards the sense of the meaning of life within the per-

[8] *Nicomachean Ethics*, X, 7, 1177b, 15.
[9] *Ibid.*, X, 7, 1177b, 15–30.

plexities of historic existence, where nothing corresponds to pure intelligibility.[10]

Stoic thought has a slightly different version of the significance of life and the meaning of history; but this different version does not seriously alter the classical interpretation of life or strategy of its fulfillment. The historical world is as rigorously equated with the natural world in Stoicism as in Plato and Aristotle. But in Stoic pantheism the emphasis lies not so much upon its inferior character as a world of change as upon its divine character by reason of its changes being under the dominion of universal law. The historical occurrences are as rigorously determined as the events of nature; and man's wisdom is exhibited in his submission to this determinism, "for it would be ridiculous to affirm that the parts of the whole are subject to change and at the same time to be surprised or vexed as if something were happening contrary to nature." [11] Everything happens "either in such a wise as thou art formed by nature to bear it or . . . as thou art not formed by nature to bear it. . . . But if it happens in such wise as thou art not formed by nature to bear it, do not complain because it will perish after it has consumed thee," [12] declares Aurelius. The advice may be regarded as a wholesome reminder of human creatureliness. Indeed Stoic wisdom is a good antidote to man's whining inclination to deny the fact of his mortality. But Stoic determinism is wholly inapplicable to the complex facts of human history where destiny and freedom are curiously compounded and responsible decisions have to be made.

There is, of course, a realm of freedom for man in Stoic thought. But it is rigorously restricted to the inner life, where the rational soul may cultivate equanimity in defiance of all outward circumstance. "Either there is a fatal necessity," declares Aurelius, "an invincible order or a kind of Providence, or a confusion without purpose and without a director. If there is an invincible necessity why dost thou resist? . . . But if there is a confusion without a governor be content that in such a tempest thou hast thyself a cer-

---

[10] *De testimonio animae,* Chs. 1 and 5.
[11] Marcus Aurelius, *Meditations,* X, 7.
[12] *Ibid.,* X, 3.

tain ruling intelligence. And even if the tempest carry thee away, let it carry away the poor flesh, the poor breath, everything else; for the intelligence at least it will not carry away." [18]

The cultivation of the life of pure reason in Stoicism is slightly different than in the thought of Aristotle. It consists not so much in the contemplation of pure being and eternal perfection as in a quiet defiance of the untoward fate of man in the world of change and decay. But it is quite clear that the Stoic scheme also gives meaning to life by a rigorous distinction between two forms of intelligibility, the one governing nature and nature-history and the other uniquely human.

The various versions of the classical idea of the meaning of life and history are sufficiently similar to justify the idea of a common classical approach to life and to history. In this approach history is equated with nature, its intelligibility is proved by its subjection to natural recurrence; and the distinctive interrelation of freedom and destiny, of human decisions and a pattern of meaning transcending human decisions, is obscured. The meaning of life is equated with a higher form of rationality which can be realized by the emancipation of the unique freedom and reason of man from the ambiguities of human history. Thus there is intelligibility on two levels; but life is not meaningful in its wholeness; and history is meaningful only in its recurrences but not in the novelties which human freedom introduces into the temporal process. Two parts of human existence are correlated to two realms of intelligibility; but the life and the history of man in the unity and the ambiguity of their freedom and finiteness are not meaningful.

This interpretation of the dominant motif in classical culture must not, of course, obscure subordinate motifs which are not in conformity to it. Heraclitus' conception of the moving flux of time and history anticipated the modern idea of time. The Greek naturalists shared with the idealists the idea of history as a realm of natural recurrence; but they did not have the escape from nature to eternity which characterizes Platonism or Aristotelianism.

The most radical departure from the rationalistic interpretation

[18] *Ibid.*, XII, 14.

of life and history is to be found in the Dionysian religious tradition which lies at the foundation of Greek tragedy. Here life is seen in its unity of finiteness and freedom. Evil is recognized, not as due to physical impulse but to the *Hybris* and boundlessness of the human spirit. Historical existence has meaning, though filled with tragic contradictions.

These profound interpretations of life in Greek tragedy chronologically precede the flowering of Greek philosophy. They are submerged by the rise of Greek philosophy, which gives a much neater account of the coherences of nature and history, but at the expense of destroying the perceptions of meaning on the abyss of meaninglessness, of coherence above and within the contradictions and antinomies of man's historic existence, which it was the achievement of Greek tragedy to portray.

III

It was the Christian faith and not modern culture which overwhelmed the classical world. Long before the modern sense of a dynamic and creative history made the classical scheme of meaning dubious, the Christian faith challenged and overwhelmed it. Origen, despite his Platonic orientation, understood the Biblical approach to life and history sufficiently to protest against the cyclical interpretation of history, the notion "that in another Athens another Socrates will be born and marry another Xanthippe and will be accused by another Anytus and another Meletus." [14] Augustine, who first fully developed the implications of the Biblical view of time and history within terms of western culture, rejected the cyclical theory of time and history contemptuously. He ridiculed classical arguments "dragging us from the straight road and compelling us to walk on the wheel . . . which, if reason could not refute, faith could afford to laugh at." [15] But we are not immediately concerned with the Christian conception of time and history, which must presently be considered more fully. Our immediate interest is

---

[14] *Contra Celsum*, iv., 68.
[15] *De civitate Dei*, xii, 17.

to compare the modern effort to reduce the meaning of life and history to a new form of rational intelligibility. In this effort historical development, the fact which classical culture obscured and modern culture discovered, becomes the new basis of intelligibility and meaning.

We have previously noted that the foundation for the modern conception of a meaningful history is laid by the emphasis upon natural cause as a sufficient explanation for the emergence of new concretions and configurations in time; and by the certainty, adduced by modern science, that there is an evolution of forms in the temporal process. These modern discoveries lead to the conception of the natural process moving along a line toward a significant future. The cycles of birth and death, of growth and decay, to be observed in specific organisms are subordinated to the line of development in the forms and structures of those organisms. These forms and structures, which classical culture regarded as eternal, are proved to be subject to growth. We have already discussed the question whether the idea of evolution is a sufficient explanation of the mystery of *Genesis,* either in natural time or in history. But whatever its inadequacies, it is certainly a part of the explanation of origin.

But if the temporal process moves forward, the question of the END toward which it moves is as important as the question of its beginning. If the historical development is distinguished as rigorously from mutations in nature as is required by the uniqueness of human freedom in the historical process, it becomes apparent that there is a level of meaning in history which is not comprehended by equating historical events with natural events. There is in every individual life a depth or a height of meaning incongruous with the natural process. In a similar fashion the collective enterprises of mankind, the cultures and civilizations, the national and imperial communities have a dimension above the necessities and limitations of nature. The question is: what is their fate? Toward what end do they move? Do they merely embody a larger cycle of growth and decay than that to which natural organisms are subject?

In answering these questions about the meaning of history modern culture accepted one part of the classical interpretation of life and radically amended another part. Most of its misinterpretations of historical reality are derived from this mixture of classical rationalism and the modern confidence in historical growth. Modern thought accepted the classical conception that evil and illusion, the frustrations to the fulfillment of life and the confusion and cross purpose in the harmony of life, are all derived from the ignorance of a mind involved in nature and, from the impotence of a will, involved in natural necessity. With classical thought it hoped for the fulfillment of life through the extension of reason. Reason would envisage inclusive purposes, rather than the narrow ends which natural necessity prompts. Reason would create larger realms of harmony in which the confusion both of natural impulses and of tribal and national ambitions would be brought under the dominion of order. The growth of reason would transmute human relations into a concurrence of mind with mind rather than a conflict between body and body and sword with sword. "Methods of force" would give way to "methods of mind." Just as the evolutionary process in nature represented the gradual ascendancy of a cosmic mind over mechanism, so the evolutionary process in history guaranteed the gradual triumph of human reason over the ignorance of the undeveloped mind, the confused impulses of natural man and the bigotries and prejudices of primitive life.

It is interesting that even the strong naturalistic emphasis in modern culture, which ostensibly prompts the modern mind to view human life from the standpoint of its dependence upon nature, does not prevent even the most consistent naturalists from envisaging an ultimate triumph of the rational over the irrational. In a recent effort to account for the irrational element in politics, John Dewey ascribed its persistence to the inadequate emancipation of culture from irrational authority. The emancipation of the intellect in the recent past, he declares, was incomplete. The battle against prejudice and authority resulted in a "compromise" in which "the world including man was cut into two separate parts. One of them was awarded to natural inquiry under the name of physical science. The other was kept in fee simple by a 'higher' and finally 'authoritative' domain of the moral or the spiritual." This compromise resulted in "dumping our actual human problems into the lap of the most immature of all our modes of knowing: politics and ethics," with the result that the division of science which is "potent in human affairs is not a science but an ideological reflection and rationalization of contentious and contending practical policies." [16]

In this explanation of the cause of interest and passion in human affairs and in this expression of the hope that a more rigorous application of the "methods of science" will lead to the subjugation of egoistic interest and the elimination of the ideological taint, modern rationalism has obviously triumphed over a naturalistic metaphysics.

The ascription of historical evil to the natural or the primitive gives modern culture its common ground with classical thought. But it has a radically different scheme of redemption from the inertia of nature. It believes that history redeems man from nature. The same history which classical culture equates with the cycles of growth and decay in nature is regarded by modern culture as a realm of indeterminate growth. It has this confidence, even though it does not distinguish history too sharply from nature, since nature is also discovered to be in the process of growth. It is growth, therefore, which is the meaning of life and the guarantee of the fulfillment of its true meaning. Growth would not have this significance of itself, if it were not assumed that growth means growth of mind or of sympathy, of the inclusive purposes which increasing reason supposedly guarantees. Even more specifically, growth means the growth of freedom; and freedom, as in classical thought, is assumed to be rational freedom. It is assumed that freedom bears within itself the principle of order. The possibility that increasing freedom over natural limitations might result in giving egoistic desires and impulses a wider range than they had under more primitive conditions seems never seriously to disturb the modern mind. It is able to recognize some provisional aggravations of social confusion through the extension of human power; but it is also quite certain that these can be overcome as soon as the "methods of mind" are applied as rigorously to human affairs as to problems of nature.

[16] "Liberating the Social Scientists" in *Commentary*, October, 1947.

A modern philosopher of religion who has sought to reinterpret religious faith in terms of this new dogma of redemption summarizes the creed succinctly: "God is growth of meaning. Meaning grows when connections do. It is clear, then, how a person can make his way to God. He must seek out and foster mutually sustaining and enriching connections between activities which make up his living and those of persons and groups and physical nature round about him." [17]

This modern creed has distilled a great illusion from an important truth. The truth is that both nature and historic institutions are subject to development in time. The truth about temporal development in nature was not known at all in classical thought; and the idea of historic development was not fully appreciated. It was recognized only obliquely in Christian thought, even though Biblical-Hebraic thought conceived of time as moving on a line rather than in a cycle. Modern culture therefore is unique in its recognition of the full significance of historic development.

The illusion which it derived from this truth was the belief that growth fulfilled the meaning of life, and redeemed it of its ills and errors. The illusion rests upon two basic miscalculations. Modern culture, despite its ostensible interest in man's relation to nature, consistently exaggerated the degree of growth in human freedom and power. To this error of overestimating the measure of human freedom it added the second mistake of identifying freedom with virtue. Both of these errors require a more careful analysis.

[17] H. N. Wieman in *The Growth of Religion* by Wieman and Horton, p. 336.

CHAPTER V

~~~~~~

The Extravagant Estimates of Freedom in the Progressive View of History

I

THOUGH all human capacities are subject to development, and the cultural achievements and social institutions of mankind are capable of an indeterminate development, the extension of human power and freedom in either individual life or in the total human enterprise does not change the human situation essentially. Man remains a creature of nature on every stage of his development. There are certain bounds of human finiteness which no historical development can overcome. The preoccupation of modern culture with the remarkable increase in human power and freedom has inclined modern men to deny and to defy these fixed limits.

The tendency to overestimate the degree of increase of human freedom expresses itself most characteristically in the belief that the development of human capacities radically alters the human situation. The final form of the modern error about history is the belief that man's ambiguous position as both a creature and a creator of history is gradually changed until he may, in the foreseeable future, become the unequivocal master of historical destiny. This final and most absurd form of *Hybris* persuades modern culture to reject all Biblical concepts of divine providence as expressions of human impotence and ignorance, no longer relevant to the modern man's situation of intelligence and power.

Actually human power over nature and history is both limited and limitless. It is limited in the sense that all individual and collective forms of life are subject to mortality. No human achievements can annul man's subjection to natural finitude. But human power is also limitless in the sense that no fixed limits can be set for the expansion of human capacities.

Human capacities and man's collective achievements are not all of the same order. The limits of growth are more fixed, or more discernible, in some levels of life than in others.

It is possible to distinguish provisionally between four categories of human capacities in which various limits of historic growth may be observed, though these categories are not to be too rigorously differentiated. The first category, in which historic development of human power seems most marked, is man's capacity to manipulate the processes of nature, to exploit its treasures and bend its forces to human ends. There is presumably some limit to the speed at which men may travel, overcoming time and space; but the limit lies considerably beyond any present achievement. The possibilities of extending the range, speed and efficacy of communications are even further beyond present accomplishments. The resources of radio communication are only beginning to be developed. The release of atomic energy will certainly increase the degree of power available for human purposes as much as electricity increased it over the use of coal and steam, and the use of coal increased it over the use of water and windmill.

It may be dubious to conclude with Lewis Mumford that "nothing is impossible" in the field of technics; but we do not know the line of demarcation between the possible and the impossible, and probably never shall.[1]

---

[1] Lewis Mumford, *Technics and Civilization*, p. 435. Mumford's able analysis of the history of technics leads him to conclusions about the possibilities of advance in non-technical fields, which illustrate how easily the sense of the limitless in man's conquest of nature is transferred to more complex problems of human culture. Mumford considers the difficulties of adjusting the cultural and moral life of man to the increased power available to him and overcomes pessimism in regard to the difficulties of such adjustments with the reassuring words: "Impossible? No; for however far modern science and technics have fallen short, they have taught mankind at least one lesson: Nothing is impos-

Technical power can not be rigorously separated from a second category of human capacities which underlies it. This comprises the whole range of human culture, including religion, philosophy, art, and social organization. There is a history of growth in each of these realms of human culture; but the advances are not as limitless as in the natural and the applied sciences. Some cultural development is due to advancing technics. The invention of writing is, in a sense, the very foundation of civilization; and the invention of printing represents a most distinctive chapter in the extension of culture. The development of technical instruments for the expression of ideas, the storing of knowledge, the discovery of facts and the projection of the artistic impulse all have contributed to evolution of culture. But there is obviously a law of diminishing returns in the relation of technics to culture. Better writing material or the invention of typewriters did not contribute to a higher quality of prose or poetry. Advanced systems of indexing historical knowledge increased the precision and quantity of historical facts but made no contribution to the imaginative grasp of the events recorded. The ubiquity of the printed word did not, as Condorcet hoped, universalize the highest achievements of culture. Condorcet did not anticipate the "comics" and other printed pabulum by which the taste of the masses is corrupted. More refined methods and tools for the expression of artistic impulses do not insure a limitless advance in the art of the sculptor or painter. It is interesting, moreover, that the instruments of art have a more fixed and limited perfection than the instruments of the scientists. The pigments used by painters and the instruments used by musicians have been improved only slightly in the past century as compared with the development of the equipment in the scientist's laboratory.

The most indubitable basis of advance in the realm of culture is the accumulation of both knowledge and experience in both the collective enterprise of mankind and in individual life. Plato and

sible." This reassurance fails to take account of the fact that the wisdom and charity by which men must come to terms with each other within ever new conditions of life involves the whole of human personality as the technical conquest of nature does not. Achievements in this field are therefore much more difficult and limited.

Aristotle neither had better instruments for their disciplines than the pre-Socratic philosophers, nor were they presumably more intelligent. But they profited from the earlier gropings after "first principles" of the first philosophers and scientists. In the same way subsequent ages have built upon their achievements. But no one would be rash enough to find "progress" in philosophy, analogous to the development of science. The fact that science is the late and final fruit, and also the realm of most unlimited possibilities in the field of pure culture, has persuaded some moderns to regard its advances as proof of the limitless growth of all culture. We have previously considered the error which underlies Comte's belief in the ability of science to penetrate more deeply into the mystery and meaning of life than philosophy or religion. Science undoubtedly elaborates the meaning of the first principles, discerned in philosophy, in more and more detail; but it may also deflect interest from the ultimate issues of life or offer false solutions for them. Pure science is obviously the nexus between the realm of pure culture and the realm of technics in which development is most nearly limitless. There is, in fact, no clear line of demarkation between pure and applied science. The intention of the scientist may be the only distinguishing mark; but the intention of the pure scientist, uninterested in pragmatic technical advances, does not preclude the appropriation of his discoveries for pragmatic purposes. The relation between the discoveries in the field of nuclear physics and the manufacture of the atomic bomb is a modern case in point.

The third category of human capacities, the historical development of which must be considered, is man's inherent rational faculty. This capacity is undoubtedly subject to historical development. Neither primitive peoples nor children are capable of consistent conceptual knowledge. But the history of thought would suggest that the development of conceptual knowledge represents primarily growth in rational experience rather than in rational capacity. There is undoubtedly a wide divergence of rational capacity between individuals within a cultural group and between groups; but this divergence does not suggest the possibility of limitless development of "mind."

Undoubtedly there are possibilities of extending the precision and profundity of the rational faculty to larger and larger numbers. It is significant, however, that the method of such extension has become a subject of debate between anthropologists who regard native capacity as a fairly fixed endowment, the development of which depends upon cultural factors, and the geneticists who would improve or extend it by selective breeding.

The project of the geneticists involves modern culture in a profound contradiction between its voluntarism and its determinism, which must be considered more fully presently. Eugenics requires on the one hand that human beings be made into guinea pigs in order that they may be subjected to a non-natural extension of natural evolution. On the other it requires an oligarchy of geneticists with such control over human life as to be able to negate and suppress natural impulses and the innate sense of human dignity which might interfere with a program of selective breeding.[2]

Human rational capacities are, in short, infinitely variable, but their limits are more fixed than the collective cultural achievements which are elaborated by these capacities.

There remains a fourth dimension of human existence which has been completely obscured in modern man's preoccupation with historical development: the dimension of man in nature. Social Darwinism has sought to derive historical progress from man's involvement in natural evolution; but Thomas Huxley's rejection of the idea that historical development is an extension of natural evolution [3] is irrefutable. The dominant schools of modern naturalism have not followed the social-Darwinist thesis. They have, however, managed to obscure the fixed limits of man's creaturely finiteness even while they pretended to understand human life in terms of its relation to the system of nature.[4]

[2] The cheerless prospect of such an effort to improve the human race is the subject of Aldous Huxley's well-known satire *Brave New World*. Julian Huxley, on the other hand, takes the idea with the naive seriousness in his *Man in the Modern World*.

[3] In his "Romanes Lecture" of 1893, *Evolution and Ethics*.

[4] Thus Roy Wood Sellars in one of the most consistently naturalistic interpretations of human life, *Evolutionary Naturalism*, closes his analysis of the human situation with this extravagant estimate of human possibilities: "Let a

The final and most irrefutable proof of man's involvement in the "coming to be and passing away" of nature is the fact of his death. The idea of a limitless growth without the incongruity of death is untrue, even when applied to the historic structures, which out-last his individual life. The conception of limitless growth is even more obviously negated by the death of the individual. But before we consider the modern effort to evade the fact of death in the conceptions of limitless growth it is necessary to call attention to other equally significant marks of man's creaturely limits, which are usually obscured in modern life.

Man as a creature is hetero-sexual. No development of human personality and no achievement of capacities, transcending sexual differentiation, can negate this fateful and irrevocable distinction between human beings. A technical society has indeed given women various forms of freedom, once enjoyed only by men. Women may reduce the responsibilities related to the biological function of motherhood to such proportions that alternative vocations become possible. And this new vocational freedom has been exploited in turn to gain a more equal position in society than obtained in traditional communities. There women were bound to the narrower sphere of family while men claimed all the rights and privileges of the larger community for themselves. The ethical significance of this emancipation can not be denied. But the more rationalistic forms of feminism have drawn some extravagant and unwarranted conclusions from this historic development. They have forgotten that the difference between fatherhood as a kind of avocation and motherhood as a vocation has a biological basis which can never be completely overcome. The mother bears the child in her body; and even when she

---

man place his hope in those powers which raise him above the ordinary causal nexus. It is in himself that he must trust. If his foolishness and his passions exceed his sanity and intelligence, he will make shipwreck of his opportunity. . . . Evolutionary naturalism does not sink man back into nature. It acknowledges all that is unique in him and vibrates as sensitively as idealism to his aspirations and passions." p. 343.

One of the many mistakes of modern naturalism is that "it vibrates as sensitively as idealism" to the foolish idea that natural evolution changes the essential human situation and finally places man in a position of freedom and power in which he can negate the conditions of his creaturehood.

no longer suckles it, the bond between the two is of a special order. Biological facts subtly but also irrevocably determine certain social and moral issues. Women may choose another vocation beside that of motherhood or they may exchange the vocation of motherhood for another vocation. But biological facts make these choices more difficult than those which a mere male faces.[5]

Ethnic particularity is in a slightly different category from sexual differentiation. Human beings are distinguished from each other ethnically but not as absolutely as they are sexually differentiated. Modern man's increasing mobility and the growing ethnic pluralism of various nations have undoubtedly accelerated the process of racial mixture. Nazism has taught us, moreover, how dangerous and perverse it is to seek a return to simple ethnic homogeneity as the basis for a modern state. Man has a wide realm of freedom in the field of race. But modern culture seems to have forgotten that a new amalgam of various racial groups in various nations will distinguish men as certainly as the purer racial distinctions. Moreover, while the typical modern dreams of some kind of universal community in which all racial distinctions are transcended, the power of a sense of ethnic uniqueness continues to manifest itself. Both the Welsh and the Scottish members of the British national community are exhibiting a strengthened awareness of their ethnic uniqueness, while Eire seeks to displace English with the Gaelic language, and the new state of Israel is born.

Language belongs to the history of culture rather than to the field of biology; and linguistic particularity is therefore even less fixed than ethnic uniqueness. The differences in language do serve to remind men of the fact that they are particular creatures and not budding angels or universal minds. The warning in the Tower of Babel myth that men, when they seek to build their towers too high into heaven, are stricken by a confusion of tongues and made con-

---

[5] The humorous magazine *The New Yorker* published this naive observation from a medical journal: "Men and women are becoming increasingly equal but there are unfortunately some anatomical differences between them which can never be eliminated." The magazine greeted this bit of wisdom with the words: "Goody. Goody."

scious of the creaturely limits of their existence, is still relevant though unheeded in our day.

In short, however much the range of the human imagination may increase, or man's mobility be enlarged, or means of communication may establish new contacts, man remains a finite creature. He surveys the world from a particular locus, betrays his particularity by his speech and physiognomy, and insinuates the partial, parochial, and unique aspects of his life into even the most ultimate insights of his mind. A naturalistic culture might have taught us this obvious fact; but it has a curious facility for extracting an impossible sense of freedom from its considerations of the finite conditions of human existence.

Sexual, ethnic, and linguistic marks of particularity are all indices of collective particularity. But the final proof of man's creaturely limit is a fact in his individual life: his death. The same man who creates and recreates historic institutions, who seeks to understand nature and history, who holds past events in memory and future events in prospect, dies just as those animals die who have no commerce with any of these wider structures of meaning. This is the final and most vivid expression of the paradox of the human situation. All non-historical religions solve that problem very simply by regarding human personality and individuality as belonging to the world of natural contingency which passes away; and believing that there is a non-personal and non-individual reality at some ultimate level of the human self which is merged at death with the divine or universal reason, life, or consciousness.

This way of solving the problem was not open to modern culture since it had inherited a Christian conception of the significance of human personality. The way of classical naturalism was also not open to a history-minded naturalism. It had found meaning in history and could not accept the pessimism of classical naturalism.

One way of solving the problem was to ignore it. The eighteenth and nineteenth century stratagem of ignoring it consisted primarily in regarding the hope of immortality as a compensation for the frustrations which men suffered in a world in which nature had not

been adequately subdued. The new triumphs over nature, promised
by science, would, according to Condorcet, prolong human life indeterminately. This was, of course, an evasion, since even the most
phenomenal advances in medical science could not promise a medicine for the cure of senility, nor could the multiplication of creature comforts finally change the fact that man's life is fragmentary
and short.

History has taken a very ironic vengeance upon a culture which
imagined that man's conquest of nature solved this problem. For
the same technical instruments by which men have gained a comparative security against the perils and caprices of nature (though
even here the security is not as absolute as they imagined) have
created a technical civilization in which men are in greater peril
of each other than in simple communities. The fear of death has
been given a new social and historical dimension. More millions
have died upon battlefields in the wars of the first half of this century than in any previous fifty years; and many millions more have
been threatened by the famines due to the dislocations of war. The
threat of atomic warfare has prompted a mood of hysteria among
many moderns, not only because it proved history to be less certainly
marching toward peace than they had imagined; but also because
the spectre of death, which they had banished from their imagination, suddenly appeared in a new and more terrible form. For a
moment they thought they might use this new fear to scare the
world into the acceptance of the authority of a world government.
But it soon became apparent that, while men feared atomic destruction *per se*, they feared even more that the Russians might hurl
atomic destruction upon America or America upon Russia. The
fear of death had become mixed with our fear of each other.

Our contemporary situation, while desperate, is not a hopeless
one. It may well be that we will solve the problem of the human
community in global terms and that we will also create tolerably
just economic and political institutions within each nation, so that
men may have a greater degree of security against the new perils of
history. But even the best possible solutions of these problems can

not give us a social order guaranteed against the decay of its stability. Thus a new social dimension has been added to the peril of insecurity and death.

II

The most comprehensive exaggeration of human freedom and denial of man's creatureliness is expressed in the widely held conviction that historical progress gradually changes the human situation, delivering man from the ambiguity of his freedom over, and subordination to, the temporal process. The thesis is that man's increasing freedom first emancipates him from subjection to natural, necessity but finally makes him master of historical destiny. The idea has served to resolve the debate between voluntaristic and deterministic versions of the modern creed. The traditional debate between voluntarism and determinism in the history of thought has been aggravated in modern culture by the fact that modern forms of determinism have annulled human freedom more completely than Christian ideas of Providence; and modern forms of voluntarism have asserted the freedom of man more absolutely than either classical or Christian theories.

The social and historical theories which took their rise in Darwinism and regarded history merely as an extension of natural evolution logically enough espoused the deterministic version of modern thought. Herbert Spencer was certain that progress was a "beneficent necessity." For him the guarantee of progress lay in the sociological corollary of the biological fact "that every species of organism, including the human, is always adapting itself to the conditions of its existence." [6] Thus men were propelled to a higher and higher form of culture by natural necessity. The British sociologist, Benjamin Kidd, had an intriguing variant of this theory. He claimed to find evidence that "natural selection is evolving a religious character in the first instance and intellectual character only as a secondary product," which was very obliging of the evolutionary process since

[6] *The Study of Sociology*, p. 346.

in Mr. Kidd's opinion intellectual character could not rise above interested action and religious character could.[7]

This deterministic view of history, which is not confined to the naturalistic version of historical progress (for Hegel elaborated an idealistic form of it), does not, however, represent the dominant mood in modern thought. That mood is voluntaristic. The early Renaissance expressed a strong voluntaristic opposition to the Christian idea of providence and to any conception of a pattern of history which would seem to make the freedom of man dubious. This protest reached a Promethean height in the words of Proudhon: "We attain to science and society in spite of God. Every progress is a victory in which we crush the Deity." [8]

According to this voluntarism history moves, not by the force of an evolutionary nature but by the extension of human freedom over nature. "The world today knows nothing more familiar," declares Eustace Hayden, "than man's success in imposing his will on the flow of events. No time is wasted by the man of affairs in anxious speculation about the supposed metaphysical controls and rigidities of the universe or human nature. He changes the face of the earth and alters the habits of men." [9] This optimistic creed contains the modern error in baldest form. The optimism is based on the erroneous assumption that the "habits of men" are in the same category of conquerable territory as the "face of the earth" and that there is therefore no difference between the conquest of nature by technical power and the management of historical destiny by the social wisdom which must deal with the "habits of men." It also assumes that the knowledge of nature and self-knowledge belong in the same category of wisdom. It is not recognized that it is man himself, and not his mind, who seeks to master historical destiny and man himself and not his body which must be mastered.

There has never been a clear resolution of the conflict between deterministic and voluntaristic versions of the idea of progress. The

---

[7] *Social Evolution*, p. 307. Kidd was not consistent. In his *Science of Power* he denied the significance of natural selection and placed his confidence in "social heredity transmitted through social culture." p. 273.

[8] *Système des Contradictions*, ch. 8.

[9] *Quest of the Ages*, p. 210.

real self, which is something more than physical impulse, had a way of confounding those who sought to equate history with nature; and the real self, which is something less than reason, confounded those who sought to achieve a clear vantage point of "scientific" or rational objectivity over the flow of events.

If, as the social Darwinists believe, progress would be best assured by allowing the struggle for survival to take its course, what was one to do about the fact that men seemed to have the freedom to interfere with that course and to enact social legislation which deflected the course of nature? Geneticists have had particular difficulty in arriving at coherent conclusions about the relation of freedom to natural necessity. What are we to do, asks one of them about the fact that "the race must be strong by a process of selective elimination and yet the individual must have an environment favorable to his life"? [10]

Or, if the "best people" have few children ought we to assume that they have become the best people because they have few children and have given them special opportunities? Such a conclusion would lead to the policy of encouraging those who are less than the "best" to limit their birth rate. Or ought we to encourage the "best" people to have more children? If so, can we change the historical trend (almost identical with a "law of nature") that men who are given the freedom to determine the birth rate through the new knowledge of birth control, exercise it invariably to limit the rate? [11] Confronted with these bewildering relations of necessity and freedom in human history, geneticists, social scientists, and biologists have arrived at equally bewildering conclusions about the relation between the two.

The most characteristic escape from this impasse between voluntarism and determinism is the belief that the historical growth of freedom, whether conceived as propelled by natural necessity or by rational development, will gradually change the human situation, making man less and less a creature and more and more a master of the historical process. This hope is succinctly expressed by J. B. S.

[10] Herbert S. Jennings, *The Biological Basis of Human Nature*, pp. 353–355.
[11] *Cf.* Edward M. East, *Heredity in Human Affairs.*

Haldane: "While man does not control his own evolution it behooves us to begin thinking what we should do when that time comes, as it probably will, when this knowledge becomes available to us. If we had discussed long in advance what we should do with nuclear energy we might have agreed in advance not to use it in atomic bombs and would have gone a long way in solving the problems we face today." [12]

The usual basis for this hope is the belief that there is no essential difference between the stuff of history and the stuff of nature and therefore no real distinction between the application of the "scientific method" to nature and to history. "Data are being gathered," declares McDougall, "by historians, biologists, and anthropologists for a science of society whose sure indications will enable us deliberately to guide the future evolution of the nation toward the highest ideal of a nation which we can conceive." [18] This faith in an ever more adequate social science, for which Comte is the most typical exponent, not only obscures the fact that the conquest of nature produces ever more complex and far-reaching historical pat-

[12] Proceedings of the Princeton Bicentennial Convocation as reported in the *New York Times*, January 3, 1947. The journal also reported that one of the biologists present challenged the optimism of the assumption that man was about to come into control of historical destiny. He believed that "mankind was being driven by an ineluctable fate to mutual annihilation." Thus despair lurks under the surface of modern optimism.

Julian Huxley in his *Man in the Modern World* speaks of "the field of human improvement" as a "battlefield between Eugenist and Sociologist." He proposes to overcome that conflict by persuading the eugenists not to think of the merely dysgenic or non-eugenic effects of social environment. In fact, Mr. Huxley is certain that modern science in every form can be made into a tool of man's mastery of his own destiny. He has a very simple voluntaristic approach to the whole problem of human fate even though he recognizes that "man can not investigate man by the same methods by which he investigates external nature. . . . When he starts investigating human motive, his own motives are involved; when he studies human society, he is himself a part of the social structure" (p. 113). But Mr. Huxley is not really worried about the bias in human judgements. He thinks it will "take generations for social science to work out the technique for discounting the errors due to bias" (p. 119). He is so certain that a group of god-like scientists can be developed that he is not afraid to turn over the improvement of the human race through scientific breeding to an oligarchy of scientists, confident that no special interests will corrupt their judgement or their power.

[18] W. McDougall, *The Group Mind*, p. 300.

terns which dwarf the human will and frustrate human decisions as certainly as did purely natural limitations in another age; but it also obscures the complexity of human nature in its unity of necessity and freedom and in its corruption of both. "The laws of nature," declares Lester Ward, "have been neutralized in the physical world and civilization is the result. They are still in force in the social and especially in the economic world but this is because the methods of mind have not yet been applied to these departments of nature." [14]

This is the same thesis with which we are already familiar from Professor Dewey's various efforts to explain the persistence of self-interest in human affairs as due to some easily corrected defect in culture which has prevented as rigorous an application of the scientific method to human affairs as to problems of natural science.

The thesis rests upon as rigorous a distinction between the self and its mind as in classical rationalism. It negates the organic relation between the self and its rational processes. This self, in the unity of its physical and spiritual life, is operative both in the stuff of the historical process which must be mastered and in the mind which is called upon to master it. The unique endowments of the human self make human nature more recalcitrant than nature when the problem is to bring human nature under control. The creaturely limitations of the self which is called upon to assume historical mastery are, on the other hand, the proof of the vanity of the imagination, which seeks to picture man as a gradually evolving god, who will ultimately come into control of all the conditions of his life.

There is a grim irony in the fact that mankind is at the moment in the toils of the terrible fate of a division between two great centers

[14] *Applied Sociology*, p. 319.

A more recent form of the same *hybris* of social science may be found in the thought of Karl Mannheim. He writes in *Man and Society in an Age of Reconstruction"* (1940): "We have now reached a stage where we can imagine how to plan the best possible human types by deliberately reorganizing the various groups of social factors. We can go on to alter those inhibitions which are the legacies of past societies. . . . Even though much remains obscure . . . we can foresee our goal which is the planned guidance of people's lives on a sociological basis and with the aid of psychology. In this way we are keeping in the foreground both the highest good of society and the peace of mind of the individual" (p. 222).

of power, one of which is informed by the communist and the other by the bourgeois liberal creed of world redemption. Both creeds imagine that man can become the master of historical destiny. The communists assume that the rationalization of particular interest will disappear with a revolutionary destruction of a society which maintains special interests. The very fury of communist self-right-eousness, particularly the identification of ideal ends with the tortuous policies of a particular nation and its despotic oligarchy, is rooted in its naive assumption that the rationalization of partial and particular interests is merely the product of a particular form of social organization and would be overcome by its destruction.

Meanwhile the liberal world dreams of the mastery of historical destiny by the gradual extension of the "scientific method" without recognizing that the objectivity and disinterestedness which it seeks by such simple terms represents the ultimate problem and despair of human existence. The two creeds are locked in seemingly irreconcilable conflict. Whether the conflict eventuates in overt hostilities or not, it has already produced an historical situation which can not be encompassed in the philosophy of history of either creed. An adequate frame of meaning to encompass it would have to contain the motif of the Tower of Babel myth of the Bible. In that myth God reduced the pride of men who wanted to build a tower into the heavens by confounding their languages, thereby reminding them that they were particular, finite, and conditioned men, who do not find it an easy matter to become simply "man."

Is it not significant that a culture which expects "man" to become master of his historical fate, and "man" to decide what direction his historical development should take, arrives at this tragic end? And that the difficulty is created by the fact that the natural scientist, who is the only scientist faintly approximating the universal *mind* which is to become master of historical destiny, discovers atomic power; and that, confronted with the necessity of bringing this new power of creativity and destructiveness under social and moral control, our generation should find *mind* dissolved into various national minds, whose social objectives are as varied as their language? And that they should find the greater difficulty in achieving a tolerable community, across this chasm of mutual fear, because each is armed with a social philosophy which obscures the partial and particular character of its objective?

When all the elements which enter our present world situation are explicated, it becomes apparent that history's pattern of meaning is more complex than either the communist or the liberal conception of historical progress. Men do not, whether by evolutionary or revolutionary means, exchange their position of creatures of historical process to that of history's masters. They remain rather in the continuous ambiguity both of being mastered and mastering the course of history. Whatever mastery they may achieve over historical processes must still operate in a wide realm of meaning in which both natural and historical factors beyond the control of any particular human will frustrate, deflect and negate, as well as fulfill, human desires and ambitions.

The modern version of an historical redemption from the human predicament of finiteness and freedom is, in short, a particularly flagrant expression of the *Hybris* which tempts man to overestimate the degree of his freedom and which Christian thought recognizes as the root of sin.

III

The general belief in modern thought, that religion is an expression of impotence, must be understood in the light of this exaggerated conception of the limitless power of man. If it should be true that history radically changes the human situation and that man's mastery over, rather than subordination to, the natural and historical process is the primary proof and fruit of that change, it would follow that religious conceptions of a providential purpose and pattern would become irrelevant through historial development. The warning of Christ, "Which of you by taking thought can add one cubit unto his stature?" (Matthew 6:27) seems from the viewpoint of modern pride a typical religious expression of impotence, which

ceases to have meaning in a day in which technics have extended the
power of the human foot in transportation, of the human hand in
manufacture, and of the ear and eye in fabulous forms of communication.

Engel's indictment of religion as an expression of weakness states
the mood of typical moderns in classical form: "All religion," he
declares, "is nothing but the fantastic reflection in men's minds of
those external forces which control their daily life. . . . Although
bourgeois political economy has given a certain insight into the
causal basis of this domination by extraneous forces, this makes no
essential difference. Bourgeois economics can neither prevent general crises nor protect the individual capitalist from losses. . . . It
is still true that man proposes and God (that is, the extraneous forces
of the capitalist mode of production) disposes. Mere knowledge
. . . is not enough. What is above all necessary is a social act. When
this act has been accomplished . . . and society has freed itself and
all its members from the bondage in which they are now held . . .
when therefore man not only proposes but also disposes, only then
will the last extraneous force which is still reflected in religion vanish
and with it will also vanish the religious reflection itself." [15]

Marxism gives the thesis, that religion is the expression of impotence, a particular color because it accuses the bourgeois world of
having emancipated man only from bondage to nature and not from
the inevitabilities of historic catastrophe. But the essential idea was
borrowed by Marxism from the liberal culture of the eighteenth and
nineteenth centuries. It was generally believed that "the illusion of
power over the external world, promised by religion, has been
achieved by science, which accounts for the decline of the religious
mentality." [16]

Mr. Calverton's observation proves that religion is subject to contrasting indictments. It is accused of seeking to give man control
over the natural world but also of expressing an attitude of impotence and defeatism toward "extraneous forces." Actually the primi-

[15] Engels, *Anti-Dühring*, Part III, v.
[16] V. F. Calverton, *The Passing of the Gods*, p. 320.

tive magic which sought to bend nature to human ends by magical formulae and incantations was a kind of prescientific science, which must be distinguished from the more typical religious attitude of reverence and awe before the power or powers of the world of nature and history which determine human destiny beyond man's contriving. While this primitive magic insinuates itself into even advanced religions of later ages; and while men do seek to use religion as a tool for a fancied manipulation of natural forces, the sense of submission toward omnipotent power is certainly more characteristically religious. It can not be denied that this religious sense of human limitations has frequently been misapplied in the realm of man's growing power and has prompted a defeatist attitude toward scientific efforts to ameliorate natural evils or toward social efforts to overcome historical evils.[17] While these errors of the religious mind prove that orthodox religions have had difficulty in appreciating the meaning of man's growing power over nature, they do not validate the curious belief of modern culture that religion is merely an expression of impotence, which man's growing power will overcome. This belief is succinctly expressed in the observation of Bertrand Russell that fishermen with sailboats incline to be religious while those who boast the possession of motorboats divest themselves of religion. "Modern technics," declares Mr. Russell, "is giving man a sense of power which is changing his whole mentality. Until recently the physical environment was something that had to be accepted. But to the modern man physical environment is merely the raw material for manipulation and opportunity. It may be that God made the world, but there is no reason why we should not make it over." [18] The modern man's sense of power does not stop with a sense of mastery over the immediate natural conditions of his life. "A cosmic process has come to consciousness," boasts Eustace Hayden,

[17] Andrew White's *History of the Warfare between Science and Religion* is a fruitful source-book of specific instances of such religious defeatism. Gandhi's opposition to surgery and projects for the arrest of the disease of leprosy is a recent example of a non-Christian religious opposition to the elimination of natural evil.

[18] *Scientific Outlook*, p. 151.

"and to the capacity for purposive self-control on the social level.
. . . The task is to impose human purposes upon the cosmic process, to shape the course of the flowing stream of life." [19]

The illusion of budding omnipotence, which inspires the charge that a religious sense of Providence is the expression of a primitive impotence, could not be stated more clearly.

[19] *Quest of the Ages*, pp. 207–209.

CHAPTER VI

~~~~~~

The Identification of Freedom and Virtue in Modern Views of History

I

THE EXTRAVAGANT estimate of the degree of freedom and power which may accrue to man through historical development is hardly as grievous an error as the estimate of the virtue of that freedom, implied in most modern interpretations of the human situation.

Since modern rationalism inherited the belief from classical rationalism that the evil in human nature is the consequence of natural finiteness and physical impulses, it naturally inclined to the conclusion that the development of rational capacities was, in itself, a process of gradual emancipation from evil. Race prejudice is generally regarded as a vestigial remnant of barbarism. Manifestations of national pride or other parochial bigotries are, in a similar fashion, thought of as forms of inertia which the ever more inclusive purposes and visions of reason will overcome. Individual and collective egotism is believed to be the consequence of a primitive ignorance which must ultimately either yield to more enlightened and therefore more inclusive forms of self-interest, or which will be brought under the dominion of the moral force implicit in man's rational faculties.

In more recent scientific forms of this identification of virtue and reason, the hope is to bring the irrational stuff of human nature under control by more adequate psychiatric technics or by estab-

lishing rational political checks upon the irrational impulses of
men.

In any event evil is always a force of the past, which must be
overcome by present and future possibilities. The triumph of virtue
is more or less guaranteed because historical development assures
both the increasing purity of reason and the efficacy of its scientific
technics. This error of identifying increasing freedom with increasing virtue is primarily responsible for the false estimates of history
by contemporary culture. The increasing evils which arose with
increasing power could be neither anticipated nor comprehended
within terms of these presuppositions.

In its most naive form modern rationalism identifies technical
competence with rational profundity and sees in the conquest of
nature a proof of man's capacity to bring the irrational stuff of
human nature under control. All that is necessary is to apply the
"methods of science" as rigorously to the world of human affairs as
to the realm of nature.[1] In forms less crude there is some recognition of the wide gulf which separates the world of history from the
world of nature; but confidence in the final dominion of reason
over this more complex world is no less sanguine.

One reason why it never occurs to the typical modern that evil
in human nature may be due to a corruption of human freedom,
rather than to some inertia of nature or history, is because the human
self in its integrity and unity has been lost.

Despite all modern protests against dualism and idealism, the
real self in its unity is dissolved into an intelligible and a sensible

---

[1] Occasionally the suggestion is made that since human nature is slightly
more complex than nature, a mastery of more varied technics is required. Thus
Alexis Carrel in *Man the Unknown* comes to the conclusion that the management of human affairs requires a thorough knowledge of "anatomy and physics,
physiology and metaphysics, pathology, chemistry, psychology, medicine, and
also a thorough knowledge of genetics, nutrition, pedagogy, aesthetics, ethics,
religion, sociology, and economics." He estimates that about 25 years would
be required to master all these disciplines so "that at the age of 50 those who
have submitted themselves to these disciplines could effectively direct the
reconstruction of human beings" p. 285.

This vision of world salvation through the ministrations of an elite of
encyclopedists is a nice symbol of the inanity to which the modern interpretation of life may sink.

self. But the intelligible self is not really a self. It is pure mind. And the sensible self is not really a self. It is a congeries of physical impulses. It conforms fairly well to Freud's "id" which is defined as a "cauldron of seething excitement." When the modern man speaks of mastering human nature, or ordering society, or manipulating historical destiny, he dismisses the real self with its anxieties and fears, its hopes and ambitions both from the concept of the man who is to become master of historical destiny, and from the picture of the stuff of history which is to be mastered. This real self as a force to be mastered has unique powers of recalcitrance not known in nature; and as the instrument of mastery it is betrayed by confusions not known in pure mind.

This dismissal of the real self in the unity of its finiteness and freedom is responsible for the note of unreality in the more theoretic disciplines of our culture, as compared either with the common sense which informs the practical life of men or the profounder insights of poets and artists, seeking to portray life in its wholeness and complexity. The common-sense of ordinary men is seldom under the illusion that the jealousies and envies which infect even the most intimate human relations are merely the defects of an undisciplined mind. They are known to be temptations for saint as well as sinner; for the wise man and fool. Practical statesmen do not regard the will-to-power of a strong man as the vestigial remnant of barbarism. All common-sense political wisdom seeks to harness and to restrain, to make use of, and to guard against, the power impulse. A common-sense regulation of economic life does not treat the economic motive as a force which is about to be eliminated from human society. It knows that motive to be one facet of the power of self-interest, which must be harnessed, deflected, beguiled and transmuted in the interest of the commonweal but which can never be completely suppressed.

The common-sense wisdom of mankind is even more aware of the recalcitrant power of egoistic interest in collective action. Nations and groups do not possess an integral consciousness as does the individual. But they do have an inchoate will; and that will is capable of only vagrant affirmations of ideals and values beyond its own interest. No one is particularly shocked by George Washington's dictum that a nation is not to be trusted beyond its own interest. That bit of cynicism is common currency in the affairs of mankind; and statesmen would be impeached if their policies ventured too far beyond its warning.

Some poets and artists, novelists and historians have been so much influenced by the modern temper as to have become incapable either of picturing human character in the complexity of its motives or of describing human relations in the bewildering confusion of interactions in which human lives impinge upon one another. Recently a few novelists have sought to do justice to the complex unity of human life by inserting psychiatric techniques into their stories, as if this little bit of science could compensate for the lack of a poetic grasp of human nature in both its grandeur and its misery. But no matter how much our imaginative literature has suffered from the illusions of our age, no respectable novel has ever quite pictured human life as vapidly as some of our more theoretic social and historical sciences. When either common-sense or poetry are not completely robbed of their art of observation they are not wholly obtuse to the reality of the human self (including an inchoate collective self) whose "ideals" are interlaced with anxieties and fears not known in the kingdom of pure reason; and whose hopes and ambitions betray a guile of spirit not known in the realm of nature.

Even the social, psychological and historical scientists are, despite their theories, unable to deny the real self, in the unity of its finiteness and freedom, completely. Thus a modern psychologist who seeks to equate the complex causation of human motives with the type of causality known in nature admits by inadvertence that a transcendent self interferes with the natural process. In L. J. Shaffer's *Psychology of Adjustment* the self is reduced to the level of nature in this fashion: "In sharp contrast to the moralistic viewpoint the objective psychological attitude places no blame or judgment upon the individual. Human behavior is the result of causes just as physical phenomena arise from certain sufficient antecedents. Not many centuries ago material events were blamed upon the wrath of deity or the perversity of nature. Conduct problems have only recently emerged in the realm of natural occurrences to be treated impartially as physical events." [2] The self, thus dismissed from responsibility for its actions, is, however, so full of guile that the same psychologist warns against placing the tools of self-knowledge too much at its disposal; for it will use them to its own advantage: "Thus one student complains of his inability to achieve because of his inferiority complex," he declares. "Another points to the fact that he is the product of his heredity and environment. Such statements must be recognized as products of rationalization rather than of reasoning." [8]

Another psychologist is rather disconcerted by the intrusion of "naive egotism" into the nicely laid plans for a rational world. William McDougall uses the lives of Woodrow Wilson and of Lord Curzon as illustrations of the "disastrous effects" of this naive egotism which makes even a great man "unwilling to dim the glory of his achievement by sharing it with others." He thinks something "drastic" must be done to break the power of this residual evil in an otherwise rational world. He suggests that nothing less than "inducing all our young people to make some study of psychology" will be adequate for the solution of this problem.[4]

Thus rationalism, defined as primarily confidence in the virtue and omnipotence of reason, can sink to a low level of unreason, if discernment of the facts of life is a mark of reason's competence.

II

The division of the self into a rational and natural, or an intelligible and a sensible, self leads to a false estimate of human virtue. The real self, in its transcendent unity and integrity, is involved in the evils, particularly the evils of self-seeking, which it commits. This self is always sufficiently emancipated of natural necessity, not to be compelled to follow the course dictated by self-interest. If

[2] P. 8.
[3] *Ibid.*, p. 543.
[4] *The Energies of Men,* p. 382.

it does so nevertheless, it is held culpable both in the court of public opinion and in the secret of its own heart. The self finds itself free; but, as Augustine suggested, not free to do good. The self seeks its own despite its freedom to envisage a wider good than its own interest. Furthermore it uses its freedom to extend the domain of its own interests. It is this use of freedom which makes the moral effect of the extension of human power so ambiguous. New technical skills become the servants of particular interest in the first instance; and come under the control of a wider community or value only by tortuous process. The ability of the self to envisage a wider world than its immediate environment is the occasion for the rise of imperialism long before it leads to the establishment of any universal concord between particular interests. It is always through some particular center of power that the human community is organized; or from some particular viewpoint that meaning is given to the course of history.

Thus the increasing freedom of the self over natural limitations aggravates and enlarges the conflicts of life with life as nature knows them. Yet the self can never use its wider freedom for itself with complete complacency. It has some knowledge of a responsibility toward life beyond itself and a vagrant inclination to be loyal to it. But there is a "law in its members" which wars against the "law that is in its mind," a powerful inclination to bend every new power to its own purposes and to interpret every situation from the standpoint of its own pride and prestige.

The selfishness of men and of nations is a fixed datum of historical science. Election results can be confidently predicted if the economic interests of the voters can be carefully enough analyzed. Yet this human egotism does not belong to nature. The eighteenth-century rationalists were wrong in asserting that men sought their own, just as every animal seeks to preserve its existence. The human self is different from other creatures in two respects: 1) It is able by its freedom to transmute nature's survival impulse into more potent and more destructive, more subtle and more comprehensive forms of self-seeking than the one-dimensional survival impulse of nature. 2) It is able to envisage a larger good than its own preservation, to make some fitful responses to this more inclusive obligation and to feel itself guilty for its failure to make a more consistent response.

Every animal will run as fast as it can from a superior foe, a strategy which subjects human beings to the charge of cowardice. Naturalists may argue that human actions have been reduced to the level of "physical events" to which no praise or blame can be attached because they always have "sufficient antecedents." But the common sense of mankind has never accepted this ridiculous denial of a unique freedom in human life and of a consequent responsibility and guilt in human action. The life and literature of the ages is replete with condemnation of cowardice and self-seeking and of praise for acts of bravery and lives of selfless devotion. Even the deterministic Marxists, who assume that moral ideals are inevitably pretentious rationalizations of self-interest, are unable to carry their determinism to its logical conclusion; for their political propaganda abounds in invectives against the dishonesty of their foes. This invective could have meaning only upon the assumption that men might be honest, rather than dishonest, and might actually seek, rather than merely pretend to seek, the good of the commonwealth rather than their own advantage.

In a similar fashion a liberal idealist who ostensibly believes that the progress of mankind depends upon the extension of the scientific method, periodically censures his fellowmen for their laziness and dishonesty, and for their inclination to make compromises with outmoded authoritarianism. "All I know about the future of progress," declares John Dewey, "is that it depends upon man to say whether he wants it or not." [5] Thus the responsible self (and the guilty self insofar as it always falls short of its highest responsibilities) peeps through even the most intricate and elaborate façades of modern thought.

The real situation is that the human self is strongly inclined to seek its own but that it has a sufficient dimension of transcendence over self to be unable to ascribe this inclination merely to natural necessity. On the other hand, when it strives for a wider good it

[5] Joseph Ratner, *The Philosophy of John Dewey*, p. 461.

surreptitiously introduces its own interests into this more inclusive value. This fault may be provisionally regarded as the inevitable consequence of a finite viewpoint. The self sees the larger structure of value from its own standpoint. Yet this provisional disavowal of moral culpability is never finally convincing. The self's ignorance is never invincible ignorance. It sees beyond itself sufficiently to know that its own interests are not identical with the wider good. If it claims such identity nevertheless, there is an element of moral perversity, and not mere ignorance in the claim. Thus the cynical attitude of all common-sense judgments toward the pretensions of nations and individuals is justified by the facts. Common sense at least touches the periphery of the mystery of original sin which uncommon sense so easily dismisses.

The common-sense of mankind, embodied in the judgments which men and nations make of each other, recognizes that there is indeed an internal debate in the life of individuals and groups between the claims of the self and the claims of some wider system of value, but that this debate is within the self and not between mind and body, or between reason and impulse. The self is indeed divided. It would do the good but does not do it; it would avoid evil but finds an inclination more powerful than its will toward the evil which it would avoid.[6] The power of this inclination to self-seeking is more potent and more mysterious than the natural impulses. The self in its totality is in the force of the inclination. Yet in moments of high reflection the self feels the inclination to be a power not its own "but sin that dwelleth in me." [7]

[6] *Cf*. Romans 7.
[7] We have previously observed how much closer to the ultimate mysteries of good and evil the poets and artists are than the psychologists and social scientists of our day. André Gide refers again and again in his journal to the mystery of evil inclinations within himself, which are his own and not yet his own. He objectifies this inclination in "the devil" though he declares, "I am utterly indifferent as to whether this name of the demon is the right name for what I mean and I grant that I give it this name out of convenience. . . . When I say: the Evil One I know what this expression designates just as clearly as I know what is designated by the word God. . . . Since he is more intelligent than I, everything he thought up to hurl me toward evil was infinitely more precious, more specious, more convincing, more clever than any argument I could have brought up to persevere in honor." *The Journals of André Gide*, Vol. II, p. 189.

The will of nations is not as clearly integrated as the "will" which symbolizes the individual self. Yet it is possible to observe this debate in the "spiritual life" of nations as well as in individuals; and to recognize that something more than a struggle between reason and ignorance is involved.

Thus American isolationism can be explained by reference to the geographic fact of the nation's seeming continental security. But though one may call attention to geographic conditions, which influence political judgements, one instinctively adds moral censure to such an analysis. If a nation ignorantly believes itself secure when it is not, it has failed to exercise its intelligence. The ignorance and finiteness of the human mind is never at a fixed limit. "We are living in a day," declared a political scientist recently, "in which knowledge of world-wide political conditions has become a possibility and a necessity. The refusal of men and nations to cultivate such knowledge has therefore become a crime." Here again the will of the self, capable of extending or restricting the knowledge required for adequate mutual relations, is revealed as a factor in a human situation, despite every effort to dismiss so incalculable an element from the rational analysis.

Though, on the whole, nations are not expected to conform to a moral standard higher than that of a prudent self-interest, yet common-sense moral judgements do cast blame upon nations for a too consistent devotion to their own interests, involving indifference to a wider good. This moral blame is justified; for though no nation will venture beyond its own interest into a system of mutual security, yet the power of even enlightened self-interest is not sufficient alone to prompt such a venture. It must be supported by a concern for a wider good, beyond its own interests. Nations are thus subject, as are individuals, to an internal tension between the claims of the self and a larger claim. Whether the second claim is tolerably met represents a spiritual issue beyond the mere calculations of prudence. Here is the responsible self in the collective life of mankind. Insofar as nations, even more than individuals, never adequately meet the wider claim the responsible self is also the guilty self.

III

The simple facts which we have enumerated are so obvious, supported by so much evidence and sustained by so many judgments of common sense in contravention to the prevailing theories of our age, that one is forced to the conclusion that something more than an honest error has entered into modern miscalculations of human behaviour and historical destiny. An honest error has indeed contributed to the confusion of our culture. It did discover the fact of historical growth and it did see that specific evils, due to specific forms of human impotence, may be overcome by the growth of human power; and that particular evils due to human ignorance may be overcome by the growth of man's intelligence; and it may well have been led astray by this evidence to the false conclusion that all human problems were being solved by historical development.

But meanwhile there was also mounting evidence that the growth of human freedom and power enlarges the scope of human problems. The problems in their larger scope are not insoluble. Proximate solutions, at least, may be found for them in time. But there is no evidence that the proximate solutions of man's perennial problems become by degrees absolute solutions. There is no evidence that highly intelligent individuals find it easier than simple folk to come to terms with their fellowmen, though intelligence may produce a social system of wider scope and greater complexity than the primitive community. There is no proof that a universal community will ever annul the partial and particular loyalties of smaller groups, rooted in nature and elaborated by history. Every wide community represents, not some simple triumph of universal over particular interest but an artful equilibration, suppression, extension, and deflection of particular interest for the sake of the wider community. Nor is there proof that history represents a gradual spiritualization or rationalization of human nature so that in some absolute sense "methods of mind" supplant methods of force. On the contrary there is mounting evidence that men act in the unity of their physical and spiritual capacities and use all resources at their command to effect what they most deeply desire or to prevent what they most profoundly abhor. In this connection the development from partial to total wars, while a culture dreamed of the gradual abolition of war, is instructive. The engagement of the total capacities of a nation for its military ventures proved to be a late achievement of culture. Precisely those technical and rational developments, which were supposed to lead to a detachment of the spiritual from the physical vitalities of men, proved to be the prerequisites for the total harnessing of all resources for the attainment of whatever end the pride or the fear, the ambition or idealism of a nation prompted.

Since there is so much proof that the development of man's power and freedom is not redemptive, the question is justified whether the modern faith in historical redemption could have been due merely to an "honest" error. The question is justified particularly because of the persistence with which modern men cling to this error in defiance of its cumulative refutation by historical experience.

These facts prompt the supposition that a more "existential" element is involved in these miscalculations. The modern interpretation of human life and history was a highly plausible evasion of some very inconvenient and embarrassing facts about human nature. It was an evasion both of the dimension of responsibility in human nature and of the fact of guilt. It made man the judge of his world and of himself and seemed to free him from the scrutiny of a higher judgement. Above all it annulled and erased the indictment of guilt contained in that higher judgement. It refuted the embarrassing suspicion that man himself is the author of the historical evils which beset him. The whole structure of the modern interpretation of life and history was, in short, a very clever contrivance of human pride to obscure the weakness and the insecurity of man; of the human conscience to hide the sin into which men fall through their efforts to override their weakness and insecurity; and of human sloth to evade responsibility.

The monotonous reiteration of the eighteenth century and of the belated children of the eighteenth century in our own age that their primary concern is to establish and to guard the "dignity of man" has the quality of a peculiar irony, when these evasions are considered.

The more consistent naturalistic versions of our culture are involved in the absurdity of ostensibly guarding the dignity of man while they actually deny the reality of a responsible self, by reducing human behaviour to the dimension of "facts of nature" about which no moral judgements can be made since every human act is the consequence of some "sufficient cause." The less consistent naturalist and the idealist do indeed exalt the dignity of the human mind; but they do not understand its involvement in finite conditions. Thus they promise a mastery of historical destiny which contradicts the permanent ambiguity of the human situation. And they construct confident "philosophies of history" as if man completely surveyed the stuff of history in his mind even as he mastered the forces of history by his power. Meanwhile man's involvement in the forces which he ostensibly masters periodically produces a shock of disillusionment in modern complacency. The vaunted master of historical destiny is subject to fits of despair when he finds himself tossed about among historical forces beyond the power of his will; and the proud interpretator of the meaning of history is periodically reduced to despair, wondering whether any truth can be known, since every truth known is known only from a special and peculiar historical locus.

Though sometimes the dignity of man is denied because the responsible self is annulled, and sometimes the dignity is exaggerated because the weakness of man is forgotten, an even more grievous error dogs all these modern calculations. The misery of man, the fact of his guilt is evaded. The fact that human power and freedom contain destructive, as well as creative, possibilities is not recognized. The responsibility of the self in the center and quintessence of its will and personality for the destructive side of human freedom is denied with particular vehemence. Even if the self is regarded as a responsible self, the idea that guilt accompanies responsibility is denied as a monstrous form of religious morbidity.

These evasions are much more serious than any of the modern rational miscalculations. They suggest that the human situation can not be understood in some simple system of rational intelligibility. Man in his strength and in his weakness is too ambiguous to understand himself, unless his rational analyses are rooted in a faith that he is comprehended from beyond the ambiguities of his own understanding. The patterns of meaning in his history culminate in a realm of meaning and mystery which, if too easily dissolved into rational intelligibility, lead to nonsense, particularly to the nonsense of contradiction. But above all there is the mystery of man's responsibility and of his guilt in failing to fulfill it. That the recalcitrance of the human heart should not be simply the lag of nature but a corruption of freedom and should not be overcome by increasing freedom: this is the mystery of original sin.

Thus an analysis of the modern conception of rationally intelligible history proves that such a conception gives history a too simple moral meaning. A profound consideration of the antinomies and mysteries which modern rationalism has been unable to digest suggests that man's life and history can be made intelligible only within the framework of a larger realm of mystery and meaning discerned by faith. In proceeding to an exposition of the Christian interpretation of life and history, in comparison with the modern one, it is necessary to disavow the purpose of proving the Christian interpretation rationally compelling, in the sense that such a comparison could rationally force modern man to accept the Christian faith. The Christian interpretation of life and history is rooted in a faith prompted by repentance. It will not be convincing except to the soul which has found the profoundest enigma of existence not in the evil surrounding it but in itself. There is therefore no simple Christian "philosophy of history" which could be set against a modern or a classical one in such a way as to prove its superior profundity through rational comparison. Yet it may be possible to prove its relevance rationally, even as it has been possible to make a rational analysis of the limits of a theory of history's rational intelligibility.

CHAPTER VII

~~~~~~

The Biblical View: The Sovereignty of God and Universal History

I

THE IDEA of a divine creation of the temporal world is not a uniquely Biblical concept. It does distinguish Biblical thought from the modern idea of a self-explanatory temporal order. But the Bible shares the idea of creation with those religions which do not regard the world of time and particularity as an emanation from, or corruption of, the eternal world. Neither is the Biblical idea of a divine sovereignty over historical destiny unique. From primitive totemism through the ancient imperial religions there is an idea of a more potent power than any human will being effective in the destiny of the tribe, nation or empire.

Yet the Biblical concept of a divine sovereignty over individual and collective historical destiny has a unique quality. This quality is given to Biblical thought by the fact that the God who is operative in historical destiny is not conceived as the projection or extension of the nation's or individual's ideals and purposes, nor as a power coextensive with, or supplementary to, the nation's power; nor as a force of reason identical with the *Logos* which the human mind incarnates.

Israel does not choose God. God chooses Israel; and this choice is regarded as an act of grace for which no reason can be given, other than God's own love (Deuteronomy 7:7-8). In Biblical thought, the grace of God completes the structure of meaning, beyond the limits of rational intelligibility in the realm of history, just as divine creation is both the fulfillment and the negation of intelligibility for the whole temporal order.

The idea of a source and end of life, too transcendent to the desires, capacities, and powers of human life to be either simply comprehended by the human mind or easily manipulated for human ends, represents the radical break of Biblical faith with the idolatrous tendencies in all human culture. This God stands over against man and nation and must be experienced as "enemy" before he can be known as friend. Human purposes, insofar as they usurp the divine prerogatives, must be broken and redirected, before there can be a concurrence between the divine and the human will.

This God is not made in any human image. The decalogue, in fact, rigorously prohibits the making of any image of God in order to guard His mystery and incomprehensibility. He is *Deus Absconditus*. The Second Isaiah reminds men in His name that "my thoughts are not your thoughts, neither are your ways my ways" (Isaiah 55:8). There is a wide gulf between His Majesty and any human sovereignty: "Behold, the nations are as a drop of a bucket, and are counted as the small dust of the balance. . . . All nations before him are as nothing; and they are counted to him less than nothing, and vanity" (Isaiah 40:15, 17).

This radical otherness of God is an offense to all rationalistic interpreters of life and history. Yet the worship of this God is the basis for the first genuine conception of a universal history; and it remains the basis for the only possible universalism which does not negate or unduly simplify the meaning of history in the process of universalizing it. This is an example of the relation of mystery to meaning in Biblical faith. Mystery does not annul meaning but enriches it. It prevents the realm of meaning from being reduced too simply to rational intelligibility and thereby being given a false center of meaning in a relative or contingent historical force or end.

Historically the prophets are responsible for this radical conception; but they could not have been capable of such a thought had it not been implicit in the idea of the covenant of God with Israel, which the prophets did not invent, though they interpreted and reinterpreted it. The idea of God choosing Israel as an act of grace, since Israel had no power or virtue to merit the choice, represents a radical break in the history of culture. It is, in a genuine sense, the beginning of revelation; for here a nation apprehends and is apprehended by the true God and not by a divine creature of its own contrivance. The proof of the genuineness of His majesty and of the truth of His divinity is attested by the fact that He confronts the nation and the individual as the limit, and not the extension, of its own power and purpose. He is the enemy and judge of every human pretension which transgresses the limits of human finiteness.[1]

Two ideas, basic to a Biblical interpretation of history, are implicit in this radical conception of the relation of God to historical destiny. One is the idea of a universal history. The other is that history is filled with man's proud and pretentious efforts to defy the divine sovereignty, to establish himself as god by his power or virtue, his wisdom or foresight.

The idea of a universal history emerges by reason of the fact that the divine sovereignty which overarches all historical destiny is not the possession of any people or the extension of any particular historical power. The other idea lays the foundation for the Biblical

---

[1] The Book of Deuteronomy constantly insists on the prophetic idea that God's choice of Israel is an act of pure grace. The transcendence of God is proved by the fact "that ye saw no manner of form on the day that God spoke to you in Horeb" (Deuteronomy 4: 15). His revelation of Himself to His people is regarded as fraught with peril to the nation: "Did ever people hear the voice of God speaking out of the midst of the fire and live?" (Deuteronomy 4: 33). The mystery of His holiness must be guarded by not permitting any symbol of Him in a force of nature "lest thou lift up thine eyes unto heaven, and when thou seest the sun, and the moon, and the stars, even all the host of heaven, shouldst be driven to worship them, and serve them, which the Lord thy God hath divided unto all the nations under the whole heaven" (Deuteronomy 4: 19). His covenant with Israel can not be explained except by His inscrutable love: "Because he loved thy fathers, therefore he chose their seed after them." (Deuteronomy 4: 37). "The Lord God did not choose you because ye were more in number than any people; for ye were the fewest of all people" (Deuteronomy 7: 7). Israel is warned against the pride of self-sufficiency which forgets the factor of grace in history. The day will come "when thou hast eaten and art full, and hast built goodly houses . . . and when thy herds and thy flocks multiply" when Israel will be tempted to say "my power and the might of mine hand hath gotten me this wealth" (Deuteronomy 8: 12–17). Such confidence in its own power and virtue will be a mark of apostasy.

conception of the complexity of history. It calls attention to the fact that the human agents do not simply conform to the divine will in history; but that they defy the divine purpose, precisely because they identify their purpose and power too simply with the divine purpose. Thereby the creativity of human freedom is turned into destructiveness. If there is a pattern and meaning in the historical drama it must be worked out against this human rebellion, which sows confusion into the order of history and makes its final end dubious. Each of these ideas must be more carefully examined.

II

It is a scandal for all rationalistic interpretations of history that the idea of a universal history should have emerged from the core of a particular historical event, whether that event be the covenant of God with Israel, or, as the New Testament conceives it, the "second covenant," instituted by the coming of Christ. Universally valid concepts of meaning must be found, according to rationalistic interpretations of history, in recurrences and forms to which all historical phenomena conform. But, as we have already noted, classical culture creates a purely negative idea of a universal history by this method. All of history is subject to the cycle of birth and death, of growth and decay. No special meaning can be assigned to the unique achievements of any individual life or culture. Modern culture, on the other hand, comprehends the meaning of history too positively as an endless development of human power and wisdom; and is driven to despair when the antinomies of good and evil manifest themselves in this development.

The "scandal of particularity" (*einmaligkeit*) in the Biblical interpretation is a necessary part of revelation in Biblical faith. The mysterious divine power, which explains the beginning, the present order and the final end of history, represents a depth of mystery and meaning which is not fully disclosed by the obvious coherences of nature and sequences of history. Yet Biblical faith is not identical with agnosticism. It believes that God does disclose His purposes. The disclosure takes place in significant events of history. The revelatory power of these events must be apprehended by faith. So apprehended they prove to be more than particular events. They are "mighty acts" of God in which the meaning of the whole drama of human life is made clear. This clarification is always an act of redemption as well as of revelation. For God reveals both His mercy and His judgement in these disclosures. If the disclosure is therefore apprehended in repentance and faith it will also lead to a reformation of life. It can not be apprehended without repentance, because the God who stands against us, "whose thoughts are not our thoughts" (Isaiah 55:8) can not be known if we do not contritely abate the pretension of reaching God by our thought or of regarding His power as an extension of our power. Thus the faith which apprehends the disclosure of the divine mercy and will implies and requires a repentance which leads to a reformation and redemption of life.

In the Old Testament every profound prophetic interpretation of God's covenant with Israel leads to the indictment that Israel has broken the covenant and that it must turn from its evil ways if it would live. The dialectical fact that the special destiny of a nation exposes it to a special peril of pride and that capitulation to this temptation subjects Israel to a uniquely severe divine condemnation is perfectly expressed by the first of the great prophets, Amos: "You only have I known of all the families of the earth; therefore I will punish you for all your iniquities" (Amos 3:2). This logic is normative for the whole Biblical interpretation of history. Though Israel never ceases to be tempted to make itself the perverse center of universal history, there is no justification for this pride and complacency in Biblical faith. The rigor of the differentiation between God and Israel, and between His Majesty and every human sovereignty, is an important element in the prophetic conception of a universal history. Prophetic universalism has its own history. Not every prophet was as loyal to it as Jeremiah and the Second Isaiah; and nationalistic motifs appear in even the profoundest of the prophets. They appear also in the apocalyptic visions of a messianic period in which history was to be both fulfilled and ended.

Nevertheless, the logic of this universalism is clear. God's special destiny for Israel implies no special security. In the ultimate instance His sovereignty over all nations expresses itself even over those nations which do not know Him. The rigor of the prophetic conception of the divine transcendence contributes to the idea of a universal history in two ways:

History is conceived as unity because all historical destinies are under the dominion of a single divine sovereignty.[2] The fact that the unity is not established empirically by tracing the interpenetration of cultures and civilizations with each other prevents a false universalism in which the destiny of a particular nation or culture is made into a false center of meaning for the whole story of mankind. While Israel does have a central place in the drama of history, it has no special security. Amos challenges the inchoate messianic hopes of a national triumph of Israel. He predicts that "the day of the Lord will be darkness and not light." In the "new covenant" or the "New Testament" the triumph of Israel as the clue to the meaning of history is even more specifically denied. The revelation of Christ as the center of and clue to history's meaning is both the negation and the fulfillment of all partial meanings in history, as they are embodied in national, imperial, and even world-wide cultures.

From the standpoint of modern interpretations of history this conception of the unity of history by faith will seem to be merely a primitive and provisional sense of a total story of mankind, transcending the separate stories of various nations and cultures. The faith which maintains it will seem to be the fruit of the immaturity of an early culture, which lacked the capacity to correlate the various historical destinies and prove them to be empirically all part of one total story. It is true that the elaboration of the historical sciences since the days of the prophets has made it possible to trace various strands of unity. Furthermore the development of technics, particularly man's triumph over time and space, has made various previously disparate and unrelated cultures contiguous. It would seem, therefore, that the story of mankind is progressively becoming

---

[2] The first explicit exposition of universal history is found in the words of the first of the great prophets, Amos: "Are ye not as children of the Ethiopians unto me, O children of Israel? saith the Lord. Have not I brought . . . the Philistines from Caphtor, and the Syrians from Kir?" (Amos 9:7).

one story, both through an actual growth in cultural interpenetration and through the development of historical sciences, able to trace and analyze such interpenetrations.

It is worth noting, however, that in all modern efforts to explicate the unity of history as a fact of historical science or as proved by the metaphysics of a philosophy of history, the correlations are too simple to do justice to the variety of historical phenomena and the richness of historical life. In the modern idea of progress, for instance, the earlier ages of mankind are debased because they are regarded merely as stepping stones for the attainment of the true life in our or in some subsequent age; and the relation between various cultures is made into a too simple rational continuum; and finally an inadequate climax is found for the drama of history in some fancied culmination either in the age of the philosopher who constructs the drama or in an immediately subsequent age. Hegel significantly regarded his attempt at universal history as a rationalized version of the Biblical idea of historical unity through divine providence. "Our mode of treating the subject is," he writes, "a theodicy, a justification of the ways of God to man . . . so that the ills which may be found in the world may be comprehended and the thinking Spirit reconciled with the fact of the existence of evil." [3] The evil which had to be reconciled was "the discord between the inner life of the heart and the actual world." This is to say that the real problem of the drama of history is misapprehended. It consists not in the discord between man's free spirit and the necessities of the "actual" world. It is rather the evil which men bring upon themselves and each other in their freedom.

Hegel constructed a drama of history which gives history an unreal unity, which found the threat of meaninglessness in natural necessity rather than in freedom, which falsified historical details to establish the idea of historical unity and which arrived at an absurd climax in the European civilization of his day. Comte, beginning with different presuppositions and boasting of a scientific, rather than metaphysical, approach to the problem, constructed a drama

[3] *Philosophy of History* (English translation), p. 16.

which is equally absurd in its details, its general scheme, and its culmination. The actual course of history has invalidated them both.

Recently Arnold Toynbee has sought to arrive at a new interpretation of the unity of history by an artful combination of the classical, the Christian, and the modern view. Basically Toynbee's pluralistic conception of history, his isolation and definition of discrete civilizations, conforms to the classical pattern. The frame of meaning is not purely classical, however, because these civilizations, according to Toynbee, do not live and die according to the laws of nature but are subject to a special historical destiny, which involves the corruption of freedom. Civilizations are ostensibly destroyed by some superior foe. Actually they perish at their own hands; and the instrument of their destruction is the pride by which they make some ephemeral technique, structure or instrument of history into a false absolute. This conception of pride as the cause of a civilization's destruction is a Biblical-Augustinian addition to the classical idea of historical recurrence.

The modern idea of progress is added to this partly classical and partly Christian interpretation by the suggestion that the rise and fall of civilizations represents the turn of the wheels of a chariot and drives the chariot forward. The chariot is high religion. "The breakdowns and disintegrations of civilizations might be stepping stones to higher things on the religious plane. After all, one of the deepest spiritual laws that we know is the law that is proclaimed by Aeschylus in the two words *'pathei mathos.'* 'It is through suffering that learning comes' . . . and in the New Testament in the verse 'whom the Lord loveth He chasteneth; and scourgeth every son whom He receiveth.' If you apply that to the rise of the higher religions which has culminated in the flowering of Christianity, you might say that in the mythical passions of Tammuz and Adonis and Attis and Osiris the Passion of Christ was foreshadowed, and that the Passion of Christ was the culminating and crowning experience of the sufferings of human souls in successive failures in the enterprise of secular civilizations. . . . If religion is a chariot, it looks as if the wheels on which it mounts towards Heaven may be the periodic downfalls of civilizations on Earth." [4]

Toynbee's effort to find a meaning for universal history in a framework for which he has appropriated Christian, as well as classical and modern motifs, belongs to one of the most impressive intellectual ventures of our age. It is nevertheless a dubious structure of meaning. A number of its weaknesses may be enumerated:

1) Toynbee's pluralism obscures the empirical unity of history as it is established by the interpenetration of cultures and civilizations. His twenty-one civilizations are not as discrete as he supposes. He seeks to do justice to their interpenetrations by concepts of "affiliation" and "apparentation"; but these are not sufficient to give an adequate picture of the complex interrelatedness of various cultures. [5]

2) The emphasis upon the classical idea of recurrence enables Toynbee to find many illuminating analogies in history which the modern idea of progress has obscured. On the other hand, Toynbee's method obscures the novelties and new emergents in history. This is particularly apparent when he compares historic facts before and after the rise of modern industrial society. He may be illuminating, for instance, when he emphasizes Russia's "Byzantine heritage" and regards the present struggles between Russia and the West as a recurrence of the old struggle between Eastern and Western Christendom. But the significant role which Marxism as a novel factor plays in this struggle is not fully appreciated. The fact that Marxism is a creed of the West, appropriated by Russia, and that part of Russia's power is derived from the appeal of this creed to the industrial classes of Europe suggests that the struggle is not so much a

[4] Arnold J. Toynbee, "Christianity and Civilization," *Civilization on Trial,* pp. 234–235. Copyright 1948 by Oxford University Press, Inc.
[5] See *inter alia,* for criticism of this pluralism: R. G. Collingwood, *The Idea of History,* pp. 159–165. Collingwood makes the interesting suggestion that Toynbee is applying the methods of natural science to historical study. The natural scientist finds himself "confronted by separate, discrete facts which can be counted. He then proceeds to determine the relations between them, these relations being always links connecting one fact with another external to it. . . . These are the principles on which Toynbee deals with history. The first thing he does is to cut up the field of historical study into a specific number of discrete sections, each called a society," p. 162.

conflict between Eastern and Western Christendom as the international projection of a civil war in the Western world.

3) The concept of religious progress through the birth and death of civilizations has the merit of calling attention to the fact that periods of historic decay may well be times of profoundest religious insights; for historic catastrophes break the power of the idolatrous worship of cultures and civilizations. They are, or may be appropriated by faith as, divine judgements upon the inclination of men and nations to regard a tenuous and tentative form of human order or justice as the final form; or to think of the stability of a moment of history as the final peace. Thus Augustine's interpretation of Christianity was profounder, not only than the interpretations of Constantine's clerical courtiers who regarded the stability of Rome as the proof of the truth of the Christian faith,[6] but it was also profounder than that of Thomas Aquinas, who subtly compounded the prestige of a seemingly stable clerical rule over the nations with the wisdom and the power of Christ.

It is nevertheless doubtful whether history conforms to any such pattern of religious growth. It is particularly doubtful whether historical catastrophes can be proved to be the instruments of such religious development. Toynbee has difficulty in fitting the religious decay in our "western post-Christian secular civilization" into his pattern. He admits that it is "at best a superfluous repetition of the pre-Christian Graeco-Roman" decay and that "at worst it is a pernicious backsliding from the paths of spiritual progress." [7]

Actually we can never dismiss the possibility that historical catastrophes may destroy religion as well as a civilization. Whenever a religious view of life and history becomes too intimately bound up with a civilization, it may be destroyed in the collapse of a civilization. If religious faith is unable to interpret historic catastrophes, so that they may be appropriated as divine judgements, men are overwhelmed by them and perish spiritually in their confusion.

There is significantly no suggestion in the New Testament of a chariot of religion mounting to higher and higher levels through

[6] *Cf.* Charles Cochrane, *Christianity and Classical Culture*, ch. V.
[7] *Ibid.*, p. 236.

the cycles of the rise and fall of civilizations. There is, on the contrary, the awesome suggestion that history remains open to all possibilities of good and evil, including the destruction of faith: "When the Son of Man cometh, shall he find faith on the earth?" (Luke 18:8). The possible destruction of faith would not mean the defeat of God, whose mercy and judgement will triumph in the end. Biblical thought recognizes the tentative and obscure patterns of meaning in history; but it never sees them consistently fulfilled in history itself.

The meaning of history is, in short, more complex than conceived in even the profoundest philosophies of history, whether classical or modern. It is significant that historians, as distinguished from philosophers of history, usually have great difficulty with these philosophical patterns of meaning because these fail to do justice to the complexity of historical patterns and the wide variety of historical facts. An eminent historian expresses his doubts as follows: "Most philosophies of history . . . appear to me to be grounded on an arbitrary and over-simplified selection of facts. I do not say that no clue to the ultimate significance of human action and suffering will ever be found in history. I can indeed see evidence of design, but *the pattern is on a scale* beyond my comprehension." [8]

There are more specific meanings in the Biblical conception of history, as we shall see presently, than merely the idea that history is potentially and ultimately one story by reason of being under one divine sovereignty. But this Biblical conception which establishes the unity of history by faith, rather than by sight, is a guard against all premature efforts to correlate the facts of history into a pattern of too simple meaning. It is indeed one of the proofs of the ambiguity of man, as an observor of the historical process who transcends but is also involved in the process, that he can not construct systems of meaning for the facts of history, whether of a particular story in it or of the story of mankind as a whole, without making the temporal locus of his observation into a falsely absolute vantage point, or without using a structure of meaning which seems to him to be absolutely valid but which is actually touched by historical relativism.

There is, in short, no possibility of preserving the sense of uni-

[8] E. L. Woodward, *Short Journey*, p. 136.

versal history, except by faith, even in a highly sophisticated culture, commanding all the resources of modern historical science. While cultures are interrelated, they remain so disparate that they can not be easily brought into a single story by empirical correlations. The Biblical faith in a divine sovereignty which unifies history is not merely a primitive conception which cultural progress outmodes. It remains a permanently necessary basis for the idea of universal history. Various religious, philosophical and scientific efforts to fill this wide frame of potential meaning with specific correlations of detailed meaning will, of course, continue to be made and must be made. But insofar as they are bound to betray man's forgetfulness that as a creature of time he is incapable of being completely the master of time, either as agent or as observor of historical destiny, they will result in schemes of meaning which will fail to do justice to the whole panorama of the historical scene.

III

The second contribution of the Biblical idea of divine transcendence to the concept of universal history is contained in the rigor with which the inclination of every human collective, whether tribe, nation, or empire, to make itself the center of universal history is overcome in principle. The God who has chosen Israel promises peril, rather than security, as the concomitant of this eminence. The God who is revealed in Christ brings all nations under His judgement. The majesty of a suffering servant and crucified Saviour will cast down "every high thing that exalteth itself against the knowledge of God" (2 Corinthians 10:5).

It is through the judgement of God, who stands against all human pride and pretension, that the inclination of men and nations to make themselves the false center of universal history is broken in principle. The scandal that the idea of universal history should be the fruit of a particular revelation of the divine, to a particular people, and finally in a particular drama and person, ceases to be scandalous when it is recognized that the divine Majesty, apprehended in these particular revelations, is less bound to the pride of civilizations and the hopes and ambitions of nations, than the supposedly more universal concepts of life and history by which cultures seek to extricate themselves from the historical contingencies and to establish universally valid "values."

Biblical faith must be distinguished on the one hand from the cultures which negate the meaning of history in the rigor of their effort to find a transcendent ground of truth; and on the other hand from both ancient and modern affirmations of the meaning of life and history, which end by giving history an idolatrous center of meaning. In the first category we must place not merely the classical culture of the western world, whose ahistorical character we have previously analyzed; but also the high religions of the Orient. In the second category belong not merely the imperial religions of the ancient civilizations of Egypt, Babylon, Persia, etc.; but also modern secularized idolatries, in which some powerful nation, whether Germany, Russia, America, Britain, or any other nation, conceives itself as the center of historical meaning; or in which a culture, such as the bourgeois culture of the nineteenth century, imagines itself the culmination of historical progress.

In contrast to ahistorical cultures, Biblical faith affirms the potential meaning of life in history. It is in history, and not in a flight from history, that the divine power which bears and completes history is revealed. In contrast to idolatrous historical cultures the revelation of the divine, which manifests itself in history, casts down everything which exalteth itself against the knowledge of God.

According to Biblical faith, the tendency toward idolatry in the interpretation of history is a part of the phenomenon of original sin; that is, of the inclination of the human heart to solve the problem of the ambiguity of human existence by denying man's finiteness. The sin is particularly evident in the collective life of mankind because nations, empires and cultures achieve a seeming immortality, a power and a majesty which tempts them to forget that they belong to the flux of mortality.[9] This inclination could be interpreted provisionally as the fruit of human ignorance. It would seem that the individual man is fooled by the greater majesty and the seeming im-

[9] *Cf.* Ezekiel 28–32.

mortality of collective man's achievements. Therefore he worships
his nation as god. But there is always an element of perversity as
well as of ignorance in this worship. For other nations and cultures
are perversely debased and become merely the instruments or tools,
the victims or allies of the nation of one's worship. There are no
strictly pluralistic conceptions of history after the primitive period of
culture, when every tribe remembers its own story without reference
to any other story or tribal destiny. Since the beginning of ancient
civilizations history is interpreted, not pluralistically, but in terms
of false conceptions of universal history. The culture which elaborates the scheme of meaning makes its own destiny into the false
center of the total human destiny.

Neither secular nor Christian nations are immune from the temptation to such idolatry. The history of Christian nations abounds in
ridiculous conceptions of nationalistic messianisms, in which a particular nation is regarded as the instrument or agent of the culmination of history.[10] In Nicolai Berdyaev's *The Russian Idea* this Christian theologian examines the various Messianic ideas in the history
of Russian culture. Instead of dismissing the very concept of nationalistic messianism as heretical from the Christian standpoint, he la-
bors diligently to find the most adequate expression of it and comes
to the conclusion that the modern secularized version of messianism,
as expressed in Russian communism, though not completely adequate, comes closer to the truth than previous messianic ideas. It
evidently has not occurred to Berdyaev that one of the most tragic
aspects of human history is that a "final" form of evil should periodically come into history by the pretension of a nation, culture, or
class that is the agent of a final form of redemption.

The virulence and truculence which flows from the Russian illusions are important reminders of the fact that secular civilizations
do not escape religious idolatries by a formal disavowal of religion.
A secular age spawns these idolatries more readily, in fact, because it
has lost every sense of a divine majesty "that bringeth the princes to
nothing" and "maketh the judges of the earth as vanity" (Isaiah

[10] For examples of such nationalistic messianism in the history of Christian
nations see Salo Baron, *Modern Nationalism and Religion.*

40:23). The concept of the "American dream" according to which America is a kind of second chosen nation, ordained to save democracy after the effete nations of Europe proved themselves incapable of the task, is a milder form of such nationalistic messianism.

While these nationalistic and imperial corruptions of the idea of universal history are the most vivid examples of the inclination of men and nations to make themselves into the false center of the vast panorama of history, they are nevertheless merely one aspect of the whole problem of historical relativism, which remains one of the unsolved problems of modern culture. The problem forces modern man, who claims to be increasingly the master of historical destiny, into periodic moods of scepticism as he analyses his dubious position as observer of history. The problem is, how a man, nation, or culture involved in the mutabilities of history can achieve a sufficiently high vantage point of wisdom and disinterestedness to chart the events of history, without using a framework of meaning which is conditioned by contingent circumstances of the class, nation, or period of the observer.

In Dilthey's profound study of historical relativism he finds escape from scepticism by the assumption that a common participation in "objective spirit" allows the observer of historical phenomena an affinity with the observed phenomena, transcending the different contingencies in which the observers and the observed are involved.[11] Kant has no difficulty with the problem because for him, history as observed belongs to the realm of nature, while the observer of history, insofar as he is rational, transcends the world of nature.

Karl Mannheim's solution of the problem of historical relativism is influenced by the modern confidence in science. He believes that it is possible to develop a "sociology of knowledge" which will, in infinite regression, refine historical knowledge by isolating and excluding the conditioned perspectives of persons, classes, interests, and periods until the real truth is reached.[12] An American philosopher, Maurice Mandelbaum, seeks to escape historical relativism by exalting "facts" and minimizing their valuation, through which the his-

[11] Wilhelm Dilthey, *Gesammelte Werke*, VII.
[12] Karl Mannheim, *Ideology and Utopia*.

torian betrays his own relative viewpoint. "Every historical fact," he declares, "is given in some specific context in which it leads to some other fact. . . . Thus when an historian makes a statement of fact it is not with an isolated fact but with a fact in a given context that he is concerned. And in that context the fact leads on to further facts without any intermediation or selection, based on the historian's valuational attitudes, class, interests, or the like." [13]

The difficulty with this solution is that every fact is both the fruit of a dozen or a hundred different historical pressures, forces, and tendencies and the root of a dozen or a hundred historical consequences. The "bare" fact is little more than a date in history. A victory or defeat in battle may be an explicit event, subject to an unambiguous description; but usually even military victories and defeats are not so explicit as to obviate conflicting interpretation. In the vast complexities of political defeats and victories, interpretations of the events depend even more obviously upon the framework of meaning from which they are observed. The larger the area of historical events which is surveyed, the more obvious is it that events in it can be correlated only within a framework of meaning, to which the viewpoint of an age, a class or a nation contributes as much as the facts themselves. There is, of course, a difference between an honest historian who changes his frame of meaning if he finds that he can not correlate the facts within it and a dishonest historian who suppresses the facts in order to preserve his frame of meaning. But when the area of inquiry is sufficiently wide and complex, even the most scrupulous honesty on the part of the historian can not prevent his viewpoint from coloring the historical picture. Historical relativism is overcome too easily if, as in the thought of Dilthey, or Kant, the involvement of the observer of history in historical mutability is denied; or if, as in the thought of Mannheim, a final scientific triumph over historical "ideologies" is presumed to be possible; or if, as in the thought of Mandelbaum, historical events are reduced to "facts" which are immune to evaluational distortion.

There is, in short, no complete rational solution for the problem of historical relativism. Insofar as the human mind in both its structure

[13] *The Problem of Historical Knowledge*, p. 200–201.

and in its capacities of observation has a vantage point over the flux of historical events, it is possible to achieve valid historical knowledge though this knowledge will never have the exactness of knowledge in the field of natural science. But insofar as men, individually or collectively, are involved in the temporal flux they must view the stream of events from some particular locus. A high degree of imagination, insight, or detachment may heighten or enlarge the locus; but no human power can make it fully adequate. That fact is one of the most vivid examples of the ambiguity of the human situation. The pretension that this is not the case is an aspect of the "original sin" which infects all human culture. Its essence is man's unwillingness to acknowledge his finiteness.

Men must observe and interpret the flow of historical events with as much honesty and wisdom as possible. Historical sciences will continue to be elaborated and scientific schemes invented to reduce conscious and unconscious ideological taints in historical observations. Philosophical disciplines will be judged and scrutinized on the basis of the adequacy of their guard against the temptation of the observer to pretend to more absolute knowledge than a finite creature has the right to claim. All such efforts belong to the legitimate improvement of human culture. But none of them can obviate the necessity of using a scheme of meaning for the correlation of the observed data of history, which is not the consequence but the presupposition of the empirical scrutiny of historical data. The more the whole panorama of history is brought into view, the more obvious it becomes that the meaning which is given to the whole is derived from an act of faith. History may have a minimal unity by reason of the fact that all of its events are grounded in the flow of time in a single world. But this minimal unity gives no key for correlating the wide variety of cultural and political configurations which distinguish history from the flow of natural events. History in its totality and unity is given a meaning by some kind of religious faith in the sense that the concept of meaning is derived from ultimate presuppositions about the character of time and eternity, which are not the fruit of detailed analyses of historical events.

Whether these ultimate presuppositions of meaning constitute an adequate framework for the correlation of all relevant historical facts is a question which can be approached rationally. It is possible, at least, to reject all concepts of the unity of history which make some vitality, event or value within history itself into a premature and idolatrous center of its meaning. If such idolatries are rejected it will become apparent that the real center of meaning for history must transcend the flux of time. To believe that the story of mankind is one story because the various disparate stories are under one divine sovereignty is therefore not an arbitrary procedure. On the contrary it prevents ages and cultures, civilizations and philosophies, from arbitrarily finding the center of history's meaning within their own life or achievements and from seeking the culmination and fulfillment of that meaning prematurely in the victory of their cause or the completion of their particular project.

Every larger frame of meaning, which serves the observer of historical events in correlating the events into some kind of pattern, is a structure of faith rather than of science, in the sense that the scientific procedures must presuppose the framework and it can therefore not be merely their consequence. The difference between structures of meaning is therefore not between supposedly "rational" and supposedly "irrational" ones. Supposedly rational frames of meaning may be irrational in the sense that an implicit and unacknowledged center and source of meaning may be inadequate to do justice to every dimension of human existence and every perplexity and antinomy in the stuff of history. A supposedly "irrational" frame of meaning may be rational in the sense that it acknowledges a center and source of meaning beyond the limits of rational intelligibility, partly because it "rationally" senses the inadequacy or idolatrous character of centers and sources of meaning which are within the limits of rational intelligibility.

CHAPTER VIII

The Biblical View: Moral Meaning and
Moral Obscurities of History

I

THE SOVEREIGNTY of God establishes the general frame of meaning for life and history, according to Biblical faith. But the first specific content of the drama of history is furnished by the assertion of divine sovereignty against man's rebellious efforts to establish himself as the perverse center of existence. Biblical faith does not deny the fact of evil in history. On the contrary it discerns that men are capable of such bold and persistent defiance of the laws and structures of their existence that only the resource of the divine power and love is finally able to overcome this rebellion. The patterns of human existence are filled with obscurities and abysses of meaninglessness because of this possibility of evil in human life.

The obscurities and incoherences of life are, according to Biblical faith, primarily the consequence of human actions. The incoherences and confusions, usually defined as "natural" evil, are not the chief concern of the Christian faith. Natural evil represents the failure of nature's processes to conform perfectly to human ends. It is the consequence of man's ambiguous position in nature. As a creature of nature he is subject to necessities and contingencies, which may be completely irrelevant to the wider purposes, interests, and ambitions which he conceives and elaborates as creative spirit. The most vivid symbol of natural evil is death. Death is a simple fact in the dimension of nature; but it is an irrelevance and a threat of meaninglessness in the realm of history. Biblical faith is, however, only obliquely interested in the problem of natural evil. It does not regard death, as such, as an evil. "The sting of death," declares St. Paul, "is sin." [1]

Nor does it regard moral evil as due to man's involvement in natural finiteness. On the contrary, moral or historical evil is the consequence of man's abortive effort to overcome his insecurity by his own power, to hide the finiteness of his intelligence by pretensions of omniscience and to seek for emancipation from his ambiguous position by his own resources. Sin is, in short, the consequence of man's inclination to usurp the prerogatives of God, to think more highly of himself than he ought to think, thus making destructive use of his freedom by not observing the limits to which a creaturely freedom is bound.

Man is at variance with God through this abortive effort to establish himself as his own Lord; and he is at variance with his fellow-men by the force of the same pride which brings him in conflict with God. The prophets of Israel seemed to sense this primary form of historical evil most immediately in its collective form. They felt that Israel was guilty of it, because it drew complacent conclusions from the fact of its special covenant with God. The great nations and empires which encircled Israel were guilty because they imagined that their power made them immortal and secure. The myth of the Fall of Adam universalizes, as well as individualizes, this theme of man's revolt against God. The influence of this myth upon the Christian imagination is not primarily due to any literalistic illusions of Christian orthodoxy. The myth accurately symbolizes the consistent Biblical diagnosis of moral and historical evil. Adam and,

---

[1] Ritschl, in common with many liberal theologians of the nineteenth century, made the mistake of believing that the Christian faith, in common with other high religions, is a way of gaining "assurance that man is not a part of the natural world, but is a cooperator with the divine purpose in the world." Faith is thus a method of man's being "sure of his spiritual uniqueness despite his subordination to the world of nature." From unpublished Dogmatik quoted by Goesta Hök, *Die Elliptische Theologie Albert Ritschl's*, p. 28. Hegel's definition of evil as the "discord between the inner life of the heart and the actual world" is prompted by the same logic.

together with him, all men seek to overstep the bounds which are set by the Creator for man as creature. St. Paul's definition of sin is in perfect conformity with this theme, even when he makes no specific reference to the Fall. Man's sin, declares St. Paul, is that he "changes the glory of the uncorruptible God into an image of corruptible man" (Romans 1:23). If men fail to penetrate to the mystery of the divine, the fault lies, according to the Bible, not so much in the finiteness of their intelligence as in the "vanity" of their imagination. They are, declares St. Paul, "without excuse" in their ignorance of God. For "the invisible things of him from the creation of the world are clearly seen, being understood by the things that are made" (Romans 1:20). It is obvious, in other words, that the world is not self-derived. It points beyond itself to its Creator. The failure to recognize this fact is not the fault of the mind but of the person who usurps the central position in the scheme of things and thereby brings confusion into his own life and into the whole order of history. Biblical faith has always insisted upon the embarrassing truth that the corruption of evil is at the heart of the human personality. It is not the inertia of its natural impulses in opposition to the purer impulses of the mind. The fact that it is a corruption which has a universal dominion over all men, though it is not by nature but in freedom that men sin, is the "mystery" of "original sin," which will always be an offense to rationalists. But it has the merit of being true to the facts of human existence.[2] A scientific age will seek, and also find, specific reasons and causes for the jealousy of children, or the power lusts in mature individuals, or the naive egotism of even the saintly individual, or the envies and hatreds which infect all human relations. The discovery of specific causes of specific forms of these evils has obscured and will continue to obscure the profounder truth, that all men, saints and sinners, the righteous and the unrighteous, are inclined to use the freedom to transcend time, history, and themselves in such a way as to make themselves the false center of existence. Thus the same freedom which gives

---

[2] "Nothing," declares Pascal, "offends us more rudely than this doctrine; and yet without this mystery, the most incomprehensible of all, we are incomprehensible to ourselves." *Pensees*, 434.

human life a creative power, not possessed by the other creatures, also endows it with destructive possibilities not known in nature. The two-fold possibility of creativity and destruction in human freedom accounts for the growth of both good and evil through the extension of human powers. The failure to recognize this obvious fact in modern culture accounts for most of its errors in estimating the actual trends of history.[8]

The tendency of modern culture to see only the creative possibilities of human freedom makes the Christian estimate of the human situation seem morbid by contrast Is not Kierkegaard morbid, even Christians are inclined to ask, when he insists that "before God man is always in the wrong"? Does such an emphasis not obscure the creative aspects of human freedom? Is it not true that men are able by increasing freedom to envisage a larger world and to assume a responsible attitude toward a wider and wider circle of claims upon their conscience? Does the Christian faith do justice, for instance, to the fact that increasing freedom has set the commandment, "Thou shalt love thy neighbor as thyself," in a larger frame of reference than ever before in history? Is it not significant that we have reached a global situation in which we may destroy ourselves and each other if we fail to organize a new global "neighborhood" into a tenable brotherhood?

Such misgivings fail to recognize how intimately the dignity and the misery of man are related in the Christian conception. The dig-

---

[3] There is a remarkable consistency in some of the ancient stories of Genesis about the growth of civilization. In a strain of tradition which Robert H. Pfeiffer distinguishes from the usual J, E and P sources and identifies as the S source, the development of mankind is traced from the Garden of Eden (Genesis 2) through use of leaves and skins as garments (Genesis 3:7 and Genesis 3:21); the cultivation of the soil (Genesis 3:17–19); the development of arts and crafts, the making of tents and invention of musical instruments, the working of metals (Genesis 4:20–22); to the age of the planting of vineyards and the making of wine (Genesis 9:20f); and finally the building of cities and the distinction of languages and nationalities (Genesis 11:1–9).

The chronicle of this development of civilization is informed by the pessimistic belief that "cultural progress is accompanied by increased wickedness and unhappiness." Pfeiffer, *Introduction to the Old Testament*, p. 163.

These ancient stories reveal a profounder understanding of the relation of freedom to evil than most modern conceptions. The Stoic idea of a Golden Age of primitive innocency and of a subsequent historical corruption is, of course, analogous to this strain of thought,

nity of man, which modern culture is ostensibly so anxious to guard and validate, is greater than the modern mind realizes. For it consists of a unique freedom which is able, not only to transcend the "laws" of nature or of reason to which classical and modern culture would bind it, but also to defy and outrage the very structure of man's existence. The dignity of man is therefore no proof of his virtue; nor is the misery of man a proof of his "bestiality." Both the destructive and the creative powers of man are unique because of the special quality of freedom which he possesses.

If the destructive, rather than the creative, possibilities of freedom seem unduly emphasized in Biblical thought, that is because in the ultimate instance (that is when men are not judging themselves but feel themselves under a divine judgement) they become conscious of the self's persistent self-centeredness. When they are judging themselves they are inclined to be impressed by the self's virtuous inclination to consider interests, other than its own.

It is worth noting that the behaviour of a man or nation, viewed from the standpoint of a critical rival or observer is invariably assessed, not as the morally complacent self judges its own actions but as the devout and contrite self judges it. The Christian interpretation of the human situation corresponds to what men and nations say about each other, even without Christian insights. But without Christian insights they bring even greater confusion into the affairs of men by assuming that only their rivals and competitors are guilty of the pride and lust for power which they behold. Only under the judgement of God do they recognize the universality of this human situation of sin and guilt.

II

The capacity and inclination of man to disturb the order and harmony of human life by placing himself, individually and collectively, perversely into the center of the whole drama of life gives the pattern of history a much greater complexity than is supposed in those interpretations which assume that man conforms naturally to whatever "laws" of life his mind discerns. The Biblical interpretation of the pattern of history must incorporate the provisional meaninglessness and obscurity which human defiance of God's laws introduces into the drama of the human story. The drama is, in essence, not so much a contest between good and evil forces in history as a contest between all men and God. In this contest God has resources of power and mercy, finally to overcome the human rebellion. He asserts His sovereignty partly by the power which places an ultimate limit upon human defiance and partly by a resource of love and mercy which alone is able to touch the source of the rebellion in the human heart. The divine sovereignty is always partly "hidden" and the meaning of life and history is partly obscure, not only because human defiance and moral evil seem to enjoy long periods of immunity,[4] thus calling the divine justice and power in question; but also because the relation of the divine mercy to the divine justice is obscure.

The climax of the Biblical revelation of the divine sovereignty over history is in the self-disclosure of a divine love, which on the one hand is able to overcome the evil inclination to self-worship in the human heart and which on the other hand takes the evil of history into and upon itself. These two facets of the divine love establish the two most important aspects of the Biblical interpretation of history. On the one hand there is a possibility of the renewal of life and the destruction of evil, whenever men and nations see themselves as they truly are under a divine judgement, which is as merciful as it is terrible. On the other hand the life of each individual as well as the total human enterprise remains in contradiction to God; and the final resolution of this contradiction is by God's mercy. From the one standpoint human history is a series of new beginnings. These new beginnings are not the inevitable springtime which follows the death of winter in nature. Life does not arise from death, as death from life, in natural cycles. Life may be reborn, if, under the

---

[4] A classical example of the doubts which assail the faithful when they behold the immunity of evil doers is found in the words of the 73rd Psalm: "But as for me, my feet were almost gone; my steps had well-nigh slipped. For I was envious at the foolish when I saw the prosperity of the wicked. For there are no bands in their death; but their strength is firm. . . . Their eyes stand out with fatness; they have more than heart could wish. . . . And they say, How doth God know? and is there knowledge in the most High?"

divine judgement and mercy, the old self or the old culture or civilization is shattered.

From the other standpoint human life and human history remain a permanent enigma which only the divine mercy can overcome. No human life has a logical or consistent conclusion within itself. It requires not only a "life everlasting" which it is unable to achieve of itself, but also the "forgiveness of sins" which it cannot earn itself. The total human enterprise is in the same case. Human powers and capacities may continue to develop indeterminately. But a "last judgement" stands at the end of all human achievements; and the "Anti-Christ" manifests himself at the end of history. This is the Biblical symbol of the inconclusive character of human history. Biblical faith is, in short, the tremendous assertion that in Biblical revelation, culminating in the revelation of Christ, man has made contact with the divine power, which is able to overcome not only the ambiguity in which all human life and history is involved but also the evils of history which are due to man's abortive efforts to overcome them himself by his own resources.

The mercy of God does not, according to the faith of the New Testament, annul the justice and wrath of God. The paradoxical relation between God's love and His justice, explicated in the doctrine of the Atonement, must be considered more fully presently. Our immediate concern is to consider the Biblical idea that judgement is one of the proofs of divine sovereignty and one (though a negative one) of the factors in the meaning of history.

The prophets believe that God's judgements are executed in history. That confidence establishes the moral meaning of history. But they sense a divine judgement above and beyond the rough and inexact historical judgements. Therein they establish a frame of reference for history beyond the obvious and observable facts of history. They look for a more perfect and exact divine retribution in a future messianic age. Thereby they establish both the attitude of expectancy toward the future, which lies at the foundation of the Biblical attitude toward a meaningful history, and toward a fulfillment of historical meanings beyond history which lies at the foundation of Biblical otherworldliness. The significance of the concept of the messianic age lies precisely in the fact that it contains both the idea of a future history which will clarify present obscurities in the moral meaning of life and of the end of history in which historical existence will be transfigured.

The trans-historical note in the prophetic sense of judgement is revealed not only in the idea of a final judgement beyond all the ambiguities of history. It is also revealed in the prophetic insistence upon an immediately felt divine condemnation, which does not require historic validation. The prophets felt Israel to be guilty before God, not because it failed to conform to some comparative historical standard or fell below the righteousness of other nations. On the contrary they assumed its superior righteousness; but this superiority did not obscure its failure to conform to the covenant it had with God. The prophet Amos predicted judgement upon Israel not because he was able to weigh historical probabilities and arrive at the conclusion that an historical catastrophe was impending. He made his prediction of doom in a period of political security and complacency. He felt, in fact, that the complacency, which falsely derived a special sense of security from Israel's unique mission, would hasten the doom.[5]

Sometimes the prophetic predictions of historical judgements upon evil rest upon shrewd analyses of the manner in which evil is punished by the operation of historical forces. "Woe to thee," declares Isaiah, "that spoilest and thou wast not spoiled; . . . when thou shalt cease to spoil, thou shalt be spoiled" (Isaiah 33: 1). Sometimes the predictions rest on erroneous estimates of historical probabilities. Thus the first Isaiah predicted the doom of Israel if it placed its reliance upon ordinary diplomatic and military strategies of security. He wanted no alliance with Egypt but a defenceless reliance upon God (Isaiah 31). He falsely promised the nation security upon that basis and thereby laid the foundation for a new, more spiritualized, version of the inviolability of Jerusalem. Jeremiah found this spiritualized version as fecund a source of

[5] "Woe to them that are at ease in Zion, and trust in the mountain of Samaria. . . . Ye that put far away the evil day, and cause the seat of violence to come near; that lie upon beds of ivory and stretch themselves upon their couches, . . . therefore now shall they go captive" (Amos 6: 1-7).

moral complacency as Amos had found grosser forms of it in his day.

Isaiah's error reoccurs perennially in the history of Christian thought and life. It consists in the belief that God's providence establishes a special immunity from disaster to a nation which makes itself worthy of such immunity by perfect righteousness. Actually the historical process is not so simply moral. Nations, as well as individuals, may be destroyed not only by violating the laws of life, but also by achieving a defenceless purity, incompatible with the necessities of survival. Ultimately New Testament faith was to revere a Christ whose perfect goodness was validated by an obvious defeat in history. But there are Christian perfectionists who still do not understand the logic of the Cross. They hope that if goodness is only perfect enough its triumph in history will be assured.

Though the prophet Jeremiah's predictions of doom were partly informed by shrewd estimates of historical factors, they were not primarily prompted by these estimates. He sensed the significance of the rising Babylonian power for the fate of Israel and regarded defiance of this new power as futile. But his counsels, which seemed, on the purely political level, to be defeatist and treasonably pro-Babylonian, were inspired primarily by a religious sense of the fate which nations deserve that exalt themselves above measure.

The hiatus between a religiously discerned judgement upon the pride and power of nations and individuals and the actual execution of such judgements in the relation of men and nations on the historical scene represents the tension between the meaning of life in the ultimate sense and the moral meaning of history. Insofar as life, in its individual or collective form, which affronts God by making itself into a perverse center for the whole of life, also affronts and wrongs the neighbor by reducing him to an instrumentality of the interests of the self, it is subject to punishment and vengeance, whenever the neighbor acquires the power to resist such encroachments upon his dignity. The fact that the historic communities of mankind have been able to devise systems of justice, capable of bringing at least extravagant forms of self-seeking and flagrant infringements upon the life and the interest of the neighbor to judgement, represents one aspect of the moral content of actual historical experience, in rough conformity with the moral meaning of life, religiously discerned. Some of the same moral meaning is experienced when tyrannical nations, who have lorded it over lesser peoples, are successfully resisted.

The processes of historical justice are, however, not exact enough to warrant the simple confidence in the moral character of history which both secular and religious theories frequently ascribe to it. Moral judgements are executed in history; but never with precision. The same governments which are the source of justice on one level of life may, by the unscrupulous use of their power, become the cause of injustice. As between nations, the cause of justice is even more precarious. Unscrupulous nations are punished, if sufficient power is aligned to implement the moral condemnation which the victims of their tyranny sense inwardly. In short, every execution of moral judgements in history is inexact because of its necessary relation to the morally irrelevant fact of power. The power which executes justice in history is never wholly non-moral. The power of a government is partly derived from justice; for the authority of government is never merely the exercise of force. The prestige of government, even in undemocratic nations, rests upon the consent and the reverence of its subjects. And that consent and reverence is generated primarily by respect for the state's justice and only secondarily by fear of the force at the disposal of the organs of government. Even in international relations power is not a complete moral irrelevance; for the possibility of organizing a successful revolt against tyrannical empires depends partly upon the feeling of a moral revulsion against the cruelties and inhumanities of tyrannical and unjust rule. Thus the sense of justice is the foundation of the power required to challenge the power of tyranny.

But these moral elements in the constitution of power can not obviate the fact that historical processes are never purely moral since the equilibria of power never correspond exactly to the necessities of justice. Arnold Toynbee may tend to obscure this moral ambiguity in history by his consistent Augustinian interpretation of the "nemesis" which overtakes the creativity of nations. Nations, cultures, and empires, declares Toynbee, are never destroyed from the outside but destroy themselves. Their self-destruction is always due to pride, or more exactly to the idolization of an ephemeral institution.[6] Either they estimate their own power too highly or they regard some form of social organization, a certain equilibrium of social forces, a given class structure, or a traditional constitutional procedure as final and absolute. Failing to recognize the contingent character of all historic forms, they are overwhelmed at some particular point in history by new forces and contingent elements, with which a fixed procedure is unable to cope. Toynbee's thesis is in perfect conformity with the general Biblical-prophetic concept of the doom which awaits proud nations, oligarchs and rulers. But "good" nations may be overwhelmed by superior power. A strategic mistake may be the cause of the defeat of a just by an unjust force.[7]

This moral ambiguity in the woof and warp of history became particularly apparent to Old Testament prophetism in the exilic and post-exilic period of Israel's history. The historic fate of Israel, though deserved in the absolute religious sense, did not seem just when the unrighteousness of the nations who defeated Israel was compared with the righteousness of Israel. The idea that God used unrighteous nations as executors of His judgement seemed particularly offensive. The Second Isaiah does not hesitate to regard Cyrus of Persia as God's "anointed" whose "right hand I have holden." Those who are religiously or morally offended by so complex and confusing a conception of the operation of divine judgement in history are warned: "Woe unto him that striveth with his maker. . . . Shall the clay say to him that fashioneth it, What makest thou?" (Isaiah 45:9). This prophet, in some respects the profound-

---

[6] *Cf.* Arnold J. Toynbee, *A Study of History*, Vol. IV.

[7] During the recent war a thoughtful soldier wrote from Italy: "The now highly probable victory of our armies over Nazism gives one a tremendous sense of the moral meaning of life. It seemed at one time so highly improbable that these tyrants would be defeated; and now their doom is sure. I confess, however, that when I realize how many strategic mistakes we have made and how we were able to cover these mistakes by the tremendous productive power of America, I become a little confused about the moral meaning of the whole thing. Is not America's fortunate productive power as morally irrelevant as any Nazi instrument used against us?"

est of all prophetic interpretors of historical destiny, insists on the hidden character of God's sovereignty over history, precisely because he is so conscious of the moral inexactness of any specific execution of divine judgement in the actual processes of history. It is significant that the disproportion between Israel's guilt and its punishment does not disturb his faith in the fact that the punishment is at the Lord's hand.[8]

The perplexity about the moral meaning of the historical process is enhanced even further by the fact that innocent individuals always suffer in the process of destroying the powerful centers of collective evil. It might well exercise the conscience of our own generation more than it does, when the fate of innocent individuals among the defeated tyrannical empires of our day is considered. The problem of innocent sufferers is presented in its most perplexing form when it is recognized that the virtuous and the innocent may, and frequently do, suffer more rather than less in the competitions of life and history, precisely because of their virtue. A man or nation which disavows the use of power as morally too ambiguous to be a means to a good end, or which refuses to press its own claims in the competitive claims and counter-claims of life, is not certain of survival. It is, in fact, almost certain to be worsted in the pressures of life.[9]

The recognition that innocency and goodness might lead to suffering rather than to security and success prompted the Second Isaiah to reinterpret the excessively severe vicissitudes of his nation. Perhaps, he suggested in a passage (Isaiah 53) which undoubtedly influenced Christ's own interpretation of his messianic mission, it was the fate of Israel to bring redemption to the nations by its vicarious suffering for their sins. Here is the beginning of transfiguration of suffering innocency from being the final perplexity of historic existence into an answer for life's moral perplexities.

[8] Isaiah 40:2: "Speak ye comfortably to Jerusalem, and cry unto her, that her warfare is accomplished, that her iniquity is pardoned: for she hath received of the Lord's hand double for all her sins."
[9] *Cf.* Habakkuk 1:13 "Thou art of purer eyes than to behold evil . . . wherefore lookest thou upon them that deal treacherously, and holdest thy tongue when the wicked devoureth the man that is more righteous than he?"

For the moment the important fact to note is that the prophets of the Old Testament correctly measured the moral problem of life in its dimensions of both height and breadth. They discerned that man, in his individual and collective experience, is finally confronted by the divine source and end of his existence; and that this experience inevitably contains the contrite sense of being judged. The conscience is guilty because the individual or the nation is discovered in this final experience of faith and revelation to be involved in a defiance of God by reason of its pride and self-seeking. The prophets saw, secondly, that this experience of judgement is neither irrelevant nor simply relevant to the experiences of history. It is relevant insofar as the individual and the collective ego is subject to pressures, punishments, vicissitudes and catastrophes which are, and which may be interpreted as, justified forms of judgement upon its sins. If they are not so interpreted the catastrophes of history are, or may become, a source of confusion and despair. If they are recognized as related to the divine sovereignty over life, they may become the occasion for the renewal of life. The prophets also recognized that the historical process represents no exact execution of a divine justice. Perhaps it would be more correct to say that it does not conform to any human notion of what the divine justice should be. There are, in short, tangents of moral meaning in history; but there are no clear or exact patterns. The moral obscurities of history must either tempt men to the despairing conclusion that there is no meaning in the total historical enterprise and that history is merely a bewildering confusion of "death for the right cause, death for the wrong cause, paeans of victory and groans of defeat," or that it is under a sovereignty too mysterious to conform fully to the patterns of meaning which human beings are able to construct. Yet this sovereignty is not pure mystery, since the experiences of life, in which egotism and self-worship are punished, are in rough and inexact relation to an ultimate judgement upon the self, perceived by the self in the experience of repentance and faith.

Finally, the prophetic interpretation of the relation of the divine to historical judgements is true to constant human experience in its discernment of two facets of the problem of man's rebellion. The moral obscurity of history is recognized as due partly to the fact that all men have the inclination and the capacity to defy the laws and structures of their existence. This fact raises the question whether there is a power great enough and good enough to overcome the confusion of this rebellion. This is the problem of redemption in its profoundest form. The moral obscurity of history is, on the other hand, recognized as partly due to the fact that rewards and punishments are not exactly proportioned to relative guilt and innocency of men and nations. This is the problem of the quality of justice in the historical process. In the final instance, it must be subordinated to the first issue, discerned by the prophets. But Old Testament prophetism had as much difficulty in subordinating it as generations of Christians have had. Both issues become the concern of prophetic messianism.

III

Old Testament prophetism and messianism established the attitude of expectancy toward the future, which lies at the foundation of modern historical consciousness, by looking toward the future for a resolution of the moral obscurities of history. In its profoundest forms Hebraic messianism hoped for an age in which the conflict between man and God would be overcome, the "stony heart" of recalcitrance would give way to a "heart of flesh" (Ezekiel 11:19) and God's people would "walk in my statutes and keep my commandments," when they "shall return unto me with their whole heart" (Jeremiah 24:7). In less profound forms messianism promised an ideal reign of justice by a messianic king. All the disbalances between the righteous and the unrighteous would be redressed, the defiance of powerful rulers and nations would be humbled by the power of the messianic king and judge. It is not necessary in this context to examine the different strains of messianic thought or to isolate those forms of messianism which regard the inexactness of historic justice as the primary problem of history from those which sense the profounder problem of the evil in which all men and nations are involved.

The important aspect of messianism for our study is that it expresses two dimensions or facets of meaning, which contain both the modern and the Christian conceptions of history in embryo. Its expectant attitude toward the future; its hope for the resolutions of the ambiguities and obscurities of history in a final messianic reign lays the foundation for the non-classical historical consciousness, which is most consistently expressed in the modern secular optimism. This attitude toward the future as a period of a significant revelation and vindication of God's sovereignty over history suggests that the obscurities of history are provisional. They are not due to history's relation to nature; and the historic future is not merely a repetition of the historic past. Prophetism and messianism did not anticipate the modern discovery of the constant emergence of novelty in history, but it did expect the future to change the human situation radically, since it would realize moral meanings of life which are only obscurely implied in the present situation.

Old Testament messianism, on the other hand, lays the foundation for the Christian, rather than the modern, attitude toward history by the fact that the expected messianic reign is always conceived as in some sense the end, as well as the fulfillment, of historic meanings. The messianic ruler, whether a glorified "Son of David" or a transcendent "Son of Man," is always more than a mere historic figure, and the messianic age is never merely the culmination of the known historical processes. It is the consequence of a radical divine intervention. The fulfillment of history requires a radical transformation of the conditions of nature underlying history. Even before messianism is transmuted into later Apocalypse, in which the scene of historical fulfillment is specifically a transfigured nature, there are suggestions in it of the destruction of the natural foundations of historic evils. The messianic age will be a reign of perfect peace and concord; and the discords of nature will be overcome to create the basis for that peace: "The wolf also shall dwell with the lamb, and the leopard shall lie down with the kid; and the calf and the young lion and fatling together; and a little child shall lead them" (Isaiah 11:6). This note of transcendence measures the hiatus between the meaning of life, as discerned in the final experiences of faith and revelation and the moral ambiguities of history. It distinguishes Hebraic messianism from modern interpretations of history which expect the ongoing historical process to clarify its obscurities and overcome its moral contradictions progressively. By that same emphasis it is both historically and logically related to a Christian interpretation of history, according to which the fulfillment of history must transfigure the actual stuff of nature-history, thereby signifying that the mere extension of the historical process does not solve history's enigmas.

Yet the New Testament faith is radically different from Old Testament messianism. That fact is signified by the rejection, by those who expect the Messiah, of a Messiah who died upon a Cross. This Messiah, whom the church accepts as the true Messiah, does not correct the moral disbalances of history. He does not establish the triumph of the righteous over the unrighteous. The perfect love which His life and death exemplify is defeated, rather than triumphant, in the actual course of history. Thus, according to the Christian belief, history remains morally ambiguous to the end. The perfect love of Christ is both the ultimate possibility of all historic virtues and a contradiction to them. Justice remains imperfect unless it culminates in this perfect love of self-giving. But every form of historic justice contains elements which place it in contradiction to such perfect love.

For the Christian faith the enigma of life is resolved by the confidence that this same love has more than an historical dimension. This love is the revelation of a divine mercy which overcomes the contradictions of human life. Suffering innocence, which reveals the problem of moral ambiguity of history, becomes in the Christian faith the answer to the problem at the point, when it is seen as a revelation of a divine suffering which bears and overcomes the sins of the world.

Thus the Christian faith does not promise to overcome the fragmentary and contradictory aspects of man's historic existence. It does claim to have apprehended by faith the divine power and mercy which will ultimately resolve life's ambiguities and purge men of the evil into which they fall because they seek so desperately to overcome them. Insofar as men abandon themselves to this power and mercy in faith and repentance, this destruction of self-hood through a too desperate effort to preserve and realize it may be overcome. New life is possible by dying to self, even as death results from a too desperate effort to live. In that sense the Christian faith promises indeterminate renewals of life in history. But on the other hand the total historical enterprise is not progressively emancipated from evil. The Christian faith expects some of the most explicit forms of evil at the end of history.[10] But nothing can happen in history to shake the confidence in the meaning of existence, to those who have discerned by faith the revelation of the ultimate power and love which bears and guides men through their historic vicissitudes.

Thus the final revelation of the divine sovereignty in New Testament faith transfigures the moral perplexity about suffering innocence into the ultimate light of meaning. It gives life a final meaning without promising the annullment of history's moral obscurities. Above all it holds out the hope of redemption from evil, upon the basis of a humble acceptance of human finiteness and a contrite recognition of the evil in which men are involved when they seek to deny their finitude.

The points of reference for the structure of the meaning of history in the Christian faith are obviously not found by an empirical analysis of the observable structures and coherences of history. They are "revelations," apprehended by faith, of the character and purposes of God. The experience of faith by which they are apprehended is an experience at the ultimate limits of human knowledge; and it requires a condition of repentance which is a possibility for the individual, but only indirectly for nations and collectives.

The character of these points of reference or these foundations for a structure of meaning make it quite clear that it is not possible to speak simply of a "Christian philosophy of history." Perhaps it is not possible to have any adequate "philosophy" of history at all because a philosophy will reduce the antinomies, obscurities and the variety of forms in history to a too simple form of intelligibility. Yet

[10] *Cf. inter alia* Matthew 24, and I Thessalonians 5.

a Christian theology of history is not an arbitrary construct. It "makes sense" out of life and history.

That the final clue to the mystery of the divine power is found in the suffering love of a man on the Cross is not a proposition which follows logically from the observable facts of history. But there are no observable facts of history which can not be interpreted in its light. When so interpreted the confusions and catastrophes of history may become the source of the renewal of life.

That life in history is meaningful though the historic growth of human power may sharpen rather than mitigate the struggle between good and evil, and may accentuate rather than modify the inclination of the human heart to idolatry, is also not a proposition which follows inevitably from an observation of the historical drama. The sense of meaning is derived from the conviction that no human rebellion can rise so high as to challenge the divine sovereignty essentially. While this confidence in the final source and end of human life is not a fruit of empirical observation, it is worth noting that the philosophies which are the fruit of empirical observation either drive men to despair by charting the growing antinomies of life or they prompt complacency by obscuring the obvious tragic aspects of life and history.

The final vision of the fulfillment of life and history in Christian eschatology transcends the canons of reason and common sense even more explicitly. Christian eschatology looks forward to an "end" of history in which the conditions of nature-history are transfigured but not annulled. This picture of the fulfillment of life involves the rational absurdity of an eternity which incorporates the conditions of time: individuality and particularity. But the alternative faiths by which men live envision an eternity which either 1) annuls the whole of history and thereby denies the significance of human life in history; or 2) falsely reduces the whole dimension of history with its partial and fragmentary meanings to the level of nature; or 3) assumes that a progressive history ceases at some point to be a history in time and culminates in an incredible utopia where unconditioned good is realized amidst the contingencies of history.

The Christian philosophy of history is rational, therefore, only in the sense that it is possible to prove that alternatives to it fail to do justice to all aspects of human existence; and that the basic presuppositions of the Christian faith, though transcending reason, make it possible to give an account of life and history in which all facts and antinomies are comprehended.

CHAPTER IX

~~~~~~

The Foolishness of the Cross and the Sense of History

I

THE NEW TESTAMENT makes the startling claim that in Christ history has achieved both its end and a new beginning. The affirmation that Christ is the end of history signifies that in His life, death, and resurrection the meaning of man's historic existence is fulfilled. The divine sovereignty, which gives it meaning, is revealed to have an ultimate resource of mercy and forgiveness, beyond judgement, which completes history despite the continued fragmentary and contradictory character of all historic reality. The affirmation that in Christ there is a new beginning, that a "new age" has been initiated in the history of mankind, means that the wisdom of faith which apprehends the true meaning of life also contains within it the repentance which is the presupposition of the renewal of life.

The New Testament claim seems equally incredible from the standpoint of either Hebraic messianism or a modern man's conception of history, because both preserve their sense of meaning for human life by the hope that its obscurities and ambiguities will be overcome in history itself. Hebraic messianism hoped for a messianic end in which the moral obscurity of history, which permitted the righteous to suffer and the wicked to triumph, would be overcome; or in which the righteous would be given a new heart so that they would deserve the victory which was assured them. In modern culture the process of historical growth is expected gradually to overcome both the inexactness of rewards and punishments in history and the inclination of the human heart to violate the laws of life. The New Testament, on the contrary, regards the defiance by man of the very structure of his existence as a permanent factor in history which is never completely overcome except by divine grace. Yet it promises a new beginning in the life of any man, nation, or culture which recognizes the depth and persistence of man's defiance of God. Where such self-knowledge is achieved both the release from sin through forgiveness and the hope of a new life are possible.

Such a faith came into the world by a highly improbable revelation and it maintains itself whenever the power of that revelation penetrates through human pretensions and discovers men in their true situation on any level of their historical development. As St. Paul insisted its acceptance could not be achieved in the first instance by "worldly wisdom." The revelation of a divine mercy in a suffering saviour was not a conclusion about the nature of God at which men might arrive if they analyzed the causes, sequences, and coherences of the world and deduced the structure of existence from these observable phenomena. Any such procedure is bound, however, to be "foolish" despite its seeming wisdom. In the case of Greek wisdom the mind which rose to the knowledge of God was separated from history. History was reduced to the level of nature. In this process man himself was lost, since man is something more than nature and something less than spirit. The problem of the meaning of history is always the problem of the meaning of life itself, since man is an historic creature involved, and yet not involved, in the flux of nature and time, but always involved in a false solution of his predicament. Thus man is always in the position either of negating the meaning of history or of completing it falsely, if he seeks to complete it from the standpoint of his own wisdom. Yet it can be completed by a revelation, the acceptance of which is possible only through a contrite recognition of the human situation of sinfulness. Such repentance is possible, in turn, only if the judgement overhanging man is known to be prompted by love and to be crowned by forgiveness.

Whether in the period when the Gospel of Christ was first proclaimed and accepted, or in our own day, the acceptance of such a gospel is always experienced as a miracle of revelation in the sense that the relation between God and man which it establishes is not the achievement of a rational analysis of life. Yet it is felt to be a new wisdom and power. From its standpoint it is possible to "make sense" out of life; whereas alternative approaches either destroy the sense of life entirely or make false sense of it.

II

In order to appreciate the seeming absurdity and the ultimate wisdom of faith in Christ as the end of history and the fulfillment of life's meaning, it will be helpful to distinguish between the form and the content of the drama, recorded in the New Testament, as the focal point of this revelation. The form is that of a story, an event in history which becomes, by the apprehension of faith, something more than a mere event. It is an event through which the meaning of the whole of history is apprehended and the specific nature of the divine sovereignty of history is revealed. It is presented as the last in a series of God's "mighty acts," and one which has a particularly definitive character. Whatever may happen in subsequent ages, nothing can occur which will shake the faith of a true believer in God's sovereignty over all history. He is "persuaded, that neither death, nor life, nor angels, nor principalities, nor powers, . . . nor height, nor depth, nor any other creature shall be able to separate us from the love of God, which is in Christ Jesus our Lord" (Romans 8:38-39). The specific content of this revelation involves the crucifixion of the Messiah. In that drama all forms of human righteousness are made problematic, except a type of perfect love which seems untenable in history. The revelatory power of this whole story, drama, event, and person requires that it be viewed not as a spectator might view an ordinary drama. Both the form and the content of the drama require that it be apprehended by man in the total unity of his personality and not merely by his reason. For it will not touch him essentially if he does not recognize that its form

as revelation challenges him as a rational though finite creature who
is incapable of giving meaning to the total dimension of his individual and collective history, whatever partial and tentative meanings he may be able to discern by tracing its sequences and tendencies.
The specific content of the revelation, on the other hand, challenges
man as a sinful creature, whose various alternative methods of bringing his history to a meaningful conclusion always involve some pretension which is revealed in the light of the Cross to be a false conclusion. Thus the claims of Christ can only be heard by man in the
unity of his personality and in the recognition of the self-contradic-
tion in which that unity is involved in actual life.

   The specific content of the Christian revelation is concerned with
the story of a Jewish teacher, rabbi, and prophet who made messianic claims for himself and yet sought to keep his messianic mission a provisional secret since his own view of the messianic end
differed radically from all current hopes. He rejected every version
of the messianic hope which involved God's miraculous intervention in history for the purpose of eliminating its moral obscurity. He
was extremely critical of the claims of virtue of the professionally
holy class or oligarchy of his day and preferred to consort with "publicans and sinners." The conclusion reached by St. Paul in the light
of the revelatory power of Christ's life, that "there is no difference
for all have sinned and come short of the glory of God" (Romans
3:22–23) is anticipated in every searching criticism made by Jesus
of all human pretensions of virtue. The Messiah would not bring
victory to the virtuous but would die and "give his life a ranson for
many" (Mark 10:45). The guiltless one would expiate the guilt of
the guilty; and that would be the only way of ending the chain of
evil in history. Thus the suffering of the guiltless, which is the primary problem of life for those who look at history from the standpoint of their own virtues, is made into the ultimate answer of history for those who look at it from the standpoint of the problematic
character of all human virtue. This suffering of the guiltless one was
to become in Christian faith a revelation of God's own suffering. It
alone was seen to have the power to overcome the recalcitrance of

man at the very center of man's personality, however successful the divine power might be to set outer limits beyond which human defiance could not go. But it alone was also the final dimension of the divine sovereignty over human history. To make suffering love rather than power the final expression of sovereignty was to embody the perplexity of history into the solution.

The actual incidents in the drama serve to add vividness to this final meaning. The Christ was not crucified by criminals or by men who fell below the ordinary standards of human virtue. Such criminals were crucified with Christ. One of the instruments of crucifixion was the Roman system of jurisprudence which rightly boasted the highest achievements of justice in the ancient world. But even a boasted system of impartial justice is sufficiently human to fear that its majesty may be challenged by one who proclaimed himself a king. The kingdom of truth is a threat to every historical majesty. Every historical majesty is more anxious and insecure than it pretends. A priestly oligarchy was also implicated in the crucifixion. This oligarchy was certain that it was merely defending a very sublime system of religious legalism against an impious rebel; but it was also defending the moral prestige of all "good" men and more particularly its own prestige and its security. That is the fate of all historic oligarchies and institutions. There is always an anxious life, individual or collective, behind the most imposing façade of ideals and principles, of values and eternal verities, to the defense of which men rise in history.

Christian piety has sometimes foolishly sought to limit the guilt of involvement in the crucifixion to the particular instumentalities depicted in the actual story. But that is to miss the real point. In its profounder moments the church has known that Pilate and the priests are symbolic of the fact that every majesty or virtue, which is tenable in history, is involved in the crucifixion of a "prince of glory" who incarnates a love which is normative for, but not tenable in, history. That love which could not maintain itself in history becomes the symbol both of the new beginning which a man could make if he subjected his life to the judgement of Christ, and of the mercy of

God which alone could overcome the fateful impotence of man ever to achieve so perfect a love.

In this double facet of the *Agape* of Christ is the point where a story in history becomes something more. It is recognized by the eyes of faith as the point where the heavens are opened and the divine mystery is disclosed and the love of God toward man shines down upon him; and man is no longer afraid, even though he knows himself to be involved in the crucifixion.

Obviously such a life and such a tragic drama could not be regarded as a revelation of divine majesty, and as concluding the meaning of man's existence, except by a faith which presupposed repentance. There is no justification in the revelation for any good man. The natural anxiety of good men about the threat which they face from evil men or from nature is forced into a subordinate position. No individual or nation is promised either moral justification or ultimate triumph. The meaning of history is not completed within itself. It is completed only from beyond itself as faith apprehends the divine forgiveness which overcomes man's recalcitrance. Thus Biblical faith, which begins with a sense of mystery, embodying meaning, and moves to a sense of meaning in history which contains perplexity and ambiguity, ends by seeing human history perpetually, and on every level of its achievements, in contradiction to the divine. It sees the possibilities of new beginnings in history only upon the basis of the contrite recognition of this contradiction. Significantly the same suffering love, the same *Agape* of Christ which reveals the divine mercy is also the norm of a new life. Men may have this new life if they discern what they are and what God is in this focal point of God's self-disclosure. Such a point in human history can be regarded both as the beginning of a new age for all mankind and as a new beginning for every individual man who is "called" by it, because both the individual and the collective realities of human existence are fully disclosed in it. If apprehended at all they are so apprehended that the old self, which makes itself its own end, is destroyed and a new self is born. That is why a true revelation of the divine is never merely wisdom but also power.

III

The form and dimension of this story of Christ, namely its revelatory significance as the point in history where the meaning of history is completed, is not presented as an afterthought to the story. On the contrary the whole story is pieced together within a Christian community, already united upon the basis of faith that this Jesus is the Christ. The Pauline theological formulations of the meaning of God's revelation in Christ actually precede the Gospel accounts chronologically. But though the story is written from the standpoint of its special significance in the eyes of faith, it still embodies the perplexities of the disciples in accepting its true significance and the tortuous path by which Jesus moved against the obtuseness of his own disciples. It is not presented as a theophany, revealing the meaning of the eternal world to finite man; nor yet merely as the story of a "God-man" who overcame the breach between the eternal and the temporal or the divine and the temporal. On the contrary it is a part of history though the claim is made that in it history has found its true fulfillment.

St. Paul recognizes the seeming absurdity of such a claim. It is as difficult for a rational man to accept the possibility and necessity of such a disclosure as for a virtuous man to accept its specific content. Its specific content challenged the virtue of the virtuous; and its form and dimension challenged the self-sufficiency of human reason. Greek rationalism had difficulty with the claim that history could be the locus of the final revelation of God and of man's true relation to God, because history belonged to nature and made such a revelation impossible; and human reason belonged to eternity and made it unnecessary. Modern rationalism has a different problem. Since it regards history as intelligible from within itself and expects that it will gradually overcome its own frustrations and moral ambiguities it combines, as it were, the objections to the Gospel of both Jews and Greeks. With the Greeks modern culture does not require the Gospel to make life intelligible; and with the Jews it does not require the Gospel to make history meaningful. Modern culture is particularly offended by the claim of finality of any disclosure of the ultimate at an antecedent point of history, partly because it believes that history itself changes the human situation radically and partly because it hopes that historical culture will be able to refine and perfect any valid solution of whatever may be perennial in the human situation. This modern objection to the Gospel seems so plausible that it has been a great embarrassment to the Gospel's theological protagonists in the past two centuries. They have done everything possible to prove that the Gospel message was practically identical with modern man's conception of a redemptive history.

Modern theology did not recognize that the new objection to the Gospel was merely an old objection in a new form. Men are inclined in every age to resist a truth which discloses the contingent character of their existence and discredits the false answer to this problem of their contingent life in which they are always involved. To make faith the requirement of the ultimate meaning of existence is to recognize the divine mystery as impenetrable by human reason. To find that revelation in an historical drama and person is to understand history as potentially meaningful rather than meaningless. To experience a divine forgiveness reaching out to man in his predicament is to recognize that the human situation, both individually and collectively, is such that man is not only unable to complete his fragmentary life but that, viewed ultimately, there is always false and sinful completion in it. Thus faith is the final expression of man's freedom; but it is an expression which involves the consciousness of an element of corruption in any specific expression of that freedom. It is the expression of his final freedom in the sense that faith achieves a point of transcendence over all the contingent aspects of man's historic existence, individually and collectively. But it must contain a recognition of the contingent and the false element in all his actual knowing. It is thus recognized as a knowledge beyond the capacity of human wisdom, as a gift of "grace." The New Testament insists that the recognition of Jesus as the Christ is possible only by the Holy Spirit.[1] And Jesus himself assures Peter that his under-

---

[1] *Cf.* I Corinthians 12:3: "Wherefore I give you to understand that no one . . . can say that Jesus is the Lord, but by the Holy Spirit."

standing of the messianic calling could have been inspired only by God.[2]

While all Gospel narratives are written in the consciousness of the revelatory significance of the story they tell, the sense of the dimension of the story influences the telling of the narrative particularly in the accounts of the resurrection of Christ. It seems fairly certain that the earlier narratives reported an experience of communion by the disciples with the resurrected Lord in Galilee (I Corinthians 15:1–8), while later narratives not only fixed this event at Jerusalem but sought to validate it by factual details of which the empty tomb was the most significant. The story of this triumph over death is thus shrouded in a mystery which places it in a different order of history than the story of the crucifixion. Yet the church as a fellowship of believers was obviously founded upon the conviction of the fact of the resurrection. This "fact" contained an alteration in the story through faith's apprehension of the significance of the story. To recognize that the Cross was something more than a noble tragedy and its victim something else than a good man who died for his ideals; to behold rather that this suffering was indicative of God's triumph over evil through a love which did not stop at involvement in the evil over which it triumphed; to see, in other words, the whole mystery of God's mercy disclosed is to know that the crucified Lord had triumphed over death and "when he had by himself purged our sins, sat down on the right hand of the Majesty

---

[2] Matthew 16:17 ff: "Blessed art thou, Simon Bar-Jonah: for flesh and blood hath not revealed it unto thee, but my Father which is in heaven." Significantly Peter misunderstands the messianic mission in the same moment in which he understands it, seeking to dissuade Jesus not to follow the logic of his messianism, which demanded the Cross rather than triumph. For Jesus "from that time forth began to shew unto his disciples, how that he must go unto Jerusalem, and suffer many things of the elders and chief priests and scribes, and be killed, and be raised again the third day." Peter's rejoinder, "Be it far from thee, Lord: This shall not be unto thee." is rebuked by Jesus in the words: "Get thee behind me, Satan, thou art an offence unto me; for thou savourest not the things that be of God, but those that be of men."

This encounter is an accurate symbolic description of the mixture of ultimate and human viewpoints which remain in the Christian church throughout the ages. Insofar as it is the community in which Jesus is acknowledged as the Lord it is a new community, different from all other human communities. Insofar as it joins in Peter's abhorrence of the Cross it is a sinful community, engulfed in the securities and insecurities of human history.

on high" (Hebrews 1:3). It is the revelatory depth of the fact which is the primary concern of faith.

The effort to certify this triumph through specific historical details may well be regarded as an expression of a scepticism which runs through the whole history of Christianity. The account of Christ's virgin birth serves the same purpose. Christ can not be known as the revelation of God except by faith and repentance; but a faith not quite sure of itself always hopes to suppress its scepticism by establishing the revelatory depth of a fact through its miraculous character. This type of miracle is in opposition to true faith.

On the other hand the belief in the resurrection is itself a miracle of a different order, and a miracle without which the church could not have come into existence or could not continue in existence. It is the miracle of recognizing the triumph of God's sovereignty in what seem to be very ambiguous facts of history. There is significantly no hint in the Gospel record of any gradual understanding even in the inner circle of disciples of the true meaning of Christ's death. Peter's confession of his Master's messianic ministry was immediately followed by a rejection of the tragic culmination of it which Christ predicted. In the Lukan account of Christ's appearance to his disciples at Emmaus they remain oblivious of the real meaning of his life, ruefully confessing, "We trusted that it had been he who would have redeemed Israel" (Luke 24:21).

The church is thus not grounded upon a slowly dawning consciousness of the true significance of Christ. It is founded in the miracle of the recognition of the true Christ in the resurrection. From the first covenant of God to the resurrection, God's revelations to a people are imbedded in history. God speaks "at sundry times and in divers manners" (Hebrews 1:1). And the revelations move toward a climax through a course of history, the climax being that He "hath in these last days spoken unto us by his Son" (Hebrews 1:2). The acceptance of that revelation in faith involves a radical break in the community in which the revelations occur. It ceases to be a particular people or nation. The revelation creates an "Israel of God" (Galatians 6:16) which is gathered together upon the basis of its acceptance of the revelation by faith.

Insofar as these various confrontations between God and His people have a history, there is also a history of revelation. But this is not the history of a broadening religious consciousness or of a more and more successful yearning or searching after God. For every step in the story requires that divine judgement be accepted in repentance against the human inclination to complete human virtue and wisdom within the historical structure; and that the divine mercy which prompts and qualifies the judgement be apprehended by faith.

The climax of the crucifixion and resurrection thus becomes not merely the culmination of the whole series of revelations but the pattern of all subsequent confrontations between God and man. They must contain the crucifixion of self-abandonment and the resurrection of self-recovery. Men must die to sin with Christ and arise with him to newness of Life.[3]

In Christian thought the resurrection of Christ is, however, not only indicative of the triumph of Christ over sin in the very Cross which seemed to make him its victim, but also is proof of God's power to overcome death. St. Paul, in fact, deduces both the resurrection from the dead and the triumph over sin from Christ's resurrection.[4]

The logic of such a faith might be expressed in the following propositions: 1) Life is fragmentary, ending in death. 2) Man seeking to live and to avoid death destroys himself in the very process of seeking to establish his life. 3) If man would truly live he must die to self; but this dying to self is no guarantee of the preservation of his physical life. 4) Men will make nonsense of life if they seek to make sense of it only upon the basis of their physical survival. But the alternative requires that they believe in the sublimation of its fragmentary character. This-worldly religions try to make sense out of life in the dimension of nature-history which man transcends. Other-worldly religions try to make sense out of life by abstracting some eternal essence of man from the fragments of history. Chris-

---

[3] Galatians 2:20. Colossians 2:12. Romans 6:3. II Timothy 2:11.

[4] I Corinthians 15:12: "Now if Christ be preached that he rose from the dead, how say some among you that there is no resurrection of the dead?" 5:17. "And if Christ be not raised, your faith is vain; ye are yet in your sins."

tianity insists upon the potential meaningfulness of man's fragmentary life in history and its final completion by a power and love not his own.

The "final enemy," declares St. Paul, is death. And the final pinnacle of the Christian faith is this confidence in the completion of life's meaning by the power of God.

This pinnacle of faith in New Testament religion is the final expression of certainty about the power of God to complete our fragmentary life as well as the power of His love to purge it of the false completions in which all history is involved. This pinnacle has no support from miraculous facts in history; neither can it be deduced from a careful observation of the general facts of human nature and history. With Plato men have always sought some rational certainty about the immortality of the soul by seeking to prove that the dimension of human existence which transcended the mortality of the body would survive the death of the body. But that which survives, according to the thought of Plato, bears no resemblance to the human self, being no more than the eternal validity of the logical faculties of the human mind. Modern Christian theories of immortality are frequently invalid mixtures of Christian conceptions of personality with this Platonic assurance.

The Biblical sense of the unity of man in his body, mind, and soul makes the Platonic escape from the contingent character of human existence impossible. If, therefore, the New Testament faith ends in the pinnacle of the hope of the resurrection this is also the final expression of a faith which sees no hope that man may overcome or escape the contingent character of his existence; yet is not without hope, for it is persuaded that a divine power and love have been disclosed in Christ, which will complete what man can not complete; and which will overcome the evil introduced into human life and history by man's abortive effort to complete his life by his own wisdom and power.

CHAPTER X

~~~~~~

The Validation of the Christian View of Life and History

I

THE Christian Gospel as the final answer to the problems of both individual life and man's total history is not proved to be true by rational analysis. Its acceptance is an achievement of faith, being an apprehension of truth beyond the limits of reason. Such faith must be grounded in repentance; for it presupposes a contrite recognition of the elements of pretension and false completion in all forms of human virtue, knowledge and achievement. It is a gift of grace because neither the faith nor the repentance required for the knowledge of the true God, revealed in the Cross and the resurrection, can be attained by taking thought. The self must lose itself to find itself in faith and repentance; but it does not find itself unless it be apprehended from beyond itself.[1]

The love of Christ thus always stands in a double relation to the strivings and achievements, the virtues and wisdoms of history. Insofar as they represent developments of the goodness of creation it is their fulfillment. Insofar as they represent false completions which embody the pride and the power of individuals and nations, of civilizations and cultures, it is their contradiction.

The truth of the Gospel is not subject to simple rational valida-

---

[1] Philippians 3:12: "Not as though I have already attained, either were already perfect; but I follow after if that I may apprehend that for which also I am apprehended of Christ Jesus."

tion because it stands beyond the ambiguities of human existence; and it negates both the complacency which denies these ambiguities; and the despair which results when they become fully known and destroy the sense of a meaningful life.

Nevertheless, a limited rational validation of the truth of the Gospel is possible. It consists of a negative and a positive approach to the relation of the truth of the Gospel to other forms of truth, and of the goodness of perfect love to historic forms of virtue. Negatively the Gospel must and can be validated by exploring the limits of historic forms of wisdom and virtue. Positively it is validated when the truth of faith is correlated with all truths which may be known by scientific and philosophical disciplines and proves itself a resource for coordinating them into a deeper and wider system of coherence.

The negative task of exploring the limits of human knowledge and the fragmentary character of all forms of human virtue is a procedure not unrelated to the experience of repentance. St. Paul distinguishes between the "foolishness of God," as revealed in the absurdity of the Cross, and the "wisdom of the world." The foolishness of God is recognized as an ultimate wisdom in comparison with the wisdom of the world. The defect of the latter wisdom is "that it knew not God" (I Corinthians 1:21). The failure of the wisdom of the world to discern the final source and end of life is due on the one hand to the fact that it seeks God too simply as the truth which supplements historic truth but does not stand in contradiction to it; which completes human virtue but does not judge it; and which guarantees some historic form of justice and does not anticipate its doom. On the other hand the wisdom of the world may be so impressed by the fragmentary character of human virtue and knowledge and so overpowered by the tragedies and antinomies of life that it sinks into despair, finding no meaning in life and history at all.

These two alternative forms of the "wisdom of the world" may be most simply defined as idolatry and atheism; and their fruits may be termed complacency and despair. Consistent atheism is rare. Most forms of ostensible atheism are merely protests against some traditional or conventional conception of the divine. They usually contain some implicit or even explicit conception of the divine in the sense that they have a system of coherence with an implicit or explicit center and source which is not explained but is the principle of explanation. Their god may be "nature" or "reason" or some particular natural or historical vitality. Thus the "god" of Marxism is obviously the dialectical process, in terms of which the coherences of both nature and history are explained. These implicit "gods" of explicit atheism place most atheistic systems in the category of idolatry, of the worship of false gods, rather than the denial of God. The gods are "false" if they make some inadequate principle of coherence into the center of meaning. The worship of false gods may lead to a hidden despair, rather than complacency, when the interpretation of life, involved in the worship, excludes a true dimension of life from the system of meaning. A consistent naturalism, for instance, which requires that man should adjust himself to the system of nature as the ultimate norm of his existence, excludes the profoundest dimension of human personality from the structure of meaning.

Idolatry is more general than consistent atheism partly because it is difficult, if not impossible, to live without presupposing some system of order and coherence which gives significance to one's life and actions. Furthermore, the idolatrous worship is usually some version of self-worship, either exalting mankind as such as an object of worship or (in more flagrant forms) exalting some historical vitality or achievement related to a particular tribe, nation or culture into the place of God, by making it the source, center and end of the meaning of life.

Idolatrous schemes of meaning are more widespread than consistent atheism also because there are always provisional and tentative structures of meaning in nature, life, and history which seem for the moment to be ultimate, if not probed too deeply. The relation of a person to his family may answer the problem of meaning so long as no great family loss or disruption disturbs this little island of coherence. In the same manner the stability of a nation or a culture may make the national life or the cultural structure appear to be the source and end of existence. It is when these seemingly "eternal" values are shaken that life is threatened with despair or is challenged to a profounder consideration of the meaning of life. Thus periods of social and political catastrophe, when idols fall, may lead men dimly to sense an ultimate Majesty "who bringeth princes to nothing and maketh the judges of the earth as vanity" (Isaiah 40:23). They may, on the other hand, also prompt men to the despairing conclusion that life has no meaning.

Biblical faith clearly recognizes complacency and despair as the two alternative fruits of the "wisdom of this world." "They that sleep sleep in the night; and they that be drunken are drunken in the night," according to I Thessalonians 5:7. "Let us, who are of the day, be sober." The complacency of sleep and the drunkenness of hysteria are regarded as the two enemies of, or alternatives to, faith.[2] They are, however, not equal enemies. Any consistent confidence in human virtue or wisdom makes faith irrelevant. A destruction of such confidence makes faith possible, but not necessary.

The preference which Christ has for the "sick" as against those "who are whole" and his ironic remark that the latter "have no need of a physician" (Matthew 9:12) is a perfect expression of the fact that despair has a greater affinity with repentance than complacency has with faith. Of course, despair is not identical with the repentance which issues in faith. It is not possible to convince men rationally of the truth of the Christian Gospel by analyzing the limits of human knowledge and virtue. The rational analysis may not penetrate through the armor of complacency; and when it does it may inflict a mortal wound. There always remains a mystery of grace in true faith which is not subject to manipulation. It is nevertheless important from the standpoint of faith to puncture the idola-

[2] Pascal's analysis of the two alternatives is the most searching in Christian literature. "Without this divine knowledge," he declares, "what could men do but either become elated by the inner feeling of their past greatness which still remains with them, or become despondent at the sight of their present weakness? . . . Some considering nature as incorrupt and others as incurable, they could not escape either pride or sloth, the two sources of all vice. . . . For if they knew the excellence of man they were ignorant of his corruption; so that they easily avoided sloth but fell into pride. And if they recognized the infirmity of nature, they were ignorant of his dignity; so that they could easily avoid vanity but it was to fall into despair. . . . The Christian religion alone has been able to cure these two vices, not by expelling one through means of the other, but by expelling both according to the simplicity of the Gospel." *Pensees*, 435.

trous pretensions of cultures and to appreciate the significance of the periodic moods of despair into which moralism, legalism, rationalism, and every other form of complacency fall. These moods of despair may be more dangerous to the ordinary stabilities of life than complacency. Self-righteous Pharisees may have a superficial sanity, superior to the inner confusion of "publicans and harlots." Civilizations and cultures which are too sure of themselves may distil a measure of stability from their self-confidence. But ultimately they hasten their destruction by being too sure of themselves; and the promise that the "halt and the blind," the "publicans and harlots" will enter the kingdom of God more easily than these who are whole, or who wrongly regard themselves as whole (Matthew 9:10–12), correctly estimates the therapeutic value of the recognition of the sickness in which all human life is involved.

The note of pessimism is always subordinate to the mood of optimism in the wisdom of the world; but it usually contains a profundity (not mixed with perverse elements) which establishes its superiority over the more popular optimism. Thus the classical age expressed its confidence in the possibility of establishing justice or of escaping from historical ambiguities through reason. But the Greek dramatists, who recognized that there are tragic antinomies in life which can not be brought into a simple rational harmony, were closer to the ultimate truth about life than the philosophers. The historian Herodotus blurts out the truth which classical philosophy and history usually evaded. "Of all the sorrows which afflict mankind," he declares, "the bitterest is this, that one should have consciousness of much but control over nothing." [8] Herodotus' conviction is typical of the insights which emerge periodically to disturb the complacency of human self-esteem.

In the history of modern culture, the romantic tradition has been the chief bearer of disillusionment about the virtue or the wisdom of man or about the stability of human institutions. We have previously noted that modern naturalism, which seeks to understand man from the standpoint of his relation to nature might be expected logically to issue in disillusionment, since it emphasizes the natural con-

[8] Herodotus, lx. 16.

tingencies which condition all forms of human culture, and since it can offer no basis of meaning for those dimensions of human existence which transcend the system of nature. Actually, however, the main stream of modern naturalism generates complacency, rather than despair. It does this by creating a very non-naturalistic confidence in the perfectability of human reason and virtue.

Death, as the final evidence of the ambiguity of the human situation, is usually evaded in naturalism by the promise of social immortality. "Within the flickering inconsequential acts of separate selves dwells a sense of the whole," declares John Dewey, "which claims and dignifies them. In its presence we put off mortality and live in the universal. The life of the community in which we live and have our being is the fit symbol of this relationship. The acts in which we express our perception of ties which bind us to others are its only rites and ceremonies." [4] Since men live in particular communities, whose existence is even more contingent than that of the individuals who are able to survey their relations to them, this is a rather inadequate triumph over life's ambiguity. It is perilously similar to Hitler's dictum: "It is not necessary that any of us should live. It is only necessary that Germany should live." On a lower plane of evasion is modern bourgeois culture's effort to rob death of its sting by the perfection of appointments for coffin, grave and cemetery in funeral rites. [5]

Modern culture has remained officially as optimistic as was classical culture, for reasons we have previously considered. The subordinate romantic stream of thought, on the other hand, usually moves on the boundary of despair. Ernest Hemingway is the only modern American novelist who deals with the problem of death basically. In typically romantic fashion he tries to rob death of its sting partly by a robust affirmation of vitality in defiance of death, and partly by the suggestion that love between a man and a woman creates a deathless realm of meaning. But this suggestion is only tentative. In Hemingway's *Farewell to Arms* death casts its shadow

[4] *Human Nature and Conduct*, p. 332.
[5] For a malicious satire of this aspect of modern culture see Evelyn Waugh's *The Loved Ones*.

upon this bit of eternity and draws the despairing cry from Hemingway's heroine, Catherine, that life is "just a dirty trick."

The profoundest expression of romantic despair in modern history was Nietzsche's revolt against the complacency of a liberal and Christian culture. Nietzsche sought to restore the classical cyclical concept of history, bound to the endless recurrences of nature, where "everything goeth, everything dieth and everything returneth." [6]

It is significant, however, that ages of Christian and modern historical consciousness in the background of Nietzsche's thought made it quite impossible for him to recapture the equanimity of the Greeks in the contemplation of the endless cycles of history. His sense of the vital unity of human personality made a simple separation between human reason and the vitalities of life impossible. His sense of the spiritual dimension of this vitality made all simple naturalistic solutions equally unavailable. His solution was to exploit the eternal dimension, the absolute meaning of every moment in defiance of history's cycles. "This, however, is my blessing," he declared, "to stand above everything as its own heaven." [7]

He regarded this as a profound affirmation of life and himself as a "yea-sayer." But the note of despair in this too robust titanism is apparent in his final formula for the assertion of human freedom. Man asserts his true freedom, according to Nietzsche, by removing death from the realm of necessity to the realm of decision and desiring consciously the fate which nature has in store for us. [8]

[6] *Thus Spake Zarathustra.* English translation, p. 245.
[7] *Ibid.*, p. 200.
[8] The inability of a culture which embodies a sense of the meaning of historic existence to return simply to a classical view without replacing classical equanimity with despair, is illustrated in an age previous to our own, in the view of life and history expressed in the Book of Ecclesiastes. Koheleth, the "gentle cynic" who is the author of this book, expresses a view of life drawn from Hellenism, in an Hebraic culture during a period when the disappointment over unrealized messianic hopes filled it with great perplexity. Koheleth interprets history in terms of the classical concept of recurrence: "One generation passeth away, and another generation cometh: but the earth abideth for ever. . . . The thing that hath been, it is that which shall be; and that which is done is that which shall be done; and there is no new thing under the sun" (Ecclesiastes 1:4, 9).

But this Hellenized Hebrew author is unable to achieve the equanimity which the classical age exhibited in contemplating the recurrences of history.

The perverse note in Nietzsche's thought has been a constant topic of sermon and essay. If modern Nazism may be regarded (though not altogether justly) as the final fruit of his moral cynicism and pessimism, it would prove very nicely that despair does not necessarily issue in repentance and newness of life but rather that, in the words of St. Paul, "the sorrow of the world worketh death" (II Corinthians 7:10).

It is nevertheless important to be mindful of the profundity of this despair as compared with the more dominant note of optimism in modern rationalism. Nietzsche is both more perverse and more profound than Kant, for instance, in his most optimistic moods: "We may reasonably say that the kingdom of God is come on earth," declares Kant, "as soon as ever the principle has taken root generally in the public mind that the creeds of the church have gradually to pass into the universal religion of reason, and so into a moral, that is, a Divine community on earth; although the establishment of such a community may still be infinitely remote from us. For this principle, because it contains the motive-force of a continual approach to perfection, is like a seed which grows up, and scatters other seed such as itself; and it bears within it invisibly the whole fabric which will one day illuminate and rule the world. Truth and goodness have their basis in the natural disposition of every human being, both in his reason and in his heart. And because of this affinity with the moral nature of rational beings, truth and goodness will not fail to spread in every direction. Hindrances arising from political and social causes, which may from time to time interfere with this expansion, serve rather to draw closer the union of hearts in the

---

Plato, Aristotle, and the Stoics felt that the meaning of life was fulfilled in the life of reason, above the change and decay of nature and history. But the Hebraic author does not have this assurance. He tries bravely to rise to the Greek confidence in the immortality of wisdom; but he is finally forced to the conclusion that the wise man dies as the stupid man. This conclusion leaves him only the alternative of clinging desperately to physical existence: "A living dog is better than a dead lion" (Ecclesiastes 9:4). The moral despair in this solution is obvious.

There is manifestly no possibility of return from a culture which embodies the sense of a meaningful history to one which equates history with nature.

good. For the good, when once it has been clearly perceived, never abandons the mind.

"This, then, though invisible to the human eye, is the constantly progressive operation of the good principle. It works towards erecting in the human race, as a community under moral laws, a power and a kingdom which shall maintain the victory over evil, and secure to the world under its dominion an eternal peace." [9]

Kant is not always as consistently optimistic. These words do not measure his ability, revealed in other writings, to measure the limits of human reason or virtue. They do betray those elements in his thought, bequeathed to him by the Enlightenment, and are expressive of the Enlightenment's complacency.

II

We have previously noted that the primary root of modern complacency is to be found in the belief that historical development insures man's triumph over whatever is fragmentary, tragic, and contradictory in human experience. A Christian (Quaker) version of this faith states the modern creed exactly: "Quietly underneath the iceberg of corruption, which causes false pessimism, the warm waves of Christian progress are doing their work; and soon it will topple over. . . . Our scepticism results from the fact that we expect immediate results and are not willing to abide the process of nature." [10]

Though the complacency is drawn primarily from the idea of progress, it has been enhanced by the characteristic circumstances of a bourgeois civilization. This civilization, in the period of its expansion, was able to obscure the conflict of interest and passion which expresses itself in even the most ordered community and in even the most delicate equilibrium of power between the nations. The predominance of economic power, which operates covertly

---

[9] *Religion Within the Limits of Pure Reason,* Book III, Section 7.

[10] Isaac Sharpless, *Quakerism in Politics,* p. 97. The identification of "Christian progress" with "process of nature" is an illuminating confession of the capitulation of Christian thought to the modern creed.

rather than overtly, gave rise to the illusion that human relations are, or will soon become, a meeting of mind with mind, in which no appeal to force will be necessary. The fragmentary and contradictory aspects of human culture and civilization were partly veiled; and insofar as they were apparent, historic development was expected to overcome them. Modern complacency was supported, in short, not only by a creed of progress, but by momentary historic circumstances which gave the creed a special plausibility.

That is why the more tragic contemporary historical facts are beginning to undermine this complacency. The hidden despair, which is never absent from complacency, is beginning to reveal itself. One development in modern culture adds a special depth of pathos to our situation; for the most obvious challenge to the complacency of our culture, Marxism, has become the source of a new and more fanatic complacency. The Marxist dialectic challenged the confidence of Hegelian rationalism in the power of reason. It saw that reason may be an instrument of interest and passion. But unfortunately it transmuted this discovery into a mere weapon of social and political conflict by attributing an ideological taint to the moral and social ideals of every group except the proletariat. The pretension that one group in human society is free of sin, naturally became the source of new and terrible fanaticisms. Marxism also challenged the bourgeois confidence in the virtue and stability of a democratic society. It discerned the social conflicts of society where bourgeois idealists saw nothing but a harmony of social interests. It predicted the doom of a civilization, when liberal society hoped to achieve ever wider and more perfect forms of social justice. Marxism became a new religion, to which not only industrial workers but a vast section of the intellectual classes repaired when the pretensions of a bourgeois culture were shaken by the realities of history. However, Marxism did not challenge the moral complacency of modern culture, essentially. It only substituted new illusions for discredited ones. It has therefore been more fruitful of a demonic idolatry than the liberal culture. It sacrificed one great source of virtue, possessed by the liberal culture: the latter's provisional recognition of the contingent and conditioned character of all forms of historic virtue. This relativism of the liberal culture is the source of the democratic virtue of tolerance. It may be superior not only to Marxism but to forms of the Christian faith which encourage a too simple identification of the goodness of Christ with whatever social value to which an ecclesiastical institution or a devout believer may be committed.

The Marxist misapplication of the discovery of the sinful taint in human knowledge and virtue leaves this problem still unsolved. The liberal culture tries to avoid disillusionment by regarding the ideological taint in human knowledge and virtue as the consequence of finite perspectives which may be progressively eliminated by a more and more astute sociology of knowledge.[11] The theory unfortunately leaves one important aspect of the process of rationalization out of account. Men are inclined to make the worse appear the better reason, not only unwittingly but wittingly. Ideology is a compound of ignorance and dishonesty. The dishonest element in it, the tendency of men to justify self-interest by making it appear identical with the common good, is an expression of the person, and not of the mind. It betrays a corrupted will, which is a mystery with which rationalism does not deal. Insofar as Freud does deal with the problem, at least in individual life, he arrives at morally cynical conclusions, thus moving toward the abyss of despair.[12]

The complacency of the liberal culture is most unshaken in America, where the social and political situation, which supported it, still bears some semblance to the stability of previous centuries. The opulence of American life and the dominant position of American power in the world create the illusion of a social stability which the total world situation belies. The absence of overt social conflict permits sentimental versions of social harmony and stability to arise, which are overtly refuted only by the fears and hatreds of racial antagonisms. The fragmentary and contradictory character of human virtues and ideals is recognized; but the abyss of meaninglessness is avoided by the confidence that a critical analysis of all historic politi-

---

[11] As, for instance, in Karl Mannheim's effort to overcome ideology by ferreting out the various bases of ideology. He hopes to lay the foundation for a rational politics by a rational purge of the irrational elements in moral and political ideals. See *inter alia* his *Ideology and Utopia* and *Man and Society*.

[12] *Cf.* Sigmund Freud, *Civilization and Its Discontents*.

cal and moral positions will gradually establish the universal truth.

In Europe the movement from complacency to despair may be seen much more clearly than in America. The rise of Nazism in the past decades was, in one of its aspects, the growth of a demonic religion out of the soil of despair. Politically men were willing to entertain the perils of tyranny in order to avoid the dangers of anarchy; and spiritually they were ready to worship race, nation or power as god in order to avoid the abyss of meaninglessness.

The military defeat of this political religion has not altered the spiritual situation of modern culture essentially. The rise of French existentialism is another manifestation of the same despair. There are fortunately no immediate political perils in this expression of despair; for it contains no effort to escape from the contingent character of the human situation by the worship of false gods. It is, in fact, a remarkably consistent effort to remain within the abyss of despair and to abjure the obvious idolatries which seem to offer an escape. Existentialism recognizes that life and history are not as coherent rationally as the liberal culture assumed. It also knows that moral ideals are contingent and fragmentary. Lacking a faith which sees a higher coherence beyond the immediate incoherences, it seeks nevertheless to assert the meaning of the present moment and the present experience in defiance of the chaos of existence. Its islands of meaning in the sea of meaninglessness are, however, tiny and periodically inundated. Existentialism is a desperate affirmation of meaning within the framework of despair. It is a very accurate index of the spiritual crisis in contemporary culture.

Perhaps a more perfect example of the movement from complacency to despair in modern culture can be found in the thought of a typical liberal optimist. H. G. Wells was, in some respects, the most representative evolutionary idealist of the past generation. After the first world war his *Outline of History* expressed the characteristic hope of our culture. The forces and processes of history were, according to his conviction, moving toward a universal community, democratically organized. By 1933 when his *Shape of Things to Come* was published, a note of desperation became apparent in his optimism. He saw no possibility of overcoming the fragmentary, parochial, and contingent elements in the various human cultures except by a desperate expedient. Modern technicians, symbolized by a group of conspirational aviators, would establish a world authority, sufficiently powerful to dictate the standards of universal truth which would inform an educational program for the whole of mankind. This educational program would ultimately create the universal mind and the comprehensive culture, essential for the stability of the universal community. The movement of his thought from democracy to tyranny is evidence of his desperation.

Shortly before his death Mr. Wells' desperate optimism had finally degenerated to complete despair. He wrote: "A frightful queerness has come into life. Hitherto events have been held together by a certain logical consistency as the heavenly bodies have been held together by the golden cord of gravitation. Now it is as if the cord had vanished and everything is driven anyhow, anywhere at a steadily increasing velocity. . . . The writer is convinced that there is no way out, or around, or through the impasse. It is the end." [18]

The despair which follows upon complacency could not be more consistently or tragically expressed. The spiritual pilgrimage of Mr. Wells is an almost perfect record in minature of the spiritual pilgrimage of our age, though in its totality it will not reveal so neat a pattern. Yet the general movement in our day is from complacency to despair. The Christian faith which "is perplexed, but not in despair" (II Corinthians 4:8), seemed completely irrevelant to a culture which had no perplexities. It has become relevant, though not necessarily acceptable, to a generation which has moved from faith without perplexity to despair. It is, in any event, the apprehension of a wisdom which makes sense out of life on a different level than the worldly wisdom which either makes sense out of life too simply or which can find no sense in life at all.

The wisdom which leads to complacency seeks both to overcome the ambiguity of human existence by the power of reason and to deny the sinful and dishonest pretension in this enterprise. The wisdom which leads to despair understands the limits of reason. It also sees something of the dishonesty by which a more idealistic culture

[18] H. G. Wells, *The Mind at the End of Its Tether*, pp. 4–5.

seeks to hide the contingent character of human knowledge and virtue, and the fanaticisms and power lusts which are the fruit of this pretension. The moral cynicism which results from this discovery is delicately balanced between complacency and despair. Insofar as it recognizes the power lusts and pretensions of other men and nations but not its own, it leads to a new and more terrible complacency. Insofar as it recognizes the sinfulness of all men, including the self, but knows of no forgiving love which can overcome this evil, moral cynicism is despair.

The Christian Gospel is negatively validated by the evidence that both forms of worldly wisdom, leading to optimism and to pessimism, give an inadequate view of the total human situation. This evidence is partly derived from the testimony which the optimists and the pessimists bear against each other. The optimists rightly insist that the pessimists do not fully appreciate the dignity of man, the integrity of human reason, and the tentative coherences of life and history which establish provisional realms of meaning. The pessimists rightly declare that the optimists do not understand the misery of man in the ambiguity of his subordination to and transcendence over nature; that they hide or wilfully deny the elements of dishonesty and pretension in human culture which are the consequence of man's effort to obscure his true situation; and that they give a false estimate of the stability of cultures and civilization because they do not understand the destructive character of human pretensions.

The Christian Gospel is thus distinguished from both forms of worldly wisdom; but its truth lies closer to the testimony of the pessimists than the optimists because it is a truth which can not be apprehended at all from the standpoint of intellectual, moral or social complacency. That is why Jeremiah condemns those prophets as false who make the "word of the Lord" to conform to the world's complacency by assuring every one "who walketh after the imagination of his own heart, No evil shall come upon you" (Jeremiah 23:17). This also is the reason for Christ's preference of the moral derelicts over the righteous of his day; for the former have some contrite recognition of the real situation and the latter have not.

Yet the truth of the Christian Gospel is not logically established from the standpoint of the position of the pessimist, the moral cynic and the social catastrophist. There is no knowledge of the true God in it, and therefore neither hope of redemption through genuine repentance, nor confidence that a power, not our own, can complete what is fragmentary and purge what is evil in human life. Since this knowledge can not be supplied by a further rational analysis of the human situation or the course of history, there is no force of reason which moves from despair to hope or transmutes remorse into repentance. Ultimately the acceptance of the truth of the Gospel is a gift of grace which stands beyond both forms of worldly wisdom and can not be achieved by the testimony of either one against the other.

III

While the negative proof of the Christian truth can not be transmuted into a positive one, which would compel conviction on purely rational grounds, there is nevertheless a positive apologetic task. It consists in correlating the truth, apprehended by faith and repentance, to truths about life and history, gained generally in experience. Such a correlation validates the truth of faith insofar as it proves it to be a source and center of an interpretation of life, more adequate than alternative interpretations, because it comprehends all of life's antinomies and contradictions into a system of meaning and is conducive to a renewal of life.

In pursuing the task of correlating the truth of the Gospel as apprehended by faith to truth otherwise known, Christian theology is subject to three temptations to error. Each error tends to destroy the redemptive power of the truth of faith. The first error is to regard the truth of faith as capable of simple correlation with any system of rational coherence and as validated by such a correlation. Thus many modern versions of Christian theism are embarrassed by the traditional Christian trinitarian definitions of God and seek to construct a theistic metaphysical system without reference to it. Trinitarian definitions are indeed embarrassing rationally; but they are necessary to embody what is known about the character of God, as apprehended in faith's recognition of the revelation of divine mercy, to what is otherwise known about God. At worst such theistic interpretations may hardly be distinguished from pantheistic systems. At best they acknowledge God as creator, thus drawing upon what may be known about God in terms of "general revelation." Thereby they acknowledge that the world we know points beyond itself to a creative ground which we do not immediately know but yet apprehend by faith. But this worship of God the Creator may still be devoid of all the deeper problems of human existence for which the "mercy" of God is the answer.

Naturally the ascription of divinity to Christ is equally embarrassing in such systems of thought. This embarrassment is overcome by fitting Christ into some general scheme of the history of culture. He becomes the great teacher or exemplar of the moral ideal or either the anticipator or the culmination of the law of moral progress. His perfect love is regarded as a simple possibility for all men, if only they are able to recover knowledge of the "historic Jesus'" persuasiveness as a teacher of the law of love or his rigor as its law-giver. The moral complacency of modern culture is supported, rather than challenged, by a faith which thus brings Christ into a system of simple historical possibilities.

The second error arises when the effort is made to guard the uniqueness of the truth of faith and to prevent its absorption into a general system of knowledge by insisting that Christian truth is miraculously validated and has no relation to any truth otherwise known. This is the error to which Protestant literalism is particularly prone. Its consequence is cultural obscurantism. The truth of faith, thus jealously guarded, degenerates into a miraculous historical fact. Miracles may be believed without the repentance which is the prerequisite of the renewal of life. The tendency to transmute a truth of faith, which can be known only by a person in the totality and wholeness of his life, into a miraculous fact, which the credulous but not the sophisticated may easily believe, accounts for the frequent spiritual aridity of Protestant orthodoxy. The whole Biblical story of redemption is not inwardly known in such orthodoxy. There is therefore no power of a new life in its wisdom and no grace in its truth. The knowledge of a series of miraculous events may be perfectly compatible with a graceless legalism or with racial and religious hatreds of every kind.

Failure to relate the truth of faith to other knowledge and experience furthermore leads to a cultural obscurantism which denies the obvious truths about life and history, discovered by modern scientific disciplines. The cultural obscurantism of this kind of literalism not only brings Christian truth in contradiction with the facts, known by natural science and indisputable on their own level. It also makes that truth completely irrelevant to the truths discovered by the social, political, psychological, and historical sciences.

Ideally there should be a constant commerce between the specific truths, revealed by the various historical disciplines and the final truth about man and history as known from the standpoint of the Christian faith. In such a commerce the Christian truth is enriched by the specific insights which are contributed by every discipline of culture. But it also enriches the total culture and saves it from idolatrous aberrations. Thus every discipline of psychology and every technique of psychiatry may be appreciated as contributing to the cure of souls provided the self in its final integrity is not obscured by detailed analyses of the intricacies of personality, and provided techniques are not falsely raised into schemes of redemption. In the same manner the social and historical sciences may give constantly more accurate accounts of cause and effect in the wide field of human relations. But without relation to the Christian truth they finally generate structures of meaning which obscure the profounder perplexities of life, offer some plan of social enlightenment as a way of redemption from evil, and lose the individual in the integrity of his spirit to the patterns of cause and effect which they are able to trace.

The third error, to which Catholic rationalism is particularly prone, is to validate the truth of faith but to explicate it rationally in such a way that mystery is too simply resolved into ostensible rational intelligibility. The rational exposition of Christian trinitarianism illustrates this difficulty from the Christological controversies of the early church to this day. It is not possible to state the truth about God, as known from the standpoint of Christian faith, except in trinitarian terms. God was revealed in Christ in actual history. The

Second Person of the Trinity thus defines that aspect of the divine power which is engaged in history, and which is known primarily by faith. The relation of the Son to the Father is most simply stated in the Scriptural word: "God so loved the world, that he gave his only begotten Son, that whosoever believeth in him should not perish, but have eternal life" (John 3:16). The relation of the Son to the Father, in which the Father's love is on the one hand the force of redemption and the Son's suffering is on the other hand the revelation of redemptive love in contrast to the "wrath" or the justice of the Father, reveals to us a partly understandable mystery, without the understanding of which either the Christian doctrine of redemption degenerates into sentimentality or the Christian conception of law and justice degenerates into legalism. This is a mystery rich in meaning. If we seek to reduce it to simple intelligibility by pretending to know too much about the relation of Son to Father and to Holy Spirit, we fall either into an impossible tritheism or a too simple monism. In the same manner the doctrine of the Holy Spirit, as the third person of the Trinity is important, if we would understand that all forms of holiness and all signs of redemption in actual history are not merely extensions of human wisdom or human virtue but are the consequence of a radical break-through of the divine spirit through human self-sufficiency. Without relating these manifestations to God's nature, Christian faith degenerates into a shallow spiritualism. Yet this fact hardly justifies the long "filioque" controversy in Christian history in which theologians sought abortively either to prove or disprove that the Holy Spirit proceeded from only the Father or from both the Father and the Son.

The effort to validate the divine nature of Christ by attributing divine omniscience to the human person is an equally abortive attempt to explicate a truth about Christ, as known to faith, in rational terms, with the consequence of reducing it to rational nonsense.

Thus a modern Anglo-Catholic theologian engages in the tortuous effort to prove that Christ both was, and was not, omniscient. He does this by supposing that there was a "stratification of knowledge in such a way that quite apart from the experimental knowledge which he acquired by the normal human use of the intellect, the Christ includes in himself, by the infusion of omniscience which the divine person possesses through its real identity with the divine nature, the possession in principle of everything that is knowable by man." But he does not always use this possession because "the exercise of his knowledge is adjusted with the most precise and exquisite accuracy to the precise needs of every situation with which he is confronted." This picture of an omniscient person who usually hides his omniscience comes into conflict with the plain Scriptural confession that Jesus did not know the "day and hour" of the final judgement. Jesus' admission of ignorance, we are told, "is neither on the one hand a mere affectation which would be difficult to reconcile with truthfulness, nor yet on the other hand the sign of the absence of knowledge in the mind considered in its totality." [14]

It is difficult to understand what could possibly be gained by such implausible efforts. The meaning of Christ's revelatory power, as apprehended by faith, is imperiled and a logical absurdity takes its place.

It is interesting that Christian piety and art are usually closer to the truth than various theologies in seeking to symbolize the true nature of Christ in both the historical dimension and in the revelatory depth or height which reveals Jesus to be the Christ. Christian art wisely centers upon the Cross in seeking to portray this deeper significance of the person of Christ and of the whole drama of his life. Other portrayals easily degenerate into sentimentality. Christian piety follows the same course, though it is not insensible to the fact that the teachings of Christ have a rigor which point beyond simple historical possibilities and that the life of Christ is filled with signs of that suffering *Agape* of which the Cross is the supreme symbol. The Cross is the symbolic point where this story most obviously ceases to be merely a story in history and becomes revelatory of a very unique divine "glory," namely the glory and majesty of a suffering God, whose love and forgiveness is the final triumph over the recalcitrance of human sin and the confusion of human history.

That history is fulfilled and ended in this *Agape* of God, as re-

[14] E. L. Mascall, *Christ, the Christian and the Church*, p. 59.

vealed in Christ, is the basic affirmation of the Christian faith. Such a love both completes and contradicts every form of historic virtue. It can not be comprehended as the completion of life, by faith, if that which stands in contradiction to it in historic forms of virtue and wisdom is not contritely acknowledged. If this truth of faith ceases to be a truth requiring such repentance, it ceases to be a truth which contains "grace," which is to say it loses its power to complete what is fragmentary and to overcome what is wrongly completed in human existence.

If the truth of faith merely becomes a "fact" of history, attested by a miracle, or validated by ecclesiastical authority, it no longer touches the soul profoundly. If it is made into a truth of reason which is validated by its coherence with a total system of rational coherence, it also loses its redemptive power. The truth of the Christian Gospel is apprehended at the very limit of all systems of meaning. It is only from that position that it has the power to challenge the complacency of those who have completed life too simply, and the despair of those who can find no meaning in life.

CHAPTER XI

~~~~~~

Beyond Law and Relativity

IN New Testament faith the same love (*Agape*) of Christ which symbolizes the suffering and forgiving love of God by which the sinful recalcitrance of the human heart is finally vanquished, is also the norm of goodness for those who seek to walk in newness of life. So St. Paul admonished: "Be ye therefore followers of God, as dear children; and walk in love, as Christ also hath loved us, and hath given himself for us an offering and a sacrifice to God for a sweetsmelling savor" (Ephesians 5:1). As the essential sin of the first Adam was pride and self-love, so the essential goodness of the "Second Adam" is sacrificial, suffering and self-giving love.

This ethic of the Cross is as certainly a "scandal" in the field of ethics as the "foolishness of the Cross" is a scandal in the realm of truth. It is a scandal from the standpoint of any common-sense or rational ethic which seeks to establish the good in human relations by some kind of balance of, or discrimination between, competing interests. Heedlessness toward the interests of the self, as enjoined in the ethics of the New Testament, would seem to imperil every discriminating concept of justice by which men seek to arbitrate conflicting claims.

On the other hand a history-minded age brings a different charge against the New Testament norm. It does not share the fear of the legalists that pure love may imperil the sanctity of law. It is afraid that the law of love represents a too fixed and inflexible conception of the final good. Since we live in an unfolding history, it hopes that another age may reveal a more perfect virtue than Christ revealed. Furthermore a culture which has learned to scan the vast varieties of social and cultural configurations in history is not certain that any law is adequate for all occasions. It is the more sceptical because it has learned to discount the pretensions of universality and eternal validity which have been made for various structures and norms of ethics in various cultures. It has learned, in short, that the so-called "self-evident" truths in the sphere of morality usually cease to be self-evident under new historical circumstances and in new occasions. The modern moral temper is naturally and inevitably relativist. The old debate between advocates of fixed rules of morality and pragmatists and relativists has taken a new turn; and this new turn gives a tremendous advantage to the relativists.

Until the rise of the modern history-minded culture the advantage was always with the advocates of fixed principles of justice. Both the ancient and the medieval world agreed with Epictetus that "there is a general standard, the discovery of which relieves from madness those who wrongly use personal opinion as their only measure." [1] Socrates vanquished the relativistic Sophists who believed that "man is the measure of all things," including the cynical form of relativism which taught that rules of justice were ideologies of the strong. Medieval Christianity incorporated both classical and Mosaic legalism into the structure of Christian morality; and has been as intent to defeat the "lawlessness" of the pragmatists and relativists as the purest rationalists. But Christian legalism, as every other advocacy of inflexible rules for shifting historical situations, is embarrassed today. It should long since have been embarrassed by the fact that the New Testament is strongly anti-legalist in tone. Traditional Christianity has appropriated little of the New Testament understanding of the limits of law. It is particularly on the defensive today because historical science has fully revealed the historically contingent elements in Old Testament moral and social standards, and because the modern conception of history challenges the classical doctrine of the changeless forms of historical cycles upon which the rationalistic version of Christian legalism rests.

[1] *Discourses of Epictetus*, Chapter 11.

On the other hand modern moral relativism is usually quite unconscious of the abyss of moral nihilism, on the edge of which it walks. Sometimes it flagrantly disregards permanent factors in the human situation in its preoccupation with the novel, and sometimes it frankly plunges into the abyss of nihilism. Thus modern French existentialism glories in an absurd denial of the fact that human freedom can not change the structure of man's being. Jean-Paul Sartre writes: "Thus there is no human nature because there is no God to have a conception of it. . . . Man is nothing else but that which he makes of himself. . . . Before the projection of the self nothing exists; not even in the heaven of intelligence. Man will only attain existence when he is what he purposes to be." [2] Thus the paradox that man must become what he truly is is resolved; and man becomes his own creator.

There must be some way of resolving this debate between legalists and relativists which will refute the legalists whenever they make too sweeping claims for fixed standards of conduct and which will, at the same time, avoid the abyss of nihilism on the edge of moral relativism. Could the "word of the Cross" be the resolution of that debate? Could the law of love, which is more than law, illumine the limits of law in prescribing rules for human freedom? Could the law of love, which rises above all specific law, refute the claims of relativists who recognize the limits of law but not the peril of lawlessness?

II

The idea that the law of love is an antidote for both legalism and lawlessness may best be tested by analyzing the human situation in both its individual and social dimensions, and considering its relevance to both the structure of the human individual and the structure and the necessities of human society. In both cases the heedlessness toward the self which is implied in the *Agape* of the New Testament seems to be an embarrassment; for it contradicts the natural and justified inclination of the self to preserve and defend

[2] Jean-Paul Sartre, *Existentialism and Humanism*, p. 28.

its own existence and it throws confusion into the nicely calculated balances and discrimination of competing interest by which society preserves a tolerable justice. Yet the relevance of the New Testament standard to the moral problem of all men in every age may lie precisely in its indirect and paradoxical relation to specific standards, as revealed in these embarrassments.

The law of love is the final law for man because of his condition of finiteness and freedom. It is not the only law of his existence because man is, despite his freedom, a creature of nature who is subject to certain natural structures. But these natural structures have negative rather than positive force. The freedom of man contains the capacity of transcending nature so that the self in the unity of its freedom and finiteness contains a bewildering degree of mixtures of spiritual freedom and natural necessity. In consequence there are not as many "things to do and not to do" which follow "in a necessary manner from the simple fact that man is man" [3] as is assumed by Christian legalists. It is at any rate apparent that Christian legalism is constantly tempted to embody historically contingent mixtures of freedom and necessity into the body of law, which is supposed to "follow in a necessary manner" from the primordial structure of human nature. On the other hand modern thought is always in danger, either of obscuring what is permanent in the structure of human nature or of denying its essential freedom by its preoccupation with the "natural" conceived as the primordial.

The law of love is the final law for man in his condition of finiteness and freedom because man in his freedom is unable to make himself in his finiteness his own end. The self is too great to be contained within itself in its smallness. The Gospel observation that "whoso seeketh to gain his life will lose it" is thus not some impossible rule imposed upon life by Scriptural fiat. It describes the actual situation of the self, which destroys itself by seeking itself too immediately. The true self dies if the contingent self tries too desperately to live.

In normal life consistent self-destruction through self-seeking, which could be defined as total depravity, is prevented by the various forces of "common grace" which serve to draw the self out of

[3] Jacques Maritain, *The Rights of Man and Natural Law*, p. 63.

itself. These family and communal responsibilities, affections, disciplines and pressures are related to the *Agape*, as the ultimate norm, since they serve to relate life to life creatively though imperfectly and to preserve the health of the self by drawing it beyond itself. But these same disciplines also stand in contradiction to *Agape* because they are fruitful sources of collective egotism, being used by the self to make inordinate collective claims after disavowing individual ones. The self-forgetfulness of *Agape* is, in short, no simple possibility in life. The self does not get beyond itself radically by taking thought. *Agape* is nevertheless the final law of human existence because every realization of the self which is motivated by concern for the self inevitably results in a narrower and more self-contained self than the freedom of the self requires. Consequently the highest forms of self-realization are those which are not intended or calculated but are the fruit of some movement of "grace" which draws the self out of itself despite itself into the love of God and the neighbor.

The law of love as we have it in the New Testament is obviously neither a simple law which states a moral obligation which the self can easily fulfill by such propulsive power as the sense of "ought" may possess; nor is it a law which requires the destruction of the self. The Christian ethical norm has little relation to mystical concepts according to which the particularity of egohood is regarded as an evil and redemption is equated with the absorption of individual consciousness in universal consciousness.[4] In contrast to such schemes of redemption from self, the Christian faith does promise self-realization. "I am crucified with Christ: nevertheless I live" (Galatians 2:20), declares St. Paul in a classical definition of the relation of dying-to-self to the realization of true selfhood in the Christian view. It must be observed, however, that the promised self-realization does not include the self's physical security or historic success. "Fear not them," declares Christ, "which kill the body, but are not able to kill the soul: but rather fear him which is able to destroy both soul and

---

[4] Modern, quasi-Buddhistic versions of such schemes of salvation may be found in Aldous Huxley's *Perennial Philosophy* and Gerald Heard's *The Creed of Christ.*

body in hell" (Matthew 10:28). Here the eschatological dimension of Christian ethics is succinctly expressed. It is recognized that the true self has a dimension, transcending its contingent historical existence, and that it could destroy itself in that dimension by trying too desperately to keep alive. In the Epistle to the Hebrews Christ is portrayed as emancipating those "who through the fear of death were all their lifetime subject to bondage" (Hebrews 2:15). Thus the root of sin (excessive concern for the self) is found in the self's concern for its contingent existence. The release from this bondage involves emancipation from anxiety about death. Thus the resurrection of Christ is always portrayed as a triumph over both sin and death. Such a faith may easily degenerate into an hysterical claim to the "right" of immortality, in which case it becomes a transcendental version of the old sin of trying too desperately to live.

It must be obvious that the triumph of faith over anxiety, which is the prerequisite of love, is no more a simple possibility than *Agape* itself. Such faith and such love are ultimate possibilities which can not be claimed as actual achievements. Yet there are partial realizations of them in history, so long as they are not proudly claimed as achievements. These impossible possibilities describe the true norms of the self in its freedom over nature and history.

If the *Agape* of the New Testament must be distinguished from the destruction of selfhood in mysticism, it must also be differentiated from the conception of love as conceived in sentimental and moralistic versions of the Christian faith. Modern liberal Christianity has sometimes sought to make suffering and sacrificial love into a simple possibility which would become progressively less sacrificial and more successful as more and more men incarnated it. Sometimes it has sought to remove the embarrassing connotations of heedlessness toward the self in the New Testament *Agape* and reduced the norm to the dimensions of the classical *Philia* or *Eros*, that is, to the level of mutual love or the love which calculates its relations to others from the standpoint of its own need of others. Walter Rauschenbusch, who was not completely oblivious to the deeper dimensions of the New Testament norm, nevertheless occasionally equated it with the idea that "man is fundamentally gregarious and his morality consists in being a good member of his community." [5] Shirley Jackson Case thinks that the heedlessness toward the interests of the self, enjoined in the New Testament *Agape*, was meaningful in the securities of an agrarian society and must be reinterpreted to fit the insecurities of an industrial society.[6] Dean Albert Knudson is embarrassed because the ethic of the Sermon on the Mount seems to "negate the right of self-defense," in which case it would be in conflict with any rational-prudential ethic, which must grant the self this right. He believes, therefore, that the injunction "Resist not him that is evil" must not be taken literally but as an Oriental extravagance intended to discourage "violence and passion in dealing with our enemies." [7]

Even when the norm of love is thus reduced to the dimension of a prudential ethic it falls under the stricture of modern psychiatry. In a significant analysis of the relation of love and self-love from the standpoint of a non-relativistic psychological theory Erich Fromm comes to the conclusion that the religious demand, "Don't be selfish," is an impossible one; and that it implies the illegitimate command: "Don't be yourself." [8] Fromm correctly discerns the weakness of a Christian moralism which regards the love commandment as the expression of a simple obligation which the self can, by sufficient will-power, obey. But in order to eliminate this error he falls into the more grievous one of making love of the neighbor a "phenomenon of abundance," a by-product of the overflowing vitality of the self which first loves itself.[9] Such a view fails to measure the freedom of the self in its dimension of transcendence over self, which makes it impossible for it to be rich within itself. Whatever spiritual wealth the self has within itself is the by-product of its relations, affections and responsibilities, of its concern for life beyond itself.

To guard against such errors in both secular and Christian inter-

[5] *Christianity and the Social Order*, p. 67.
[6] *The Social Triumph of the Early Church*, pp. 223–226.
[7] *The Principles of Christian Ethics*, p. 229.
[8] *Man for Himself*, p. 127.
[9] *Ibid.*, p. 126.

pretations of love, Anders Nygren wrote his monumental work on *Agape* and *Eros*, the thesis of which is that a rigorous distinction must be made between the "unmotivated" self-giving love which the Gospels ascribe to a merciful God and the classical idea of *Eros* which, according to Nygren, is always a calculating love, seeking to complete the self from the standpoint of the self and which therefore makes love the servant of self-love. Nygren fails, however, to take the paradox of self-realization through self-giving, as we have it in the New Testament, seriously. Consequently his *Agape* is really a complete impossibility and irrelevance for man. It describes the character of God but has no real relation, as source and end, toward *Philia* and *Eros*, toward either mutual love or expressions of love, tainted with self-interest, which are the actual stuff of our human existence.

Nygren's thesis has been challenged by the Jesuit scholar, Father M. C. D'Arcy.[10] D'Arcy points out that the *Agape* of Nygren's conception can not be related to actual human experience at all, whereas in a true Christian life the grace of *Agape* prevents self-seeking love from degenerating into a consistent egoism and thus has a creative relationship to the whole range of human experience. D'Arcy falls into the opposite error, however, of finding a natural ground for *Agape* in a certain type of *Eros* which does not seek its own but seeks to abandon itself.[11]

The perpetual relevance of the norm of *Agape* to the structure

[10] In *The Mind and Heart of Love.*

[11] D'Arcy astutely compares the *Eros* of classical thought as outlined in Denis De Rougemont's *Love in the Western World* with the classical *eros* as defined by Nygren. De Rougemont centers his attention upon that aspect of the *Eros* motif in classical thought through which the self seeks to be lost in the other or through which the lovers seek death together. This, he rightly declares, is not identical with the more rational *Eros* doctrine which seeks the completion of the self from its own standpoint. In the one case the self seeks escape from self; and in the other case the self completes itself too simply through its intellectual love. D'Arcy finds a natural ground for *Agape* in the *Eros* of self-abandonment, described by De Rougemont.

Actually an erotic love which flees from self in despair is as near and as far from true *Agape* as an erotic love which seeks to complete the self from its own standpoint. It may be significant that the ablest Protestant treatise on this subject should separate the grace of true *Agape* too radically from the realm of "nature" while the ablest Catholic treatise should find a too simple basis in human nature for the grace of *Agape*.

of human existence lies in the fact that it is both the fulfillment of the self's freedom and the contradiction of every actual self-realization insofar as every actual self-realization is partly an egoistic and therefore a premature closing of the self within itself. *Agape* is thus, as the final norm of the self as free spirit, a perpetual source of judgement upon every other norm which may be used tentatively to describe the self's duties and obligations. At the same time it refutes the lawlessness of those theories which imagine that the freedom of the self entitles it to have no law but its own will. Such a proud assertion of the self's freedom and disavowal of its finiteness leads to self-destruction.

III

Since the human self is not simply free spirit, transcending its finite conditions in indeterminate degree, but a creature subject to natural and historical limitations, it is subject to other law, subordinate to the law of love. In defining this law Christian legalism continually involves itself in the error of fixing and defining "immutable" norms, which a modern history-conscious culture is able to refute. For while human nature has, in one sense, an immutable structure, it belongs to the freedom of man to create new configurations of freedom and necessity, which are not as easily brought under fixed norms as Christian legalism imagines. The worst form of legalism has been that of Protestant literalism, which frequently insists upon applying certain Scriptural injunctions, as absolutely normative for the ethical life under all conditions, even though it is quite obvious that the injunctions are historically contingent.[12] Liberal Protestantism has usually fled from such literalism into the opposite error of assuming that Christians could live purely by the law of love without any other normative principles. In comparison with such literalism and such sentimentality Catholic moral theory is remarkably sane and circumspect. Yet its efforts to derive an immutable

---

[12] A flagrant example of such a literalistic legalism was the authority of the Biblical injunction, "Thou shalt not suffer a witch to live" (Exodus 22:18) in our early New England Calvinism.

moral law from "reason" ultimately betrays it into quite obvious absurdities.

The "natural law" of Catholic moral theory which Thomas Aquinas defines as "nothing else but the rational creature's participation in the eternal law" [13] of which "each rational creature has some knowledge" [14] derives law from reason in two ways. Sometimes it would seem that the natural law consists of moral judgements which reason knows intuitively, or as "self-evident" deductions from the primary proposition that "good is to be done and promoted and evil is to be avoided." [15] Usually the "self-evidence" of more detailed requirements of the natural law consists in their derivation in a "necessary," that is logical, manner from the primary proposition that good is to be done and evil avoided.[16] About the hazardous character of these specific norms of the moral law we must speak presently. At the moment it must be observed that reason, according to the theory, sometimes seems to arrive at the truths of the moral law inductively and analytically, rather than deductively. It seeks to discern the permanent structure of human existence. For there is "an order or a disposition which human reason can discover and according to which the human will must act." [17] In this sense the law is "natural" not so much because it embodies the self-evident truths of practical reason as because reason discerns analytically the permanent structure of human nature, it being assumed "that there is a human nature, and that this human nature is the same in all men." [18] There is indeed a permanent structure of human personality, which modern relativists are usually unable to recognize in their obsession with the changing aspects in the human situation. There are, however, always historically contingent elements in the situation which natural-law theories tend falsely to incorporate into the general norm; and there are new emergents in the human situation which

[13] *Summa theol.* I, Quest. 91, Art. 2.
[14] *Ibid.*, Quest. 93, Art. 6.
[15] Thomas Aquinas writes: "Hence this is the first precept of law, that good is to be done and promoted and evil is to be avoided. All other precepts are based upon this." *Ibid.*, Quest. 94, Art. 2.
[16] *Cf.* Joseph Rickaby, *Moral Philosophy*, pp. 138–140.
[17] Jacques Maritain, *The Rights of Man and Natural Law*, p. 61.
[18] *Ibid.*, p. 60.

natural-law theories tend to discount because their conception of an immutable human nature can not make room for them.

The attitude of modern relativism and of Catholic moral theory toward the ethic of sex will serve as an example of the limitations of each. Bertrand Russell, a typical exponent of historical relativism in the morals of sex, argues that modern technics of birth control justify promiscuity when parenthood is not intended. Such a theory obviously disregards one important immutable aspect of the human situation, namely, the organic unity between physical impulses and the spiritual dimension of human personality. This organic unity means that sexual relations are also personal relations and that when they are engaged in without a genuine spiritual understanding between persons and without a sense of personal responsibility to each other, they must degrade the partners of the sexual union.[19]

Catholicism, on the other hand, prohibits birth control, even in marriage, on the ground that it is "intrinsically against nature."[20] The entire argument against birth control in Catholic theory rests upon the second use of the word "nature"; for it could not possibly be maintained that the prohibition follows as a direct and necessary deduction from the primary proposition that good should be done and evil avoided. Nature in this context really means the primordial nature, which has the obvious purpose of perpetuating the species through sexual intercourse. But it is also a characteristic of human nature that its freedom endows all natural impulses with new dimensions, relates them to other impulses in complex formations and enables men to discriminate between various ends of the same impulse. Birth control is a new freedom, gained by technical society, which makes sexual intercourse without procreation possible. Even Catholic theory admits that sexual intercourse may have "secondary ends such as the cultivation of mutual love and the quieting of concupiscence."[21] The satisfaction of these secondary ends is permitted "so long as they are subordinated to the primary ends." But the

[19] Bertrand Russell, *The Scientific Outlook*, Ch. XVI.
[20] Encyclical *On Christian Marriage in Our Day*, by Pope Pius XI, par. 55.
[21] Encyclical *On Christian Marriage in Our Day*, by Pope Pius XI, par. 60.

primary end is not guaranteed, according to theory, by an adequate number of children. It is secured only if actual intercourse has the possibility of procreation. Yet it is not regarded as contrary to nature to indulge in sexual intercourse if "on account of natural reasons either of time or of certain defects new life can not be brought forth." (*Ibid.*) It is not even contrary to nature to seek to avoid conception by limiting intercourse to periods in which conception is least likely. When all these exceptions are granted, it becomes the more arbitrary to insist that the artificial prevention of contraception is contrary to nature. It remains arbitrary even if one recognizes that the new freedom of contraception creates new temptations to vice and makes marriages possible in which the primary aim of marriage is not fulfilled. But this fact is merely an example of the sinful possibilities in the exercise of all forms of human freedom. In the same manner modern industrial methods have increased the temptation to avarice and modern means of warfare have increased the temptation to cruelty. It is precisely because human freedom introduces sinful as well as creative elements into the various historic configurations of human vitality that it is so dangerous to define the "human nature which is the same in all men." It is certainly dangerous to fill the "natural law" with too many specific injunctions and prohibitions.[22]

Catholic legalism has obviously elaborated a standard in this instance which makes a loving consideration of the problems and perplexities of parenthood, particularly under circumstances of poverty, very difficult. In actual practice it operates to lighten the burden of parenthood among those classes which may avail themselves of birth control information through private means and to deny this

[22] It is worth noting in this connection that Thomas Aquinas had less specific content in his natural law than is found in modern Catholic theory. Aquinas said: "Although there is necessity in common principles, the more we descend to the particular the more we encounter defects.... Truth or practical rectitude is not the same for all as to what is particular, but only as to the common principles.... The greatest number of conditions added the greater number of ways in which the principle may fail." *Summa theol.* I, Quest. 94, Art. 4. This warning, if taken seriously, would challenge some of Thomas' own elaboration of specific rules of conduct but even more some of those which have been subsequently elaborated.

advantage to those classes who depend upon public clinics, which Catholic pressure upon public law suppresses. The Catholic standard may come in increasing conflict with the wise policy since modern medicine reduces infant mortality to such a degree that increase in populations has been enormous in the industrial era. Malthusianism, which had presumably been reduced to irrelevance, has therefore become, once more, a plausible theory. Mankind may be breeding too prolifically for its own good, despite the knowledge of birth control.

There is not much that is absolutely immutable in the structure of human nature except its animal basis, man's freedom to transmute this nature in varying degrees, and the unity of the natural and the spiritual in all the various transmutations and transfigurations of the original "nature." Man's social nature is derived from both his natural gregariousness and from the requirements of his spiritual nature, previously discussed. But no particular form of human society can be defined as according to the laws of nature. The most immediate limitations of man as a creature of nature are immutable; but any particular historic expression of them is mutable. Most of the natural or creaturely limits of human nature, such as his heterosexual character, his survival impulse, and his ethnic particularity are only negatively operative in the construction of norms. Eighteenth-century rationalism involved itself in confusion when it tried to raise the survival impulse to a primary norm of ethical life. Nazi racism became involved in perversity when it sought to raise the natural fact of ethnic particularity into a positive law of ethics. Even Reformation moral theory led to confusion when it sought to deal with historic structures and institutions, such as marriage and the state, as belonging to the "order of creation" (*Schoepfungsordnung*).

There are many norms of conduct, validated by experience, between the conditions of man's creatureliness and the law of love, which is the final norm of man's freedom. But they must be held with some degree of tentativity and be finally subordinated to the law of love. Otherwise the norm of yesterday becomes the false standard of today; and lawlessness is generated among those who are most conscious of, or most affected by, the historical changes in the human situation.

IV

The *Agape* of Christ, which the New Testament regards as the final norm of human life, would seem to have an even more problematic relevance to the structure of human society than to the structure of individual existence. Can the idea of sacrificial love be anything but an embarrassment when the community's need of social harmony, justice, and peace are considered? The justice of a community requires a careful and discriminate judgement about competing rights and interests. The admonition to be heedless of the interests of the self introduces confusion into such discriminate judgements. In the collective relationships of mankind ruthless aggression must be countered by resolute defense; and the impulse of dominion must be resisted, if slavery is to be avoided. A sacrificial submission to a ruthless antagonist may mean a noble martyrdom if the interests of the self alone are considered. But if interests other than those of the self are sacrificed, this nobility becomes ignoble "appeasement." This fact our Christian perfectionists learned (and sometimes failed to learn) in the tragic decades of recent history. The justice of even the most perfect community is preserved partly by the rational elaboration of principles of equity in which the non-calculating, non-prudential and ecstatic impulse of *Agape* would seem to have no place. Justice is partly maintained by balances of power in which the push and shove of competing vitalities in society is brought into some kind of stable or unstable equilibrium. Unwillingness or inability to put in one's claims amid the vast system of claims and counter-claims of society means that one's claims will not be considered. A saintly abnegation of interest may encourage the ruthless aggrandizement of the strong and the unscrupulous. These facts are so plain that every effort to introduce suffering love as a simple alternative to the complexities and ambiguities of social justice must degenerate into sentimentality.

For this reason the main streams of Christian thought have re-

served the norm of love for the realm of personal and intimate relations, above and beyond the structures of justice by which society
preserves a tolerable harmony. Catholic moral theory places these
ultimates of *Agape* in the realm of "counsels" of perfection, which
may be fulfilled more perfectly in the life of the dedicated ascetic
than in the market place. Luther makes a rigorous distinction between the realm of grace and the realm of law. Forgiving love has
a place in the one realm; but in the other realm nothing is known
of it. In this realm of "Cæsar" nothing is known but "chains, the
sword and the law."

This distinction is provisionally justified by the fact that there is
obviously a more direct relevance of the norm of love to the relation, particularly the intimate relations, of persons than to the rough
and ambiguous methods by which a community preserves a tolerable
harmony and justice. The most direct relationship of love to the
problems of community would seem to be the purifying effect of
sacrificial love upon mutual love. Mutual love and loyalty are, in a
sense, the highest possibilities of social life, rising above the rational
calculations and the power-balances of its rough justice. The grace
of sacrificial love prevents mutual love from degenerating into a
mere calculation of mutual advantages. If mutual love is not constantly replenished by impulses of grace in which there are no calculation of mutual advantages, mutual relations degenerate first to the
cool calculation of such advantages and finally to resentment over
the inevitable lack of complete reciprocity in all actual relations.

But this is not the only relation of *Agape* to the structures of
justice in society. If love is removed from its position as final, though
indirect, norm of all human relations, by what standard are the
structures of justice measured? Did not Luther's rigorous distinction
between the realm of grace and the realm of law destroy the ultimate criterion for judging the moral quality of the positive law of
historic states? The result was that the order of the state became an
end in itself; and the lack of justice in that order was accepted too
uncritically. Perhaps justice degenerates into mere order without
justice if the pull of love is not upon it.

Catholic moral theory had the advantage over Lutheran theory

because it subjected the justice of positive law and of historic structures more consistently to the criterion of "natural law." But Catholic theory assumes that the requirements of natural law are absolute
and inflexible, being contained in the reason which the creature
has from God. But this claim for the absolute validity of rational
norms must be questioned from the standpoint of New Testament
doctrine as well as from the standpoint of historic experience. Here
is the very point at which the New Testament norm of *Agape*
may resolve the debate between legalism and relativism. The question which must be raised is whether the reason by which standards
of justice are established is really so pure that the standard does not
contain an echo and an accent of the claims of the class or the culture, the nation or the hierarchy which presumes to define the standard. May not the scruple that we ought not to enter our own claims
in the balances of justice [23] represent a profound consciousness of the
contingent character of our claims and the taint of interest in the
standards by which we regard our claims as justified? One need
only consider how every privileged class, nation, or group of history
quickly turns privileges into rights, to be stubbornly defended against
other claimants in the name of justice, to recognize the importance of
this final scruple about our schemes of justice from the standpoint of
Christian love.

It is important to note that modern relativism challenges Christian
and other forms of legalism not merely on the ground that their laws
are too inflexible to be adequate for all, particularly for novel, situations; but also on the ground that the norm of justice is frequently
actually a rationalization of the interests of one party to the dispute
which the standard is to adjudicate. Karl Marx's jeer at legalism
contains this charge in simplest form: "You transform into eternal
laws of nature and reason the social forms springing from present
modes of production and forms of property. What you see clearly in
the case of ancient property, what you admit in the case of feudal
property you are, of course, forbidden to admit in the case of your

---

[23] *Cf.* I Corinthians 6:7: "Now therefore there is utterly a fault among you,
because ye go to law one with another. Why do ye not rather take wrong? Why
do ye not suffer yourselves to be defrauded?"

own form of bourgeois property." [24] Marx is right, even in the description of the unconscious form in which rationalizations of interest express themselves. It is always possible to see a problem of justice more clearly when our own interests are not involved than when they are. In the latter case we are "forbidden to admit" the truth because interest is subtly compounded with our reason.

This jeer at bourgeois legalism and moralism did not prevent Marx from elaborating new, and supposedly "eternal," principles of justice in which equality became the absolute rather than the guiding principle of justice. Thereby liberty was subordinated to a too great degree. Furthermore, the socialization of property became too simply the condition of justice, supplanting the previously too simple confidence in property as the instrument of justice. The new Marxist legalism, springing from a provisional moral cynicism, is characteristic of the spirituality of our age beyond the confines of Marxism. Moral cynicism, scepticism and relativism are usually only provisional. There are consistent moral sceptics such as E. Westermarck who believes "that moral standards are based upon emotions which necessarily vary with different individuals." [25] But usually the relativism of both the older romanticism and of modern pragmatism is only provisional. Thus Herder protested against the false universals of the rationalists of the Enlightenment and suggested that each culture and age had its own standard. But his relativism was relieved by his certainty that "constant development is the purpose of God in history" and that "history is a stream which flows unceasingly toward the ocean of humanity." [26] In the same fashion John Dewey's pragmatism is quite innocent of the taint of moral cynicism which is frequently levelled at it by the advocates of law. Like Herder and all modern believers in development, he seems at times to believe that growth and development are themselves a norm to which life may conform. "Since there is nothing in reality to which growth is relative save more growth," he declares, "there is nothing to which education is subordinate save more education. . . . The criterion of value

[24] *Communist Manifesto.*
[25] *Christianity and Morals*, p. 411. See also his *Ethical Relativity.*
[26] Johann Gottfried Herder, *Werke*, Vol. 5, 512.

in education is the extent to which it creates the desire for more growth." [27] Actually this confidence in growth as a norm of life is qualified by the belief that historical development moves in a particular direction. For Dewey the direction includes both freedom and justice. If one were to make a charge against modern evolutionary relativists it would be that they usually implicitly accept some version of the Christian norm which they explicitly deny. Very frequently, also, they fail to recognize that the two values of freedom and order which are involved in the Christian norm of love are not easily reconciled, when the effort is made, as it must be made, to embody the law of love into norms of justice. Failing to recognize the complex relation of freedom to order, they frequently end by sacrificing the one to the other. Thus Joseph Needham is convinced not only that "history is on our side" but that what puts it on our side is the growth toward communism. "The question is not whether communism will come or no," he declares; "the question is how much culture can be saved from fascist barbarism." [28] Needham's belief that history is moving toward communism can be matched by equally simple beliefs that it is moving toward a libertarian democracy. In each case the ultimate norm, supposedly supported by the actual processes of history, either sacrifices freedom too simply to order or order and equality to freedom.

Moral cynicism and scepticism is almost as rare in moral theory as atheism is in religious theory. For every Sartre or Westermarck there are a hundred provisional moral sceptics who end with a new, and usually too simple, statement of the norms of social justice or with an inadequate estimate of the structure of selfhood.

Christian legalism is, therefore, in error when it seeks to support its too rigid and inflexible rules by raising the spectre of moral anarchy. It is doubly wrong if it denies that its supposedly absolute norms of justice may become the bearers of injustice in specific situations. The principles of "natural law" by which justice is defined are, in fact, not so much fixed standards of reason as they are rational efforts to apply the moral obligation, implied in the love commandment, to

[27] John Dewey, *Democracy and Education*, pp. 60–62.
[28] Joseph Needham, *History is on Our Side*, p. 34.

the complexities of life and the fact of sin, that is, to the situation created by the inclination of men to take advantage of each other. The most universal norms are also significantly the most negative, such as the prohibition of theft and of murder. They define our obligation to the neighbor in such minimal terms that they have achieved almost universal acceptance in the conscience of humanity. There are, however, "self-evident" moral propositions included in most summaries of moral intuitions which have neither such "self-evidence" or unanimous acceptance in history as the prohibition of murder. Aquinas points out, for instance, that the proposition that "contracts ought to be kept" is a generally valid rule but is nevertheless subject to contingency. There are situations in which contracts ought not to be kept.

Any definition of moral rules beyond those which mark the minimal obligation of the self to the neighbor are discovered, upon close analysis, to be rational formulations of various implications of the love commandment, rather than fixed and precise principles of justice. All principles of justice are designed to arbitrate and adjudicate competing claims and conflicting rights. In this adjudication the Aristotelian principle that everyone is to have his due defines the spirit of justice, but the formula contains no indication of what each man's due is. It is equally impossible to derive any specific criteria from the general Thomistic proposition that we ought to do good and avoid evil.

The most frequent general principle of justice in the thought of modern as well as Stoic and Catholic proponents of natural law is the principle of equality. The dominant position of the principle of equality in all natural-law concepts is significant. Equality stands in a medial position between love and justice. If the obligation to love the neighbor as the self is to be reduced to rational calculation, the only guarantee of the fulfillment of the obligation is a grant to the neighbor which equals what the self claims for itself. Thus equality is love in terms of logic. But it is no longer love in the ecstatic dimension. For the principle of equality allows and requires that the self insist upon its own rights and interests in competition with the rights and interests of the other. Therefore equal justice is on the one hand the law of love in rational form and on the other hand something less than the law of love. The heedlessness of perfect love can not be present in the rational calculations of justice. The self's lack of concern for its own interests may have to be reintroduced into the calculations of justice, however, when and if it becomes apparent that all calculations of justice, however rational, tend to weight the standard of justice on the side of the one who defines the standard.

This existential defect in definitions of justice becomes apparent just as soon as it is recognized that equality is a guiding, but not an absolute, standard of justice. If, as in Marxism, equality is made into an absolute standard, it bears the ideological taint of the "lower" classes in society. They rightly resent unequal privileges but they wrongly fail to appreciate the necessity of inequality of function, without which no society could live. Undoubtedly the classes in society who perform the more important functions appropriate more privileges than the proper performance of function requires or deserves. Yet on the other hand the function does require some special privileges. It is possible and necessary to correct this ideological taint in Marxist equalitarianism. An adequate social theory must do justice to both the spirit of equality and to the necessities of functional inequality. But such a social theory can not possibly have the validity of what is usually meant by "natural law." It will be filled with speculative judgements on just how much special privilege is required for the performance of certain functions in society. It will certainly contain as many ideological taints as any Marxist theory.

It must be obvious that, as one moves from the primary principle of justice to more detailed conclusions, judgements become more hazardous, and conclusions should be regarded as the fruit of social wisdom rather than of pure logic. Most of the propositions which are presented to us in the name of "natural law" are in fact in the category of what Aquinas defined as "secondary principles which . . . are certain detailed proximate conclusions drawn from first principles" [29] and which he admitted to be subject to change. Others might well be placed on the even lower level of practical applications

[29] *Summa theol.* I. Quest. 94, Art. 5.

to particular problems about which Aquinas admits that "the more we descend toward the particular the more we encounter defects," for "in matters of action truth or practical rectitude is not the same for all." [30]

The right to the possession of property as defined in Catholic natural-law theory is a good illustration of the defects of a too inflexible legalism. "Every man has by nature the right to possess property of his own," declares Leo XIII in the encyclical "On the Condition of the Working Man." Property is "natural," according to the theory, in both meanings of that word. "Natural" means, on the one hand, that man, as distinguished from animals, has both the ability and the inclination to appropriate instruments, goods and land and "make them his own." It is "natural," on the other hand, in the sense that reason justifies this extension of the power of the person as logically implied in his power over himself and because it contributes to social peace and justice since "we see that among those who hold anything in common and undivided ownership, strifes not infrequently arise" (Aquinas). The social wisdom of regarding property as a relatively effective institution of social peace and justice can not be challenged. It is a "remedy for sin" in the sense that it gives the person power to defend himself against the inclination of others to take advantage of him. It endows him with instruments for the proper performance of his function and grants him a measure of security in an insecure world. But both Catholic and Protestant social theory tended to make the right of property much too absolute. The wisdom of some of the early church Fathers was forgotten. They understood that the power of property could be an instrument of injustice as well as of justice; and that it could be the fruit of sin as well as remedy for sin.

These scruples of the early Fathers achieved a new relevance in an industrial age in which new and dynamic aggregates of economic power developed. They were too inordinate to come into the category of defensive power; and they obviously encouraged the temptation to injustice in men. For great inequalities of power always tempt the strong to take advantage of the weak. Resentment against rising

[30] *Ibid.*, Art. 4.

injustices in an industrial society gave birth to a new and heretical religion of social redemption. According to this Marxist religion, property was the very root of sin in human nature; and its abolition would redeem society from sin, ushering in a utopian harmony of all interests and vitalities. This heretical religion blew the half of the truth which the early Fathers of the church had recognized (namely that property could be the fruit and bearer of sin) into a monstrous error.

The error should have been countered by a profound reconsideration of the whole problem of the relation of property to justice. Instead it was met by a hard and fast Christian legalism, proclaiming "eternal" principles of natural law, which daily experience continued to prove problematic and contingent, rather than eternal.

Even Pope Leo XIII, despite his interest in and understanding of the problems of justice in an industrial age, declared categorically that proposals for the socialization of property "are emphatically unjust because they would rob the lawful possessor, bring the state into a sphere not its own and cause complete confusion in the community." [31]

Less than a century later the Vatican made a much more qualified judgement on the problem of property; for Pius XI declared: "It may well come about that the tenets of a mitigated socialism will no longer differ from those who seek to reform society according to Christian principles. For it is rightly contended that certain forms of property must be reserved to the state since they carry within them an opportunity for dominating, too great to be left to private individuals." [32] The difference in accent between the two encyclicals can hardly be denied. Some rather tragic social history in western civilization accounts for the difference. One is tempted to speculate whether some of that history might have been avoided if the earlier encyclical had contained the wisdom of the second.

In any event the difference between them is not to be accounted for by a difference in the logic by which reason moves from primary to secondary principles of justice. It is a difference in social wisdom,

[31] Encyclical: "On the Condition of the Working Man," par. 3.
[32] Encyclical: "Restoring the Christian Social Order," par. 114.

determined by differences in social experience. The difference proves that the application of general principles of justice to particular situations includes not merely the application of general rules to particular instances and persons, but to particular epochs and to particular types of general institutions. The institution of "property" is not one but many. Property in land may mean the power of the landlord over the peasant and it may mean the security of the peasant in his own land. Property in industry may mean inordinate power; and it may mean the right of an inventive genius to profit from his inventions.

There are, in short, fewer specific principles of justice with "eternal" validity than is assumed in almost all theories of natural law.

Rules of justice do not follow in a "necessary manner" from some basic proposition of justice. They are the fruit of a rational survey of the whole field of human interests, of the structure of human life and of the causal sequences in human relations. They embody too many contingent elements and are subject to such inevitable distortion by interest and passion that they can not possibly be placed in the same category with the logical propositions of mathematics or the analytic propositions of science. They are the product of social wisdom and unwisdom. Reason itself is not the source of law, since it is not possible to prove the self's obligation to the neighbor by any rational analysis which does not assume the proposition it intends to prove. Yet reason works helpfully to define the obligation of love in the complexities of various types of human relations.

If the *Agape* of New Testament morality is the negation as well as the fulfillment of every private virtue, it is also the negation and the fulfillment of all structures and schemes of justice. It is their fulfillment in the sense that the heedlessness of perfect love is the source and end of all reciprocal relations in human existence, preventing them from degenerating into mere calculation of advantage. It is also the source of the principle of equality and may be a complement to it in all intimate and private relations.

Yet *Agape* stands in contradiction to all structures, schemes and systems of justice, insofar as all historic schemes of justice embody sinful elements, because they contain implicit rationalizations of spe-

cial interests. This sinful corruption is as obvious in rational definitions of justice as in the positive laws of justice which are historically
enacted in given states.

Thus a Christian morality, inspired by the spirit of the New Testament, must be as ready to challenge legalism as relativism. Against
relativists it must insist that no man or nation, no age or culture can
arbitrarily define its own law. Against legalists it must insist that
there is no virtue in law as such (Romans 7:7-25). It does not have
the power within itself to compel obedience. All genuine obedience
to law is derived from the grace of love, which is more than law.
Neither does law have the virtue to define the interests of the self
and the neighbor with precision, since there is no completely disinterested intelligence in history. If the faulty criteria of law are
not corrected by love, law is always in danger of becoming the instrument of sin.[33]

The Pauline admonition against legalism, "Stand fast therefore
in the liberty wherewith Christ hath made us free, and be not en-
tangled again in the yoke of bondage" (Galatians 5:1), is inspired
not merely by a consideration of the moral defects in any specific
system of law but by the limits of law as such. The admonition has
been shockingly disregarded by most versions of the Christian faith.

[33] In recent Protestant moral theory Emil Brunner, in his *Justice and the
Social Order,* tends to revert to an almost pure Thomism in seeking after a
"justice which transcends human caprice and convention" (p. 85) in the resources of reason. Karl Barth, on the other hand, deals realistically with the
existential factors revealed in the justice of an actual community in his
Christengemeinde und Buergergemeinde. But he is rather unnecessarily cryptic
and embarrassed about the fact that there are implied standards of "natural
law" in his discussion of the justice of a state. He declares that he is not
ashamed of possible affinities between his thought and "natural law" concepts
but declines to elucidate the point further. Ultimately he comes to some rather
curious conclusions about the source of justice in the civil society. "The
divine ordinance of the state," he declares, "makes it quite possible that it
may in its own sphere come to quite correct theoretic and practical conclusions and decisions, even though one might, considering the dubious source of
the judgement, expect nothing but error and misadventure" (p. 31). This
means that the standards of justice in any society are so corrupted by sin that
only a mysterious overruling providence achieves the kind of social harmony
and peace which we know in some states. Actually the justice of the most
healthy human communities is not as mysterious as that. It is a revelation of
man's residual capacity for justice, despite the corruptions of self-interest in
his standards and in his practices.

They have found some way of making law, whether derived from Scripture or from the supposed absolutes of reason, too binding. The only exception to this legalism is found in modern sentimental forms of Christianity which assume that the supremacy of the law of love makes it possible to dispense with subordinate laws of justice. It is not possible to dispense with them; but it is important to recognize the historically contingent elements in every formulation of the principles of justice.

It is specially important to reaffirm the New Testament spirit of freedom over law in our own day because the task of preserving justice in the rapidly shifting circumstances of a technical society and of preserving personal integrity under conditions of growing human power require that the spirit of love be freed of subservience to traditional codes. It is not wise to alter social customs and traditional restraints upon human expansiveness lightly. The more the historical root of social restraints is known, the greater must be the inclination to deal conservatively with any viable structure of the human community. But no historic structure or traditional restraint deserves the sanctity which is usually ascribed to it. A truly religious morality must appreciate the virtue of historic and traditional forms of justice against attack by abstract forms of rationalism; but it must at the same time subject every structure of justice, whether historically, rationally, or Scripturally validated, to constant scrutiny.

CHAPTER XII

~~~~~~

False Absolutes in Christian Interpretations of History

I

WHILE the Christian interpretation of history has achieved a new relevance through the obvious inadequacies of modern interpretations, it would be wrong to present the truth of the Christian view without a contrite recognition of the errors which have crept into various Christian interpretations. One of the most tragic aspects of human life is that the profoundest truth may become the source or bearer of grievous error. The self-worship of individuals and nations, of civilizations and cultures, may express itself more plausibly through facets of truth, embodied in a truly universal religion, than by obviously idolatrous religious ideas. There is therefore never an absolute defense against the corruption of Christian truth through the pride and pretension of nations and cultures. The sad history of fanaticism in Christian civilizations proves that no version of the Christian faith has been completely immune to the error of claiming absolute and final significance for contingent, partial, and parochial moral, political and cultural insights.

It is therefore necessary to subject Christian interpretations of life and history to constant reexamination, in order to detect the errors which become compounded with its truth in various stages of history. In our own day this reexamination has become the more important because it is necessary to incorporate what is true in the modern discovery of a moving time and a development in history into the final truth of the Christian Gospel. There is nothing incompatible between a Biblical conception of a dynamic history and the modern view of historical development if the modern errors of regarding historical development as self-explanatory and of equating it with redemption are avoided. If the affinities which exist between the two views are fully explored, some insights, drawn from the modern view, may, in fact, serve to correct some of the errors which have crept into traditional statements of the Christian view.

The core of the Christian view of life and history is embodied in the twofold significance of the love of Christ. It is on the one hand the symbol of the norm of man's historical existence. Man must realize himself not within himself but in a responsible and loving relation to his fellowmen. The insufficiency of man as a finite creature requires his fulfillment beyond himself; and the freedom of man as spirit means that no limits set by nature and history upon his obligation to his fellows are final. Insofar as human history represents an extension of human freedom the discovery of this fact accentuates the this-worldly emphasis of the Christian faith. The fact that his responsibility to his fellowmen in a global community has become an historic urgency underscores the potential meaningfulness of historic existence.

But the love of Christ has another dimension in Christian faith. The self-realization through love which is promised does not carry the guarantee of historical survival. It makes historical survival more problematic, for it points to the fact that the highest form of human goodness embodies a heedlessness of self which endangers the self in its physical security. Thereby it points to a dimension of existence transcending physical existence but involving the existential self rather than merely timeless mind, the *Logisticon* of Plato or Aristotle's *Nous*. In sentimental forms of Christianity such a love is regarded as a simple possibility. In classical Christianity it is understood not only that such love can be fully realized only at the expense of life itself (the simple moral meaning of the Cross) but also that all historic forms of life, individual and collective, embody a positive contradiction to it. The contradiction to it is not the animal survival impulse of man but the spiritualized survival impulse, the will-to-power and the pride by which men seek to overcome their finiteness and actually aggravate the competition between life and life. This contradiction is recognized as a permanent element in man's historic situation, the permanence being symbolized by the vision of the most explicit defiance of the law of love appearing at the end of history in the Anti-Christ. The human situation is not, however, regarded as hopeless; for wherever men recognize the reality and the power of self-love and stop pretending the possession of a goodness which they do not have, the power of self-love may be broken. Insofar as it persists men live in the hope and faith that God will overcome what they can not overcome. The meaning of life is completed in principle whenever it is recognized that all human completions are not only imperfect but contain positive contradictions to its true meaning. It is in this sense that a love which transcends the possibilities of history becomes also the pledge of the completion of life beyond human possibilities. Such a faith can, of course, be held only on the ground of a view of life which makes all human virtue problematic and sees all historic achievements as ambiguous. Its basis is repentance. Yet it can be negatively validated by the simple process of recognizing the problematic character of all human virtue and the ambiguous character of all historic achievements, by methods of ordinarily objective analyses of human history, particularly by analyses of segments of human history which are bereft of the façades which are erected in periods of historic stability.

This Christian conception of life and history is obviously not some simple bit of wishful thinking. It embodies the most tragic conception of historic realities into its universe of meaning. But it must be frankly admitted that this truth was subject to various forms of corruption. Some proponents of the Christian faith frequently seek to press these very errors upon modern man as alternatives to the error of his religion of progress.

One error in Christian thought arises from the fact that the individual is always able to achieve a purer realization of meaning than can be realized communally. The brotherhood which is achieved in human society is stabilized by such institutions as government and property, which contradict as well as support the justice which is the institutional approximation of the law of love. This fact has tempted some versions of the Christian faith, particularly Protestant versions, to betray a defeatist attitude toward the social existence of mankind, to exclude the possibility of redemption and a new life in man's social existence and to confine redemption to individual life. The thought of Martin Luther certainly contains this error. Luther believed that "the world is far too wicked to be worthy of good and pious lords. It must have princes who go to war, levy taxes and shed blood and it must have spiritual tyrants who impoverish it with bulls and letters and laws. This and other chastisements are rather what it deserves and to resist them is nothing else than to resist God's chastisements." [1] Insofar as Luther believed in the possibility of perfecting the social life of man he placed an undue reliance upon the virtues of rulers rather than upon the reform of social structures and institutions. "I know of no state," he declared, "which is well governed by means of law. If the magistrate is wise he will rule more prosperously by natural bent than by laws. . . . More stress ought therefore be placed upon putting good and wise men in office than on making laws, for such men will themselves be the best laws and will judge every variety of case with lively justice." [2]

This negative attitude toward the structures and institutions of social and political life is integral to a wide tendency in Christian thought which may express itself in the optimism of the American social Gospel as well as in the pessimism of Luther.[3] It fails to understand that the moral ambiguity in all social structures and institutions does not destroy the possibility of an indeterminate improvement in them. Luther's defeatism on social life is implicit in his rigorous separation of the realm of grace from that of "civil policy." "The way to discern the difference between the law and the Gospel," he declared, "is to place the Gospel in heaven and the law upon earth." This "heaven" was actually the interior life of the individual. "If the matter be a question concerning faith and conscience let us utterly ex-

---

[1] *A Treatise Concerning the Ban, Works,* II, p. 51.
[2] *On the Babylonian Captivity of the Church, Works,* II, p. 263.
[3] *Cf.* Francis Peabody, *Jesus Christ and the Social Question,* p. 320ff.

clude the law and leave it on earth. . . . Contrariwise in civil policy
obedience to law must be severely required. There nothing must be
known concerning the Gospel, the remission of sins, or heavenly
righteousness or Christ himself but only Moses with the law and the
works thereof." [4]

The indeterminate possibilities of a higher justice in the social
structures of human society, which modern culture has discovered,
refutes this defeatism, even though the modern hope in the gradual
elimination of all moral ambiguities in the political and economic
institutions of mankind is an error. No form of property or government can be made into a simple instrument of pure justice; but
neither can a society without property or government achieve a
perfect accord of life with life. An individualistic and pietistic version of the Christian faith obscures the moral and social meaning of
human existence and evades man's responsibility for achieving a tolerable accord with his neighbors. The rapidly shifting circumstances
of a technical civilization require the constant exercise of this responsibility, not merely in order to achieve a more perfect justice but
also to reconstitute and recreate older forms of justice and community which the advent of technics tends to destroy and disintegrate.

II

If Lutheranism gives a classical expression of the error in Christian
thought, derived from the fact that the individual transcends every
social structure and community and is therefore tempted to regard its
moral ambiguities as proof of the unredeemable character of man's
social existence, both Catholicism and Calvinism are safe against this
error. They have a lively sense of the individual's responsibility for
the whole of his common life. Each seeks in its own way to bring the
social structure under the dominion of justice, though neither assumes, as does sectarian Christianity, that sinful elements in the social
structures, in the economic and political institutions, could be wholly
eliminated. But both Catholicism and Calvinism are tempted to an
opposite error. They seek to guarantee the justice of the social institu-

[4] *Commentary on Galatians.*

tions of the community by bringing them under the sovereignty of some unambiguously righteous will. In the case of Catholicism this righteous power is the church and in Calvinism it is the "rule of the saints." In both instances new evils are introduced into history by the assumption that there is in either the church as a redeemed community, or in the "saints" as redeemed individuals, a source of pure goodness and justice, which can guarantee the justice of the state established under the aegis of either. This assumption obscures the relative character of historical forms of virtue and justice and thereby tempts Christians to the fanaticism which the pretension of righteousness generates. Christ ceases to be, in these forms of the Christian faith, a source of judgement upon the church or the "holy commonwealth" but becomes its secure possession. The faith may therefore continue to generate humility and charity in the lives of individuals; but it becomes a source of collective pride.

Beginning with Augustine's definition of the church as the only society in which perfect justice prevails, Catholicism consistently obscures the contradiction between the historical and the divine which exists, and is bound to exist, within the redeemed community insofar as that community is related to all the natural stuff of human history. Despite all the Augustinian reservations about the imperfections of the historic church, the basic assumption of its perfection is established by him and tends to become more unqualified. It is significant, furthermore, that an uncritical attitude toward the church is also transferred to a Christian state, that is, a state in which God is explicitly acknowledged as Lord. While there is an undoubted difference between a pagan community which acknowledges no sovereignty beyond its own will and knows no majesty beyond its own pride and a "Christian" state which recognizes an ultimate Majesty and Judge, it is the general tendency of Catholic political thought to over-estimate this explicit acknowledgement and to obscure the fact that all particular communities in history, as indeed all individuals, tend to an idolatrous self-worship, even when they are officially or formally "Christian." Thus the inclination of Catholicism to exempt the church from involvement in sin tends to political views in which Christian states partly participate in this exemption.

The pretensions of perfection for the church as a redeemed community become the more intolerable whenever explicit authority of the church over political communities is claimed. For such authority, whether conceived as direct or indirect, is in the context of a culture which accepts the Catholic faith, a source of political power. Thus a particular form of political power is derived from the pretension of a sanctity, ostensibly transcending all particular and competing forms of power in history.

From Hildebrand's subtle, or perhaps not too subtle, transformation of Augustine's conception of the spiritual authority of the *civitas Dei* in the *civitas terrena* into a claim of the supremacy of the *sacerdotium* over the *regnum* the Catholic church has never varied in its insistence that the church which claims authority over the "ultimate end" of human life must have supremacy over the state which seeks the lower end of civil justice.[5]

The claim of a direct authority of the church over civil government, elaborated in the Middle Ages, has been modified in recent centuries. The authority is now claimed to be "indirect." All Catholic authorities are declared by the Catholic scholar, Joseph Mausbach, to be unanimous "in thinking that the church has indirect authority over temporal matters and temporal life, since in all that concerns religion and morals in the highest questions of life, she is and must be the court of last resort." [6] That there is little difference between the claim of "direct" and of "indirect" authority is attested by a Catholic scholar who thinks that "this controversy turns on the

[5] Aquinas, or his disciple, states the argument in *De regimine principum* as follows: "Since man, by living virtuously, is . . . ordained to a higher end, which consists in the enjoyment of God . . . then human society must have the same end as individual man. . . . But because man does not attain this end, which is the possession of God, by human power but by divine power . . . therefore the task of leading him to that end does not pertain to human government but to divine. Consequently government of this kind pertains to that king who is not only man but also God, namely to our Lord Jesus Christ." It is further claimed that the "ministry of this kingdom is entrusted not to earthly kings but to priests and in the highest degree to the chief priest, the successor of St. Peter, the Vicar of Christ, the Roman Pontiff to whom all kings and peoples are subject as to our Lord Jesus Christ Himself. For those to whom pertain the care of intermediate ends should be subject to him to whom pertains the care of the ultimate end and be directed by his rule." Bk. I. ch. 14.

[6] *Catholic Moral Teachings and Its Antagonists*, p. 367.

name rather than the thing. In essentials the two kinds of authority seem to be identical." [7] Pope Leo XIII, in his encyclical *Sapientiœ*, to cite but one of dozens of possible Papal affirmations of this claim, asserts that "it belongs to the Pope to judge authoritatively not only what the Sacred Oracles contain but also what doctrines are in harmony and what are in disagreement with them; and also for the same reason to show forth what things are to be accepted as right and what are to be rejected as worthless."

It is difficult to know what is more dubious in this claim of final authority over all human authorities, whether it is the usurpation of the Divine Majesty by a human dominion or the effort to derive the authority of a sacerdotal institution from the powerless power of the perfect love of a crucified Lord. In any event the fragmentary and sinful character of all historic reality is falsely transcended. The consequences of this error are apparent wherever the church seeks to protect either itself or its "Christian" civilizations from the fury of new forces in history. In all such efforts enmity against the church is falsely interpreted as enmity against God and against Christ. A special pathos is revealed in these historic situations because the human anxieties of priestly oligarchs and the anxious survival impulses of an historic institution are so patent in the polemics of the church even when, and precisely when, it claims to be dealing only with eternal verities.

The Calvinist theocratic impulse is not as consistently pretentious as the Catholic effort at dominion. But Calvinism's various theocratic experiments, in which not the church, but the "rule of the saints" or the "holy commonwealth" was accorded an idolatrous sanctity, have all proved how dangerous it is for the Christian faith to equate any form of historic virtue or power with the sanctity of Christ. The Calvinist holy commonwealth is sometimes assumed to be holy because it has drawn its constitution from the Scripture and has thereby avoided the corruption of the world. By "receiving from the Lord both the platform of their civil polity as it is set down in the essentials of it in the Scripture, and also their laws, which they resolve by His grace to fetch out of the word of God, making that their only

[7] J. Hergenroether, *Katholische Kirche und Christlicher Staat*, I, p. 448.

Magna Carta and accounting no law, statute or judgement valid than it floweth or appeareth to arise from the Word of God," [8] the saints hoped to avoid the sins and corruptions of the world, unmindful of the fact that many institutions which "appear to arise from the Word of God" are just as surely touched by special interest as those which have a less sacred derivation. Moreover, no one can guarantee that the institutions "which appear" to arise from the Word of God, may not become the vehicles of a special oligarchy, seeking power, or in any event becoming corrupted by the power which accrues to its special function in society. Priestly oligarchies, including those which have transmuted the prophets of yesterday into the priest-oligarchs of today, have a rather odious repute in human history, precisely because their religious claims and pretensions have been particularly successful in obscuring the power impulses of the oligarchs, both from themselves and their victims. One need only think of the very good opinion which the religious oligarchy of the Massachusetts theocracy had of itself and the indictment which Roger Williams makes of its Pharisaic pretensions to measure the difference between appearance and reality in every theocratic system which endows religious leadership with political power or derives political power from the religious function.

Calvinistic theocrats sometimes took particular pains to guarantee the probity of the "saints" who were to rule the holy commonwealth. But even the most rigorous "blue laws" could not establish the wisdom or charity which true statesmanship requires.[9] Furthermore, the tendency of a religious oligarchy to use civil power for the suppres-

---

[8] John Elliott, *The Christian Commonwealth*, 1660, Ch. 1. Part 2.

[9] Richard Baxter sought in his *A Holy Commonwealth* (1659) to assure the virtue of the electors by the following provisions: "The Moral Qualification of Electors must be this, that no man choose but those that have publicly owned the Baptismal covenant, personally, deliberately and seriously, taking the Lord for their only God, even the Father, Son and Holy Ghost, the Creator, Redeemer and Sanctifier; and that lyeth not under the guilt of any of those sins for which God would have men put to death or cut off from his people . . . viz., for Balshemy, Idolatry, persuading to Idolatry, Murder, Manstealing, Incest, Sodomy, Adultery, presumptuous sinning and obstinate refusal to obey Magistrate, Priest, or Parent, in case of Gluttony, Drunkenness and the like: all wizzards and those that turn after wizzards and more such like, which may easily be collected,"

sion of religious dissidence inevitably introduces the evil of religious fanaticism into the administration of the civil community.[10]

Both the Catholic and the Calvinistic efforts to overcome the moral ambiguities of human history by bringing political power under religious control, whether under an explicit ecclesiastical authority or a "rule of the saints," or through a constitution derived from Scripture, must be honestly designated as dismal failures, which justify the indictment which both secularists and Christian sectarians have brought against them. They prove the error of transmuting the Christian faith, which in principle does not believe in the possibility of any human or historic force or agency standing above or beyond the human predicament, into a false support for theocratic experiments. There is a profound pathos in these failures. They prove that just as sin is the corruption of man's creative freedom so also the ultimate form of sin is a corruption of man's quest for redemption. Wherever the longing, expressed by St. Paul in the words "that I may gain Christ" is not accompanied by the Pauline reservation "and be found in him, not having mine own righteousness, which is of the law" (Philippians 3:8, 9) and wherever the final virtue is claimed as a secure possession, rather than as intention and hope, and the contradiction between even the most disciplined historic vitalities and the divine will is obscured, there new evils are created. If the effort of modern culture to make history itself into a false Christ is to be refuted, the Christian faith must allow modern culture to bring its evidence against Christianity itself, wherever the Christian life or thought has created false Christs of political power.

III

Neither Catholicism nor Calvinism has any illusion about the inevitability of sin in all human striving. Their religious pretension

---

[10] The debate between John Cotton and Roger Williams on this issue illumines the whole problem of theocratic government. *Cf.* Roger Williams, *The Bloody Tenent of Persecution* (1644). John Cotton answered in the tract "The Bloody Tenent washed white in the Blood of the Lamb," and Roger Williams' rebuttal, "The Bloody Tenent yet more Bloody" (1652), rigorously exposes the perils of theocratic persecution.

arises from the fact that in the one case the church and in the
other the Holy Commonwealth is given a too absolute authority
over the affairs of men. It remained for sectarian Christianity to
seek a complete freedom from sin in society and thereby to lay the
foundation for even more monstrous evils. The Anabaptist sectarianism of the Continental Reformation and the sectarian movement
of the Cromwellian period of England are one-sided expressions of
the facet of hope in Biblical faith, expressed in the petition, "Thy
kingdom come, thy will be done on earth as it is in heaven." They
are justified protests against failures of orthodox Christianity to
challenge the moral evils in particular social situations and against
the dissipation of the true Christian impulse toward the realization of the will of God in history. The desire that "not only
heaven shall be our Kingdom but this world bodily" [11] is a true and
necessary aspiration of the Christian life. But the hope that human
life in history can be freed of every taint of sin, and that man's social
existence can be emancipated from every moral ambiguity, inevitably
generates evil in a pathetic effort to overcome the inexorable relation
of sin and freedom in human life.

There are forms of pietistic sectarianism which have no interest
in the social realities of man's existence. They seek for an individual
bliss and perfection at the price of denying the social dimension of
human personality and the social responsibilities of the Christian life.
They usually breed a Pharisaic self-righteousness which may be an
unlovely caricature of Christian love but which lacks the social
power or interest to be of special peril to human society. Our concern
is with those forms of sectarianism which seek for the unqualified
realization of the Kingdom of Christ in history, which usually
means the reconstruction of human society into a commonwealth of
perfect love or perfect equality or perfect liberty. But not all forms
of socially radical sectarianism breed the fanatic fury which makes
the pretension of perfection so dangerous. We must, in fact, make
a sharp distinction between the soft and the hard utopianism of
various forms of sectarianism.

The soft utopians do not set themselves in array against an evil

[11] In *Glimpse of Zion's Glory*, 1641.

world, or claim their cause to be the perfect embodiment of the divine will. On the contrary they are usually pacifistic, holding to the conviction that if only all individual Christians did live perfectly by the law of love, all strife and contention would be progressively eliminated and a universal kingdom of love established. The Mennonites of continental Europe and the Quakers of Cromwellian England represent the soft utopian wing of radical sectarianism. Mennonite perfectionism is less inclined to the belief than Quakerism that sin can be progressively eliminated by perfect love. It is content, rather, to seek after the perfection of love for each individual Christian life and leave the total problem of the completion of history to God. Quaker perfectionism, on the other hand, usually indulges in the hope that suffering love will gain progressive victories in human history until it becomes triumphant love. One reason why the whole of modern liberal Christianity has become infected with the illusions of soft utopianism is because the modern idea of progress seemed to reinforce all the hopes for the progressive triumph of pure love which the soft utopians cherished. The spread of the pacifist movement in modern liberal Christianity, particularly in the Anglo-Saxon countries, to the point where it seemed that the perfectionist hopes of the small sectarian churches would be shared by the whole of Protestantism was undoubtedly due, primarily to the substitution of the idea of progress in liberal Christianity for the truth of the Gospel. In the words of a typical exponent of the American "social gospel" "the new social order will be based not on fighting but on fraternity . . . not simply because the cooperative fraternal life is the highest ideal of human living but because the spirit and method of cooperation is the scientific law of human progress." [12]

At its best, sectarian perfectionism seeks to raise symbols of the perfect *Agape* of Christ in history, without making any claims that the character of human history will be changed thereby but rightly insisting that such symbols remind Christians of the peril as well as

---

[12] Harry F. Ward, *The New Social Order*, p. 104. For the effect of the modern idea of progress upon Quaker thought, see Isaac Sharpless, *Quakerism in Politics*.

the necessity of using instruments tainted with sin to fight evil. At their worst, sectarian Christianity, liberal Christianity, and modern secular liberalism have all become united in the errors and sentimentalities of a soft utopianism, which manages to evade the tragic realities of life and to obscure the moral ambiguity in all political positions. These evasions are achieved by hoping for a progressive alteration of the character of human history. This soft utopianism is free of the sin of fanaticism but it is not without its dangers. The recent encounter of the democratic world with tyrannical forces might have proved fatal to civilization had not the common sense of children of this world outweighed the illusions of the children of light. For the soft utopians were prepared to meet malignant evil with non-resistance, hoping that kindness would convert the hearts of tyrants.

The soft utopians represent only a negative peril to society in comparison with the positive peril which the fanaticism of hard utopianism engenders. The hard utopians create a fighting community which regards itself as the embodiment and champion of an ideal commonwealth of perfect justice or perfect love, for which it is ready to do battle against all enemies. The hard utopianism of the Continental Anabaptist movement in the Reformation period was perhaps too fantastic in its claims and too romantic in its ventures to reveal the real peril which inheres in these pretensions of hard utopianism. Nor can one speak of too great a peril to society from the hard utopianism of the fighting sects of seventeenth century England, when Diggers and Levellers and Fifth Monarchy Men, who constituted the left wing of Cromwell's army, sought to establish a communist or an anarchist society. The Diggers may have defined the ideal commonwealth too much in equalitarian terms and the Levellers too much in libertarian terms,[18] failing to recognize, as per-

[18] The libertarianism of Cromwellian army radicalism expressed itself in wide range of thought from the anarchism of the "Fifth Monarchy Men" who would have no other ruler except Christ himself and hoped that the destruction of the English monarchy would bring this "fifth" monarchy of Christ into existence, to the individualism of the "Levelers" who believed that no civil covenants could ever destroy the individual's innate rights. In the words of Richard Overton in *An Appeal from the Commons to the Free People* (1647): "It is a firm law and radical principle in nature, engraven in tables of the

fectionists always do, that perfect liberty and perfect equality are harmoniously united only in that love (*Agape*) which transcends all law. Some of the sectarians sought to achieve perfect brotherhood through the abolition of government and others through the abolition of property. But the error of regarding either government or property as the root of all evil could be considered as a necessary corrective to orthodox Christianity's blindness to the moral perils in the institutions of both government and property. The Cromwellian sects made very great contributions to the development of Anglo-Saxon democracy, despite their errors. But they also laid the foundation for the civil war in western civilization, when the half-truth for which the sect stands was set in violent contradiction to the half-truth propounded by orthodox Christianity.

The real perils of the "fighting sect" did not develop fully so long as this form of utopianism remained within the general framework of the Christian faith. The perils became more apparent as the Marxist movement of the nineteenth century presented a secularized version of sectarian perfectionism. In this version the working class, more particularly the class of industrial workers, were constituted into a messianic class whose triumph over their foes would prove, according to their faith, to be not merely a triumph over particular foes but the final triumph over evil in history. The "saving remnant" of this messianic class would be the "vanguard" of "class-conscious" workers, the members of the Communist party, whose purposes were so identical with the very purposes of history

---

heart by the finger of God in creation, for every living, moving thing, wherein there is the breath of life to defend, guard, and deliver itself from all things hurtful, destructive, and obnoxious. . . . Therefore from hence is conveyed to all men in general and to every man in particular an undoubted principle of reason: by all rational and just means to deliver himself from all oppression, violence, and cruelty."

The equalitarianism and communism of the "Diggers" is rooted in the belief that the earth was originally a "common treasury." Gerrard Winstanley, in words which establish the historical nexus between Christian radical sectarianism and Marxism, insists that "you have Scripture to support you in making the earth a common treasury." Winstanley also anticipated the Marxist theory of the "withering away of the state." "When once the earth becomes a common treasury again, as it must," he writes, ". . . this enmity in all lands will cease. For none shall seek dominion over others, . . . nor desire more of the earth than another." In *The True Leveller's Standard Advanced*, 1649.

that every weapon became morally permissible to them and every vicissitude of history was expected to contribute to the inevitability of their victory.

The Christian myth of the Fall was reinterpreted so that an original state of innocency was posited as existing before the rise of private property. In this state man had not lost the communal essence of his existence. The rise of private property constituted the Fall, and the socialization of all property was therefore expected to usher in the kingdom of perfect love on earth, in which, when fully developed, everyone "would give according to his ability and take according to his need." The state was regarded as merely an instrument of class domination. It would "wither away" after all the enemies of this new commonwealth were defeated. An anarchistic millennium would crown the final triumph of the proletariate. Meanwhile a "dictatorship of the proletariat" was morally legitimatized both to practice a tyrannical rule over the faithful and to conduct ruthless conflict against all enemies. There is no question about the religious character of this whole program, despite its ostensible scorn for religion and its pretension to a "scientific" interpretation of the "laws of motion" in history. A "dialectical" process becomes surrogate for the absent God. This process guarantees the victory of the cause which the faithful deem to be unqualifiedly just. Everywhere the sense of the ultimate which characterizes religion reveals itself. It is furthermore a religion indirectly related to Biblical faith but perverted at two points. The first perversion is that it has no sense of a conflict between all men and God. It knows only of a conflict between the righteous and the unrighteous. This conflict is existentially interpreted, with considerable justification, as one between the privileged and the poor. Marxism is thus a secularized version of messianism without the knowledge of the prophets that the judgement of God falls with particular severity upon the chosen people.

The other perversion of Christian faith lies in the expectation of the complete realization of the kingdom of perfect righteousness in history. This utopian hope, partly derived from sectarian Christianity and partly from the general utopian temper of the eighteenth and nineteenth centuries, completely obscures the fact that corruptions of the meaning of life are bound to appear on every level of history, so long as human freedom is real freedom and therefore contains the possibility of evil.

The combined impact of these two perversions generates the fanatic fury of orthodox Marxism. Its non-prophetic messianism endows a particular social force in history with unqualified sanctity and its post-Christian utopianism prompts the illusion of the appearance of a kingdom of perfect righteousness (i.e., a classless society and an anarchistic brotherhood) in history. The self-righteous fury, prompted by these two errors, constitutes the real peril of orthodox communism. Most of the conventional objections to Marxist "materialism" and "atheism" are beside the point. Its materialism is, on the whole, a justified reaction to pietistic religions which do not understand the social character of life and to "spiritual" versions of Christianity which do not understand the unity of individual and collective man in the material and spiritual dimensions of his life. Its ostensible atheism is less significant than its idolatry. It worships a god who is the unqualified ally of one group in human society against all others.

The fanaticism of this new religion rent the social and cultural unity of western society and helped to create the social confusion out of which the even more primitive political religion of Nazism emerged. The fact that this religion gained a foothold in one particular nation has created an almost fantastic religious situation in the western world. For thousands of intellectuals and millions of workers, particularly in continental Europe, desperately seeking for a sense of meaning in life, after the utopianism of a bourgeois culture had ended in disillusionment, were willing to invest all their spiritual capital in this new hope, though it was made even more implausible by the fact that the messianic pretensions of a particular nation were compounded with the messianic pretensions of a particular class. There are still numberless people in the western world who cling to this hope desperately, even though it becomes increasingly difficult to regard the tortuous politics of an anxious dictatorship as the strategy which will usher in a kingdom of perfect righteousness. That so desperate a hope and faith should still be regarded as credible by many is an indication of the desperation of modern man about the meaning of life.

The new evils which have been introduced into modern history by this new fanaticism must not, however, obscure the fact that Marxism is the perversion of a profound truth. It understands, as the purely progressive view of history does not, that civilizations and cultures do not merely grow but that they must die and be reborn if they are to have a new life. Its program of the socialization of property is a proximate answer to the immediate problem of achieving justice in a technical age. The validity of this answer to an immediate problem would have been the sooner recognized had it not been falsely made into an absolute answer to the immediate problem and in addition into an ultimate answer to the ultimate problem of human existence itself. European civilization will undoubtedly resort to increasing socialization of property on pragmatic and experimental terms. But it can do so now only after devastating wars which were caused in part by the social confusion generated by the fanaticism of this new political religion. The struggle between rich and poor, between the owners and the workers in modern industrial society, is a fact which Marxism illumined, and which both orthodox Christianity and liberalism were inclined to obscure. But Marxism falsely made it into a final fact of history which was supposed to bear within itself the possibility of an ultimate redemption of history. The illusions of Marxism are thus the end-products of a Christian civilization which either failed to realize the highest possibilities of life in history or which claimed the realization of a perfection which can never be achieved in history. The fact that some modern political conflicts should be between quasi-feudal social and political organizations, given undue sanctity by the Catholic faith (as, for instance, in Spain) and revolutionary political organizations which are involved in the pretension of being the protagonists of a perfect social order, is a nice indication of the confusion and evil brought into history in a Christian culture which in both its orthodox and heretical forms fails to recognize or fear the divine judgement which remains over all historical achievements and realizations of meaning. The goodness of Christ must be embodied in the stuff of history. But it can never be so embodied that it does not also stand in contradiction to history in judgement and become the completion of history only by divine mercy rather than by human achievement.

~~~~~~

CHAPTER XIII

Fulfillments in History and the Fulfillment of History

I

THE fact that the grossest forms of evil enter into history as schemes of redemption and that the Christian faith itself introduces new evils, whenever it pretends that the Christian life, individually or collectively, has achieved a final perfection, gives us a clue to the possibilities and the limits of historic achievement. There are provisional meanings in history, capable of being recognized and fulfilled by individuals and cultures; but mankind will continue to "see through a glass darkly" and the final meaning can be anticipated only by faith. It awaits a completion when "we shall know even as we are known." There are provisional judgements upon evil in history; but all of them are imperfect, since the executors of judgement are tainted in both their discernments and their actions by the evil which they seek to overcome. History therefore awaits an ultimate judgement. There are renewals of life in history, individually and collectively; but no rebirth lifts life above the contradictions of man's historic existence. The Christian awaits a "general resurrection" as well as a "last judgement."

These eschatological expectations in New Testament faith, however embarrassing when taken literally, are necessary for a Christian interpretation of history. If they are sacrificed, the meaning of history is confused by the introduction of false centers of meaning, taken from the contingent stuff of the historical process; new evil is introduced into history by the pretended culminations within history itself; and tentative judgements are falsely regarded as final. Whether dealing with the *Alpha* or the *Omega* of history, with the beginning or with the end, the Christian faith prevents provisional meanings, judgements, and fulfillments from becoming ultimate by its sense of a final mystery of divine fulfillment beyond all provisional meanings. But it does not allow this ultimate mystery to degenerate into meaninglessness because of its confidence that the love of Christ is the clue to the final mystery.

There are forms of the eschatological hope which tend to deny the provisional meanings, the significant rebirths and the necessary moral judgements of history. They reduce historical existence to complete darkness, illumined only by a single light of revelation; and they reduce historical striving to complete frustration, relieved only by the hope of a final divine completion. This type of Christian eschatology is as false as the optimism which it has displaced; for it destroys the creative tension in Biblical faith between the historical and the trans-historical. When followed consistently, the Biblical faith must be fruitful of genuine renewals of life in history, in both the individual and the collective existence of man. These renewals are made possible by the very humility and love, which is derived from an awareness of the limits of human virtue, wisdom and power.

We have previously considered the Christian interpretation of the possibility and necessity of the renewal of the life of the individual. Christian faith insists that "except a man be born again . . . he cannot enter into the kingdom of God" (John 3:5). The question to be answered is what light this Christian doctrine of the renewal of life throws upon the fate of civilizations and cultures. Can they escape death by rebirth? Is the renewal or rebirth of individual life an analogy for the possibilities of man's collective enterprises? The individual is promised new life if he dies to self, if he is "crucified with Christ." The self which seeks the realization of itself within itself destroys itself. Does this fate of self-seeking individuals give us a clue to the self-destruction of cultures and civilizations? And does the promise of a new life through the death of the old self hold also for the life of nations and empires?

The classical view of the fate of civilizations and cultures makes no distinction between these historic organisms and the organisms of nature. The former are, as the latter, subject to nature's cycle of birth, growth, decay, and death. This analogy is obviously mistaken, since human freedom is mixed with natural necessity in all historical enterprises. Civilizations come to life and prosper by the ingenuity of human freedom. Presumably they die by the misuse of that freedom. Perhaps they can be reborn by the renewal of that freedom. The modern interpretation of history does not understand the cycle of birth and death of civilizations and culture at all because its conception of the indeterminate possibilities in history leaves no room for death or judgement. Yet civilizations do die; and it may be that, like the individual, they destroy themselves when they try too desperately to live or when they seek their own life too consistently. Thus neither the classical nor the modern interpretations of historic reality conform to the observable facts. Does the Christian interpretation of life in history, though primarily applied to the life of the individual, also conform to the facts of man's collective existence and does it illumine those facts, where they are obscure?

In answering these questions it is necessary to begin by defining the most important differences between individual and collective organisms in human history. One obvious difference between them is that there are no discrete or integral collective organisms, corresponding to the life of the individual. One may speak of cultures and civilizations as "organisms" only inexactly, for the purpose of describing whatever unity, cohesion and common purpose informs the variegated vitalities of a nation, empire or civilization. The political forms of collective life have a higher degree of inner integrity than the cultural forms. Nations are organized through organs of government, which integrate their common life and, within limits, articulate a common will. But political communities are overarched by structures of culture and civilization, less discrete and definable than the political communities, but nevertheless possessing a common ethos, distinguishable from competing forms. But these forms and structures are so intertwined and may be viewed on so many different levels that the two outstanding historical pluralists of our day, Spengler and Toynbee, can give plausible reasons for tracing their history in such completely different dimensions that Spengler finds only four cultures in the history of the world while Toynbee counts twenty-one.

To speak of our Western civilization as "Christian" is to analyze it on a different level than when we speak of it as democratic. It may die as a Christian civilization and yet live as a democratic one, or vice versa. Is modern secularism in the West the executor of judgement upon, or the inheritor of, a "Christian civilization"? And is the current communism of what Toynbee identifies as "Eastern Christendom" the fulfillment or the annulment of the ethos of that civilization? Shall one regard modern communism, transcending the confines of Eastern and Western Christendom as an integral culture or civilization with its own peculiar fate, rather than an aspect of the fate of those cultures and civilizations which become involved in civil war? Such questions reveal how various are the dimensions of the cultures and civilizations which one must seek to interpret.

Even if the inquiry is limited to political organisms, one faces complex formations. Imperial structures overarch national entities and the fate of one need not be identical with that of the other. The British Empire might perish and the British Commonwealth of Nations still endure; or even that might perish and the United Kingdom preserve health comparable to that of Sweden, for instance, after the heyday of its imperial ventures. There are, furthermore, no simple distinctions between life and death in collective organisms. Nations may persist in a coma, or a kind of living death, which has no counterpart in the destiny of individuals. These differences between the individual and the collective life of mankind make it impossible to reach as precise conclusions about the fate of nations and empires as about the destiny of individuals. They make generalizations about cultures and civilizations even more hazardous.

But such differences must not obscure the obvious similarities between individual and collective life, which create analogies between the fate of individuals and nations. It is particularly significant that the interpretation of human destiny in Old Testament prophetism was first concerned with nations, rather than individuals.

The most important similarity between the life of individuals and collective organisms is that the latter, like the former, have the same sense of the contingent and insecure character of human existence and they seek by the same pride and lust for power to hide or to overcome that insecurity. Though nations and empires have a longer life-span than individuals they are all, as the prophet observed, "delivered unto death" (Ezekiel 31:14). They seek, just as the individual, to overcome their mortality by their own power. This effort invariably involves them in pretensions of divinity, which hastens the fate which they seek to avoid. They "set their heart as the heart of God"; but the vicissitudes of history prove the vanity of this pretension. The "terrible of the nations" shall "draw their swords against the beauty of thy wisdom." They will be proved to be "men and not God" "in the hands of him that slayeth" them (Ezekiel 28:6–9). These words of the prophet Ezekiel to Tyrus are a succinct interpretation of the whole Biblical approach to the destiny of nations. Men seek in their collective enterprises, even more than in their individual life, to claim an absolute significance for their virtues and achievements, a final validity for their social structures and institutions and a degree of power which is incompatible with human finiteness. Since the collective achievements of men are more imposing than those of individuals, their power more impressive and their collective stabilities less subject to the caprice of nature, the idolatrous claims which are made for them are always more plausible than the pathetic pretensions of individuals. The plausibility of these pretensions delays the *Nemesis* upon human pride; yet the death of nations and empires is more obviously self-inflicted than that of individuals. For the collective enterprises of men are not physical organisms and are therefore not subject to natural fate. They are created by the ingenuity of human freedom and are destroyed by corruptions of that freedom.[1] This moral and religious content of historical destiny must not be insisted upon too consistently. Nations may become the victims of historical caprice, even as individuals may have their physical fate sealed by a caprice of nature. Nations may perish simply because they lie in the path of the superior forces of advancing empires. Yet the prophets were certainly right in interpreting the destiny of their nation in another dimension than one which would have made the weakness of Israel, in comparison with the circumambient empires, the clue to its historical fate. Nations, like individuals, may defeat superior power by special measures of spiritual grace. They may also, within limits, achieve a spiritual victory in the agony of physical defeat. Such victories in defeat have historical significance as well as an absolute significance, transcending history.

II

Human communities are exposed to both external and internal dangers. All historic communities have a limited and particular character. They are bounded by this ocean and that mountain or a line of demarcation, drawn by this or that historic victory or defeat. They live in partly cooperative and partly competitive relation with other communities. The superior power, skill in battle or geographic advantage of a competitive community may threaten it with defeat; and defeat may lead to enslavement. To ward off such dangers the community makes itself as powerful as possible. It also faces the peril of internal disintegration. The ideal possibility of any historic community is a brotherly relation of life with life, individually within the community and collectively between it and others. This ideal possibility is marred by competitive conflict with other groups and by the coercive character of its internal peace.

The internal peace of a community is always partly coercive

[1] It is the great achievement of Arnold Toynbee's *Study of History* that he finds the clue to the fate of civilizations in the use and abuse of freedom, and does not, after Spengler's manner, seek to equate historical with physical organisms. The difference between Toynbee and Spengler is the difference between a classical and a Christian interpretation of historical cycles.

because men are not good enough to do what should be done for the commonweal on a purely voluntary basis. There are both organic and moral forces of inner cohesion; but they are not sufficient to obviate the necessity of coercion. Ideally the coercive power of government is established by the whole society and is held responsible to it. Actually the ideal is never completely attained even in the most democratic societies. The oligarchy which helps to organize a community gains its position either by the military prowess by which it subjugated the community or by some priestly prestige which gave its will and law an authority beyond its own power or (as in modern states) by some special measure of power or skill with which it organized the vital forces of the community. Government is thus at once the source of order and the root of injustice in a community. Thus the external peace between communities is marred by competitive strife and the internal peace by class domination. Both forms of sin are related to the insecurity of the community. It must make itself powerful to ward off the peril of the external foe; and it must allow an oligarchy to arise within it to ward off the peril of anarchy.

The indictment of the nations by the prophets of the Old Testament was concerned with these two facets of collective sin. Israel was indicted for seeking its own ends, rather than the will of God. The prophets sought to make nations as well as individuals conform to the absolute and final possibilities of human existence. The other facet of the prophetic indictment concerned the "elders," the "princes" and the "judges" of Israel. They were accused of subverting justice and justifying "the wicked for a reward" (Isaiah 5:23), of crushing the needy (Amos 4:1), of having the spoil of the poor in their houses (Isaiah 3:14), of living in complacent luxury (Amos 6:4); in short, of exploiting their eminence in the community for their own advantage. This second indictment calls attention to the inevitable corruption of government because the coercive power required to maintain order and unity in a community is never a pure and disinterested power. It is exercised from a particular center and by a particular group in society. In the modern period the liberal society assumed that it had destroyed every specific center of power in the community by the democratic checks which were placed upon the organs of government. But this proved to be an illusion. The proletarian revolt against bourgeois society was prompted by resentment against the injustices which arose from the inordinate power of the commercial and industrial oligarchy of modern society. The new communist society made the same mistake in turn. It assumed that the destruction of an oligarchy whose power rested in ownership would create an idyllic society without oligarchic power. But this new society came under the tyrannical power of a new oligarchy of political overlords, who combined economic and political power in a single organ. These modern errors prove the persistence of the tendency of the organs of order in a community to become instruments of injustice. The same power required to establish the unity of a society also becomes the basis of injustice in it because it seeks its own ends, rather than the common weal.

The basic pattern of man's collective life thus corresponds to Augustine's description of the *civitas terrena,* the concord of which is alternately or simultaneously corrupted by conflict and domination. The conflict is the inevitable consequence of the tendency of partial and particular communities to make themselves their own end; the domination and injustice in the internal structure of particular communities is the consequence of the idolatrous self-worship of the oligarchies which have the responsibility for the order and unity of the community. Thus man's collective, as his individual, life is involved in death through the very strategies by which life is maintained, against both external and internal peril. But there is life as well as death, virtue as well as sin in these social and political configurations. St. Augustine's Christian realism errs in its too consistent emphasis upon the sinful corruptions of the world's peace. Civilizations and cultures do rise and prosper; and they have periods of creativity and stability before the destructive elements in them overcome the creative ones. Augustine may, in fact, have made the mistake of taking his analogies for the *civitas*

terrena from the Roman Empire in the period of its decay, thus failing to do justice to the creative achievement of the *Pax Romana* at
its best.

The creative and virtuous element in historic communities and
in the ruling oligarchies within them are of two types: 1) The
virtues which a community exhibits in its genuine concern for life
beyond its borders and which an oligarchy in a community achieves
by a creative interest in the welfare of the community. 2) The
virtues which communities and ruling groups within a community
have "by grace" rather than by moral achievement. The latter form
of virtue is historically the more important. It is the virtue which
arises not from pure disinterestedness but from the provisional
coincidence between the interests of a ruling group within a nation
and the interests of the total community, or from the coincidence
between the interest of a powerful imperial community and the
wider community of nations which its power helps to organize.
A too moralistic approach to the collective life of mankind usually
fails to do justice to this important "righteousness which is not our
own," this virtue by grace of providence and coincidence rather
than by goodness.

Arnold Toynbee's profound analysis of the fate of historic civilizations and communities finds the cause of the disintegration of
an historic community in the change of its ruling group from that
of a "creative" to that of an "oppressive" minority. His analysis is
informed by a genuine Biblical-Augustinian understanding of historic destiny. But the distinction between the "creative" and the
"oppressive" period in the life of a minority is too moralistically
conceived. Ruling oligarchies within a national community and
hegemonic nations within an imperial community are never purely
creative, even in their heyday, except "by grace." The grace which
makes them creative is the historic coincidence between their will-to-
power and the requirement for wider unity within a nation or community of nations which that will-to-power serves. The priestly
oligarchs of Egypt and Mesopotamia who, with or without the
cooperation of military confederates, organized the first great civi-

lized communities, were "oppressive" from the beginning, in the sense that their justice was always corrupted by a lust for power. They appropriated more privileges in payment for their service to their community than their contributions warranted at the very beginning of their rule. Every community of history has paid a high price in injustice for its wider cohesion. Modern imperial communities, in which an advanced nation has helped "backward" peoples to come in contact with the larger world, have never been free of exploitation, even though imperial powers may have evinced a certain degree of responsibility for the weak, which the weak did not appreciate until the hour of their emancipation. (Modern India, involved in internecine strife, may yet discover that the order imposed upon a people, incapable of avoiding anarchy by its own resources, is not as unmixed an evil as it had supposed in its resentment against foreign rule). But on the other hand no imperial power is quite as perfect a "Father" to its immature children as it pretends.

The capitalistic oligarchy of the modern bourgeois society had a creative period, not because it was prompted to develop modern technical power out of motives of disinterested love of science. It was creative because the profits it claimed for its services did not completely annul the benefits it bestowed upon the modern community by the extension of the community's technical power. There is a period in the life of nations when the exercise of even irresponsible power makes for peace and order, however unjust the order and however tentative the equilibrium of its peace.

Yet it is possible to distinguish between "creative" and "oppressive" periods in the life of an oligarchic minority within a nation or an hegemonic nation within a community of nations. An analysis of the historic process of this decay will bring us closer to the secret of the possibilities of both "death through life" and of "new life through death" in the destiny of civilization. It is this alternative which constitutes the relevance of the Biblical concept of the renewal of life through the death of the old self, for the collective experience of mankind.

III

Ruling groups within a nation and hegemonic nations in a community of nations face the alternative of dying because they try too desperately to live, or of achieving a new life by dying to self. This alternative is offered when their power, prestige and pride are challenged by the emergence of new social forces in history. The emergence of these new forces is the historic execution of the absolute judgement which constantly hangs over them by reason of their "sin." In history God always chooses "the things which are not, to put to nought things that are" (I Corinthians 1:28). A traditional equilibrium of power, an established structure of justice, a hallowed system of social norms, comes under historic judgement when the emergence of new classes or nations, or the acquisition of new technics or powers in the hands of previously subject groups, challenges the established hierarchical structure of power. Such new elements and forces are constantly arising in history. That fact has been clearly discerned in the modern view of history. But the new forces of history do not merely complete and perfect the old and established forms. They are forced to enter into competition or even into a life-and-death struggle with the old forces. History is, for this reason, not a realm of indeterminate growth and development. It is a realm of conflict. In this conflict new forces and forms of life challenge the established powers and orders. They are a reminder to the established forms and powers of the contingent character of all historic configurations and a judgement upon the pretension which denies this contingency.

It is precisely at the point of challenge by new forces that the old structures, powers and forms of life either atrophy and are destroyed, or submit to judgement and are renewed. They atrophy and are destroyed if and when the challenge of new competing forces in history tempts them to make even more extravagant claims for the absolute validity of their power and justice than they have previously made and to regard the competitor and foe merely as an interloper or as a foe of all order and justice. From the standpoint of pure morals, as we have previously noted, no oligarchy in society is ever purely disinterested. But it becomes excessively oppressive when the challenge of new forces tempts it to increase its idolatrous claims rather than be persuaded of the ephemeral and contingent nature of its rule. Thus the landed aristocracy of medieval Europe created an order of society in which "Christian" concepts of justice and charity were used to create the illusion of an absolutely valid and stable form of social organization. These absolute claims became increasingly insufferable and untenable as they were asserted against the challenge of a rising middle class. The forms of moral and political control of an agrarian economy did not fit the necessities of a commercial age; and the social and political supremacy of the landed aristocracy, which was always unjust from the standpoint of the peasants, became untenable from the standpoint of the rising middle class. This new class had effective power to challenge the rule of the aristocrats, while the peasants lacked such power. The longer the power of the landed aristocracy remained unchallenged the more absolutely valid it seemed to those who wielded it. But when it was finally challenged the new sense of insecurity tempted the holders of it to make even more extravagant claims for its validity. One may note something of the same desperation in the attitude of the white overlords in South Africa and the American southern states, as they meet the challenge of a once impotent colored world, now growing in strength.

The institution of monarchial absolutism was the apex of the pyramid of power in the agrarian world of Europe and Asia. In non-Christian cultures the claims of absolute monarchs were unashamedly idolatrous. The "divine right" which kings claimed in Christian cultures were only slightly less idolatrous. Wherever the power of monarchy was completely broken by new social forces, the self-delusion, caused by idolatrous religious claims, proved to be the chief cause of its blindness in recognizing the validity of competing claims upon power and of its inflexibility in dealing with new social forces.

The culture of the middle classes, which supplanted the civilization of a Catholic agrarianism, has been prevailingly secular rather than specifically religious. But this secularism did not prevent the institutions of modern capitalism from claiming as absolute a moral and social validity as the more pious aristocratic world claimed for itself; and from meeting the competitive challenge of the industrial workers with the same religious rigidity as that with which the aristocrats met the challenge of the capitalist. The Babylons of this world always declare: "I sit a queen; and am no widow, and shall see no sorrow." And this self-assurance is always the primary cause of their undoing: "Therefore shall her plagues come in one day, death, and mourning, and famine" (Revelation 18: 7, 8). The death and famine in the life of man's social institutions and cultures is thus never so much the fruit of a natural mortality as the consequence of a vain delusion which seeks to hide the contingency and mortality of every power and majesty in human history.

But there is fortunately another possibility in history. The powers and majesties, the institutions and structures of human contrivance do not always meet the challenge of competitive forces by increased rigidity and idolatry. Sometimes the competitive challenge serves to moderate the idolatrous claims. Judgement leads to repentance. There is not as clearly defined an experience of repentance in the life of communities and social institutions as in that of individuals. Yet there is a possibility that old forms and structures of life may be renewed, rather than destroyed by the vicissitudes of history. These experiences establish the validity of the Christian doctrine of life through death for the collective, as well as for the individual, organism.

The history of the institution of monarchy gives us a simple example. Absolute monarchy has been destroyed in every nation in which modern conditions prevail. But the institution of constitutional monarchy has proved to be a most efficacious instrument of democracy in many of the most healthy of modern nations. Its virtue lies in its capacity to symbolize the permanent will of the national community in distinction to the momentary and shifting acts of will which are expressed and incarnated in particular governments. The political wisdom incorporated in constitutional monarchy is literally a wisdom vouchsafed to men "by grace." For neither the traditional proponents of monarchism nor its opponents had the wisdom to conceive the institution of constitutional monarchy. The former wanted to preserve its power unchanged and the latter wanted to destroy the institution. The emergence of this old institution in a new form did require that its defenders yield, however reluctantly, to new social forces in society. The monarch was shorn of his power; whereupon it was discovered that his powerlessness provided the community with a new form of power, which was completely compatible with the requirements of a more democratic justice.

In the same manner those national communities in which aristocratic and agrarian economic and political institutions yielded to, rather than defied, the power of rising middle classes, and subsequently of the industrial classes, have been able to preserve both a cultural and a political health which has been denied communities in which the old and the new forces clashed in mortal combat. Their health is superior to that of even those communities in which new forces have been able to gain complete victory over the old. The clear cut victory of the rising middle classes in the French Revolution and of the working classes in the Russian Revolution has not resulted in a saner or healthier life of the community. Nor has the fact that the political life of the United States began on an unchallenged bourgeois basis, without the irrelevance of a feudal past, made American life healthier than that of the best democratic nations of Europe. It has rather contributed to an uncritical acceptance of bourgeois ideologies which robs our culture of the flexibility required for dealing with new social forces and configurations in the latter days of the bourgeois disintegration.

IV

The fact that a clear cut victory for advancing social forces is no better guarantee of social health than their defeat is particularly instructive. It proves that the advancing social forces of history, which are, from the absolute viewpoint, instruments of divine judgement upon all established institutions, are always involved in the same idolatries as the forces against which they contend. They are not content to be instruments of providence. They claim god-like qualities for themselves. It is particularly significant that the liberal idealism of the commercial classes and the Marxist ideology of the industrial classes, both essentially secular, should have exhibited increasingly clear evidences that the taint of idolatry is upon the idealism of the challengers as well as of the challenged in history. Utopia is, as Karl Mannheim has insisted, the ideology of the dispossessed.[2] They are not content to prove that the rule of the past has been unjust and that their own rule would be more just. They insist rather that their rule will establish absolute justice, and furthermore that it will be free of coercion. There is an implied anarchism in the liberal-bourgeois theory of government, and communism indulges in the fatuous hope that a revolutionary use of force will finally destroy the necessity of coercion in society. Thus the executors of divine judgement in history forget that they are also under judgement, and thereby they increase the measure of new evil which attends the abolition of traditional injustice.

The fact that there are no disinterested executors of judgement in history prevents the historical process from issuing in the progressive abolition of evil, which modern culture had hoped for. The fact that there should be increasingly pretentious claims of such disinterestedness among the executors of judgement upon established historical forces creates the possibility of more monstrous evils arising through the effort to abolish evil. Of this the history of modern communist tyranny is a vivid example. But even if communist utopianism had not created the corruptions of communist cynicism, there would be no absolute guarantee in history against the possibility of such aberrations. These new evils in the renewals and rebirths of the collective life of man are analogous to the evils which arise in individual life through the spurious claims of perfection among redeemed sinners. It is thus as true for human institutions as for individuals that, in the ultimate instance, they are "justified by faith and not by works lest any man should boast." The more uncritically a civilization or culture, a nation or empire

[2] *Ideology and Utopia.* ch. 4.

boasts of its disinterested virtue, the more certainly does it corrupt that virtue by self-delusion. It belongs to the deepest tragedy of our age that the proletarian revolt against a bourgeois civilization should have been informed by even more explicit pretensions of divinity and perfection than previous civilizations and that it should have, upon the basis of such pretensions, spawned a new oligarchy, more uninhibited in its power lusts than any oligarchy since the rise of prophetic religion brought the majesties of history under the judgement of a divine Sovereign over history.

It would be wrong, however, to attribute these modern idolatries altogether to the secular character of our modern culture and to its explicit denial of a Majesty which "maketh the judges of the earth as vanity." It is significant that when "God-fearing" nations of our own day pretend to defend a Christian civilization against the ridiculous priest-kings of Russia's secular religion, they involve themselves in dishonesties and pretensions almost as ridiculous as those of the latter. They pretend, for instance, that they must destroy the industrial equipment of a vanquished foe in the interest of peace. Yet it is quite apparent that this destruction is prompted only partly by the desire to lame the aggressive power of the beaten foe. It is primarily intended to destroy his competitive power in the rivalries of peace. These dishonesties are too patent to be denied; yet nations engage in them as if they were plausible.

The stubbornness of these pretensions of collective man raises the question whether "the word of God" ever reaches the heart of nations and cultures, whether they ever discern a judge beyond themselves; or anticipate the doom to which their self-seeking exposes them in the end; or whether they interpret the defeats to which they are subject from an ultimate standpoint. The "vain imaginations" of collective man are so plausible from the standpoint of the individual, the mortality of nations is so shrouded in the seeming immortality of their long life, and the pomp and power of the community is so impressive in comparison with the individual's impotence, that the final words of judgement and mercy scarcely penetrate to the heart of nations. They are furthermore

involved in a despair which the individual does not know. They
have no other life than their life in history, since they lack those
organs of self-transcendence which place them within reach of a
meaning of existence beyond their physical life. Collective man
clings more desperately to this life than the individual because
he is not certain of a deeper dimension of meaning. There are,
therefore, no martyr nations, though there may be martyr individuals. It is not impossible, as we have seen, for nations and cultures, rulers and communities to interpret their vicissitudes as
judgements upon their pride and thus to be reformed, rather than
destroyed, by the bludgeonings of history. There are, in fact, indeterminate possibilities of such renewal; so that no culture or civilization need die by a fateful necessity of its sin. But the judgements of God are not so clear to nations or cultures that they could
escape a final *Nemesis*, when some final triumph or some extraor-
dinary period of stability, or some phenomenal success tempts them
to a final form of *Hybris*.

The significance of the contest of the prophets of Israel with the
pride of their nation lies precisely in the fact that in the contest it
became more and more apparent that only a "saving remnant"
within the nation could finally understand the ultimate issue. The
prophets warned the nation to "beware that thou forget not the
Lord thy God, . . . lest when thou hast eaten and art full, and
hast built goodly houses and dwelt therein . . . thou say in thine
heart, my power and the might of my hand hath gotten me this
wealth," in which case "as the nations which the Lord destroyeth
before your face, so shall ye perish" (Deuteronomy 8:11–20).

Such warnings were heeded only relatively. In the absolute sense
Israel, as every other nation, defied them. This is why the messianic hopes for the renewal of the nation became more and more
a hope for the redemption of the whole of history. Ideally the
Christian community is "the saving remnant" which calls nations to
repentance and renewal without the false belief that any nation
or culture could finally fulfill the meaning of life or complete the
purpose of history.

V

The knowledge that "the world passeth away and the lusts thereof" and that every *civitas terrena* is a city of destruction does not, however, negate the permanent values which appear in the rise and fall of civilizations and cultures. A feudal civilization may be destroyed by its inability to incorporate the new dynamism of a commercial and industrial society. But there are qualities of organic community, including even the hierarchical organization of the community, in a feudal society, which transcend the fate of such a civilization. In the same manner a bourgeois society, though involved in a self-destructive individualism, also contributes to the emancipation of the individual in terms of permanent worth. There are thus facets of the eternal in the flux of time. From the standpoint of Biblical faith the eternal in the temporal flux is not so much a permanent structure of existence, revealed in the cycle of change, as it is a facet of the *Agape* of Christ. It is "love which abideth." An organic society may achieve a harmony of life with life without freedom. Insofar as it is without freedom it is not a perfect incarnation of *Agape*. But insofar as it is a harmony of life with life it is an imperfect symbol of the true *Agape*. A libertarian society may sacrifice community to the dignity of the individual. But insofar as it emancipates the individual from social restraints which are less than the restraints of love, it illustrates another facet of the full dimension of *Agape*. Thus the same civilizations which perish because they violate the law of love at some point may also contribute a deathless value insofar as they explicate the harmony of life with life intended in creation.

If this be so, the question arises why the process of history should not gradually gather up the timeless values and eliminate the worthless. Why should not history be a winnowing process in which truth is separated from falsehood; and the falsehood burned as chaff, while the wheat of truth is "gathered into the barn." In that case *die Weltgeschichte* would, after all, be *das Weltgericht*. There is one sense in which this is true. Yet this conception of history as its own judge is finally false. It is true in the sense that history is actually the story of man's developing freedom. Insofar as increasing freedom leads to harmonies of life with life within communities and between communities, in which the restraints and cohesions of nature are less determinative for the harmony than the initiative of men, a positive meaning must be assigned to growth in history. There is, certainly, positive significance in the fact that modern man must establish community in global terms or run the risk of having his community destroyed even on the level of the local village. To establish community in global terms requires the exercise of the ingenuity of freedom far beyond the responsibilities of men of other epochs, who had the support of natural forces, such as consanguinity, for their limited communities. The expansion of the perennial task of achieving a tolerable harmony of life with life under ever higher conditions of freedom and in ever wider frames of harmony represents the residual truth in modern progressive interpretations of history.

But this truth is transmuted into error very quickly if it is assumed that increasing freedom assures the achievement of the wider task. The perils of freedom rise with its promises, and the perils and promises are inextricably interwoven. The parable of the wheat and the tares expresses the Biblical attitude toward the possibilities of history exactly. The servants who desire to uproot the tares which have been sown among the wheat are forbidden to do so by the householder "lest while ye gather up the tares, ye root up also the wheat with them. Let both grow together until the harvest: and in the time of harvest I will say unto the reapers, Gather ye together first the tares, and bind them in bundles to burn them: but gather the wheat into my barn" (Matthew 13:29-30).

There is, in other words, no possibility of a final judgement within history but only at the end of history. The increase of human freedom over nature is like the advancing season which ripens both wheat and tares, which are inextricably intermingled. This simple symbol from the sayings of our Lord in the synoptics is supplemented in the eschatology of the Epistles, where it is Christ himself who becomes the judge at the final judgement of the world.

History, in short, does not solve the enigma of history. There are facets of meaning in it which transcend the flux of time. These give glimpses of the eternal love which bears the whole project of history. There is a positive meaning also in the ripening of love under conditions of increasing freedom; but the possibility that the same freedom may increase the power and destructiveness of self-love makes it impossible to find a solution for the meaning of history within history itself. Faith awaits a final judgement and a final resurrection. Thus mystery stands at the end, as well as at the beginning of the whole pilgrimage of man. But the clue to the mystery is the *Agape* of Christ. It is the clue to the mystery of Creation. "All things were made by him; and without him was not any thing made that was made" (John 1:3). It is the clue to the mystery of the renewals and redemptions within history, since wherever the divine mercy is discerned as within and above the wrath, which destroys all forms of self-seeking, life may be renewed, individually and collectively. It is also the clue to the final redemption of history. The antinomies of good and evil increase rather than diminish in the long course of history. Whatever provisional meanings there may be in such a process, it must drive men to despair when viewed ultimately, unless they have discerned the power and the mercy which overcomes the enigma of its end.

The whole history of man is thus comparable to his individual life. He does not have the power and the wisdom to overcome the ambiguity of his existence. He must and does increase his freedom, both as an individual and in the total human enterprise; and his creativity is enhanced by the growth of his freedom. But this freedom also tempts him to deny his mortality and the growth of freedom and power increases the temptation. But evils in history are the consequence of this pretension. Confusion follows upon man's effort to complete his life by his own power and solve its enigma by his own wisdom. Perplexities, too simply solved, produce despair. The Christian faith is the apprehension of the divine love and power which bears the whole human pilgrimage, shines through its enigmas and antinomies and is finally and definitively revealed in a drama in which suffering love gains triumph over sin and death. This revelation does not resolve all perplexities; but it does triumph over despair, and leads to the renewal of life from self-love to love.

Man, in both his individual life and in his total enterprise, moves from a limited to a more extensive expression of freedom over nature. If he assumes that such an extension of freedom insures and increases emancipation from the bondage of self, he increases the bondage by that illusion. Insofar as the phenomenal increase in human power in a technical age has created that illusion, it has also involved our culture in the profound pathos of disappointed hopes, caused by false estimates of the glory and the misery of man.

To understand, from the standpoint of the Christian faith, that man can not complete his own life, and can neither define nor fulfill the final mystery and meaning of his historical pilgrimage, is not to rob life of meaning or responsibility.

The love toward God and the neighbor, which is the final virtue of the Christian life, is rooted in an humble recognition of the fragmentary character of our own wisdom, virtue and power. The forgiveness which is the most perfect expression of that love, is prompted by a contrite recognition of the guilt with which our own virtue is tainted. Our faith in the faithfulness of God, and our hope in His triumph over the tragic antinomies of life do not annull, but rather transfigure, human wisdom. For they mark the limit of its power and purge it of its pretenses. For "God hath chosen the foolish things of the world to confound the wise; and God hath chosen the weak things of the world to confound the things that are mighty . . . that no flesh should glory in His presence."

CHAPTER XIV

~~~~~~

The Church and the End of History

I

OUR study has frequently taken note of the fact that the New Testament envisages a culmination of history which is not, literally speaking, within time-history. It looks forward to a final judgement and a general resurrection, which are at once both the fulfillment and the end of history. They imply an end in the sense of *Finis*; but the end in the sense of *Telos*, that is, as the moral and spiritual culmination of the meaning of history, is not within history itself. We have called attention to the significance of the symbol of the Anti-Christ at the end of history, as indicative of the belief in New Testament that history remains open to all possibilities of good and evil to the end.

The "Anti-Christ" can be, and has been, interpreted in two ways. The symbol can be interpreted as meaning that the most explicit form of evil, the most obvious defiance of God appears at the end of history. It can also be interpreted as meaning that the evil which appears at the end is the assertion of selfish ends in the name of Christ or in the name of God. It is not possible to choose absolutely between these two interpretations; but it is important to recognize that both are legitimate interpretations of the final evil. It is particularly important for the church not to disavow the second interpretation, because it is the form of the evil to which the church is tempted. It is not tempted to defy God explicitly; but it is tempted to insinuate historical evils into the final sanctity. It succumbs to that temptation whenever it identifies its own judgements with God's judgements; or whenever it pretends that the meaning of history has culminated in the church as an historical institution.

The New Testament looks toward the end of history with faith and hope, rather than with fear, despite its anticipation of increased antinomies and contradictions between good and evil in history. Fear has been banished by the faith that this final climax, as well as the whole drama of history, is under a sovereignty of divine love, which has been revealed in Christ.

Nothing is added to, and much may be subtracted from, the power of this faith by idle speculations about the character and the time of the end of history as *Finis*. Speculations based upon the second law of thermodynamics would seem to make the actual end of history certain but very remote. The certainty of an historical end may tempt all those to despair who find the meaning of life only in the historical process. Against such despair the Christian faith insists that the end as *Finis* is not identical with the end as *Telos*. The *Telos* is in the Resurrection. Against the complacency to which men may be tempted by the temporal remoteness of the end, New Testament faith introduces a note of urgency and insists that "the time is short" (I Corinthians 7:29). It derives this sense of urgency from the feeling that the ultimate judgement and the ultimate issues of life impinge upon each moment of time.

There is a natural inclination to transmute this qualitative judgement into quantitative speculations and to derive from it the belief that the end is temporally imminent. This tendency is not lacking in the New Testament itself. As a consequence the first two Christian centuries were involved in the illusory hope of an imminent return of Christ as final judge and redeemer. Many subsequent generations were beguiled into the expectation of an actual end of history at an imminent point in time, whenever some particularly flagrant form of evil seemed to conform to the Biblically predicted final evil which was to herald the end of history. The eschatological fears of our own atomic age are similarly derived. It is now fairly certain that atomic destruction is not likely to rise to the height of imperiling the global structure. But since it has brought the destruction of the whole of civilization into the realm of possibilities, sensitive spirits naturally feel that this form of destruction is really the final evil. Since human decisions are involved in this new historical fate, more obviously than in any previous impending catastrophes, the sense of eschatological urgency is morally justified. But speculations about the end derived from it are not only scientifically implausible but religiously wrong. Against all such speculations about the *Finis* Christ's observation that "of that day and hour knoweth no man, no, not the angels of heaven, but my Father only" (Matthew 24:36) is a pertinent reminder of the limits of knowledge about the end of history from within history.

If, then, it is impossible to define the end of history as a particular event in history and since the end as *Telos* lies outside of history, the question arises why the Biblical symbols should be taken seriously at all. The answer is that without them Biblical faith degenerates either into Platonism or utopianism. In Platonism eternity becomes a *totum simul* which gathers up all historical events and annuls their unique significance in the eternal moment. The significance of the drama of history with its fateful decisions, its cumulative effects, and its unique events is lost. By the symbol of the Resurrection the Christian faith hopes for an eternity which transfigures, but does not annul, the temporal process.

The symbol of the Last Judgement, on the other hand, emphasizes the moral ambiguity of history to the end. It negates utopian illusions in progressive interpretations of history as rigorously as the symbol of the Resurrection rejects the Platonic flight into an eternity of "pure" being. These eschatological symbols transcend the rational; but they do justice to the temporal and the eternal dimensions of man's historic existence. Platonism and modern utopianism are only superficially, but not ultimately, more rational. For in elaborating frames of meaning in which eternity exists without time or time without eternity, they tear the two dimensions of human existence asunder.

II

The Christian church is a community of hopeful believers, who are not afraid of life or death, of present or future history, being persuaded that the whole of life and all historical vicissitudes stand under the sovereignty of a holy, yet merciful, God whose will was supremely revealed in Christ. It is a community which does not fear the final judgement, not because it is composed of sinless saints but because it is a community of forgiven sinners, who know that judgement is merciful if it is not evaded. If the divine judgement is not resisted by pretensions of virtue but is contritely accepted, it reveals in and beyond itself the mercy which restores life on a new and healthier basis.

Ideally the church is such a community of contrite believers. Actually the church is always in danger of becoming a community of the saved who have brought the meaning of life to merely another premature conclusion. It is in danger of becoming a community of the righteous who ask God to vindicate them against the unrighteous; or, even worse, who claim to vindicate God by the fruits of their own righteousness. In that case the church loses the true love of Christ, which is the fruit of a contrite heart, by claiming that love as a secure possession.

In short, the church is always in danger of becoming Anti-Christ because it is not sufficiently eschatological. It lives too little by faith and hope and too much by the pretensions of its righteousness. There is a modern form of eschatological Christianity, particularly upon the European continent, which goes to the length of disavowing the Christian's responsibility for the weal of the world in its frantic flight from the moral pretension of the Pharisaic church. Ideally the faith and hope by which the church lives sharpen rather than annul its responsibility for seeking to do the will of God amid all the tragic moral ambiguities of history. This faith and hope are the condition of a true love "which seeketh not its own." They are the condition for a courageous witness against "principalities and powers," which is untroubled by punitive strength in the hands of these powers and which does not mistake the judgements of the church as an historic institution for the final judgement of God.

Without such a faith and hope the church seeks to vindicate itself by the virtue of its martyrs and its saints. This vindication never avails in the end because the "godless" are always able to find for every martyr and saint in the church a score of pious frauds or religiously inspired bigots or self-righteous Pharisees. Without the final eschatological emphasis the church claims to be the Kingdom of God. Actually it is that community where the Kingdom of God impinges most unmistakably upon history because it is the community where the judgement and the mercy of God are known, piercing through all the pride and pretensions of men and transforming their lives.

The church which claims to be itself the end of history, the fulfillment of history's meaning, seeks to prove the truth of its message by the continuity of its traditions, the "validity" of its order and the solidity and prestige of its historic form. There is an obvious pathos in this attempt to achieve a transcendent perfection within history. The traditions and continuities by which the church seeks security before the final judgement can be proved by any rigorous scholarship to be more dubious than the church admits. The "orders" or the "order" by which it establishes its claims of catholicity obviously reflect historical contingencies of Roman or of Anglo-Saxon or of some other history. An actual historic unity and geographic universality of the Roman church gives such claims a momentary plausibility; but this only serves to make the claims of absoluteness more pretentious and therefore more implausible.

There are fragments of the church which find these claims of absoluteness for the church's means of grace so intolerable that they seek to live by unmediated grace, dispensing as far as possible with theological, liturgical and other traditions and disciplines. But this merely leads to a crude immediacy in which the aberrations of the hour are not checked by the insights of the Christian ages. The worship of the church becomes cheap and banal, lacking the full treasure of the Christian testimony; the teachings of the church become sentimental and moralistic, lacking the discipline of long experience; and the life of the church becomes lawless, lacking the discipline of a Christian consensus. Nor are the claims to perfection which the saints make on the basis of unmediated and direct grace any more tolerable than the claims of absoluteness made for the means of grace by other parts of the church.

There are fortunately signs of a greater humility in the church, which may lead to the vision of a truly Catholic church above the fragments which now claim to be the whole church. The unity of this one church will be the more certainly realized if neither the fragments, nor yet the sum total of the fragments, claim absolute truth or grace as a secure possession. The church, as well as the individual Christian, must live by faith and hope if it would live by love; for it, as well as the individual, is involved in the ambiguities of history. If it pretends to transcend them absolutely, rather than by faith and hope, it is subjected to the more terrible judgement. One form of this judgement is the scorn of the "godless" who find no difficulty in discrediting these pretensions.

III

A community of grace, which lives by faith and hope, must be sacramental. It must have sacraments to symbolize the having and not having of the final virtue and truth. It must have sacraments to express its participation in the *Agape* of Christ and yet not pretend that it has achieved that love. Thus the church has the sacrament of baptism in which "we are buried with him by baptism into death: that like as Christ was raised from the dead by the glory of the Father, even so we should also walk in newness of life" (Romans 6:4). The admonition that "we should" walk in newness of life is a nice indication in Pauline thought of his consciousness of the Christian's having and yet not having that new life which is the fruit of dying to self. The Christian participates sacramentally and by faith in Christ's dying and rising again; but he must be admonished that he should walk in that newness of life which is ostensibly his assured possession. He is assured that he is free from sin and yet admonished:

"Let not sin therefore reign in your mortal body" (Romans 6:12).

The supreme sacrament of the Christian church, the Lord's Supper, is filled with this eschatological tension. It is instituted with the words: "This do in remembrance of me." St. Paul declares that "as often as ye eat this bread, and drink this cup, ye do shew the Lord's death *till he come*" (I Corinthians 11:26). Thus in this Sacrament the Christian community lives by a great memory and a great hope. The present reality is different because of that memory and hope. What lies between the memory and the hope is a life of grace, in which the love of Christ is both an achieved reality in the community and a virtue which can be claimed only vicariously. The Christian community does not have the perfection of Christ as an assured possession. It will show forth that love the more surely the less certain it is of its possession.

Ideally the community of grace knows nothing of class or race distinctions: In Christ "there is neither Jew nor Greek, there is neither bond nor free" (Galatians 3:28). Yet there is no community of grace in which there are not remnants and echoes of the world's pride of race and class. If there is no sacramental agony in the church about this corruption, the religious community easily becomes a seed-pot of racial pride and bigotry. It would be ridiculous, however, if the church dispensed with the sacrament until such time as it could prove itself free of every racial prejudice. It is equally ridiculous that fragments of a divided church are unable to have a common observance of the Lord's Supper until the divisions are absolutely healed. The divisions can never be absolutely healed, unless all fragments of the church submit to the fragment which makes the most extravagant pretensions. The pride of race and class, the cultural and national divisions of the human community, the contingencies of various histories can never be completely excluded from the human and historic life of the church; and yet they can not be accepted with an easy conscience.

Ideally the sacraments save the Christian life from moral pretension because they emphasize that the Christian community is always involved in having and yet not having the final truth and grace. The

very fact, however, that the sacraments may be the instruments of
the final pretension of various fragments of the church proves that
they are also subject to corruption. They easily degenerate into a
magic which gives an unrepentant heart an even cheaper security
before the final judgement than any simple moralism. When the
eschatological tension disappears from the 'sacraments, sacramental
piety becomes a source of a particularly grievous religious complacency. That is why a truly Catholic church would require a considerable degree of patience with the periodic rebellions in the Christian community against sacramental piety. These revolts are based
upon the realization that means of grace may become corrupted.
That understanding belongs to a truly Catholic church; even as a
truly Catholic church would finally persuade the advocates of unmediated grace that these historic means are as necessary as they are
perilous. If the full eschatological meaning of the sacraments, as we
find it in the Gospels, were restored, the tension between these two
forms of piety in the total church might be eased.

It is obvious, in short, that the church may become involved in
a more grievous error than the world, precisely because it is the
bearer of a Gospel according to which all human truths and virtues
are rendered problematic. One may question whether any fragment
of the modern church understands as well as the prophets of Israel
understood how severely the judgement of God falls upon the community which is the bearer of the judgement. It falls with particular
severity upon the mediator of the judgement because the mediator is
always tempted to claim an unproblematic security as a reward and
consequence of his mediation. It is this temptation which makes Mr.
Toynbee's hope implausible, that the self-destruction of pretentious
empires and cultures will finally lead to the victory of a universal
church in actual history. It is indeed promised that the gates of hell
shall not prevail against the church; but the church which has that
security can not be any particular church with all of its historic ad-
mixtures of the grace of Christ and the pride of nations and cultures.
The secure church is precisely that community of saints, known and
unknown, among whom life is constantly transformed because it is
always under the divine word.

The truth of the Gospel must be preached today to a generation which hoped that historical development would gradually emancipate man from the ambiguity of his position of strength and weakness and would save him from the sin into which he falls by trying to evade or deny the contradiction in which he lives. Experience has proved that mode of salvation to be an illusion. But a Gospel which can penetrate through this illusion and save men from the idolatrous confidence in history as a redeemer will also shake the false islands of security which men have sought to establish in history in the name of the Gospel.

If the "weapons of our warfare are not carnal, but mighty through God to the pulling down of strongholds; casting down imaginations, and every high thing that exalteth itself against the knowledge of God, and bringing into captivity every thought to the obedience of Christ" (II Corinthians 10:4–5), they will also pull down many a stronghold which has been ostensibly erected in the name of Christ. If God can take the "things which are not, to bring to nought things that are: that no flesh should glory in his presence" (I Corinthians 1:25), He will surely not exempt priest or prophet or any community of the "saved."

SCRIPTURAL INDEX

GENERAL INDEX

Printed in the United States
136581LV00001B/69/A